Supervision of Sandplay Therapy

D0224204

Supervision of Sandplay Therapy, the first book on this subject, is an internationally based Jungian-oriented approach that describes the state of the art in supervision of sandplay therapy. Recognizing that practitioners are eager to incorporate sandplay therapy into their practice, Harriet Friedman and Rie Rogers Mitchell respond to the need for new information, and successfully translate the theories of sandplay therapy into supervision practice.

This book provides a meaningful connection and balance between theoretical principles, practical application, and ongoing therapeutic encounter involved in sandplay. Divided into six sections, contributors cover:

- Original supervision models
- Contemporary supervision models
- Special challenges in supervision
- International sandplay supervision
- Supervision of special groups
- Connections with other arts therapies

With the wealth of information provided, this volume better equips supervisors to help their supervisees understand the many complexities when using non-verbal therapy. It expands the vision of what is possible in supervision and will be vital reading for those studying supervision and sandplay therapy, as well as for those wanting to provide a depth-oriented approach during supervision.

Harriet S. Friedman, Jungian analyst, is a founding member of Sandplay Therapists of America, and former board member of the International Society of Sandplay Therapists. She co-authored (with Rie) *Sandplay: Past, Present and Future* (Routledge, 1994). She also lectures nationally and internationally on integrating sandplay and Jungian psychology, and has supervised sandplay practitioners for over 25 years.

Rie Rogers Mitchell is professor of educational psychology and counseling at California State University, Northridge. She is a certified sandplay therapist and teacher, vice president of the International Society of Sandplay Therapy, and co-president of Sandplay Therapists of America. She supervises internationally and has published extensively in sandplay and counselor education.

Supervision in the Arts Therapies
Series Editor: Joy Schaverien

'This splendid series breaks new ground in its depth, breadth and scope, guided by Joy Schaverien's recognition that the time is right for a comprehensive, multi-faceted study of supervision in the arts psychotherapies. With each volume, the reader is invited to imagine, explore, and reflect on the expressive qualities of a particular art form in clinical supervision, turning special attention to art, music, dance, drama, and sandplay through contributions by leading experts from different parts of the world. These five volumes will make a lasting contribution as essential reading for supervisors and supervisees across the psychotherapies. The series also contributes towards a deeper understanding of the mentor–student relationship and the healing power of the arts.'

Joan Chodorow, Jungian Analyst and former President of the American Dance Therapy Association

'This new series of *Supervision in the Arts Therapies* is both timely and necessary. Now that all the arts therapies are established as state registered professions in their own right, there is a lack of resources that can support both the more advanced practitioner and the student. The writers of these individual titles are leaders in their respective fields both as researchers and practitioners. These publications make very important and innovative steps, and should be read by everyone in related fields of work.'

Dr Sue Jennings, Consultant Dramatherapist and Supervisor

'Each volume will not only communicate across the arts therapies but also to colleagues in other psychotherapies and health professions, to our mutual benefit.'

Diane Waller, Professor of Art Psychotherapy, Goldsmiths College University of London, President of the British Association of Art Therapists

This innovative series comprises five edited volumes, each focusing on one of the arts therapies – art, music, drama, dance or sandplay – and reflects on the dynamic nature of the presentation of that art form in supervision. The series reveals similarities and differences encountered in the theory and practice of supervision in each modality and within a range of contexts, and with diverse client groups.

Supervision in the Arts Therapies makes a timely contribution to the literature and will be essential reading for experienced practitioners and students of the arts therapies, as well as psychotherapists and other professionals engaged in supervision.

Titles in the series

Supervision of Art Psychotherapy
Joy Schaverien and Caroline Case

Supervision of Music Therapy
Helen Odell Miller and Eleanor Richards

Supervision of Dramatherapy
Phil Jones and Ditty Dokter

Supervision of Dance Movement Therapy
Helen Payne

Supervision of Sandplay Therapy
Harriet Friedman and Rie Rogers Mitchell

Supervision of Sandplay Therapy

Edited by Harriet S. Friedman
and Rie Rogers Mitchell

Routledge
Taylor & Francis Group

LONDON AND NEW YORK

First published 2008 by Routledge
27 Church Road, Hove, East Sussex BN3 2FA

Simultaneously published in the USA and Canada
by Routledge
711 Third Avenue, New York, NY 10017

Routledge is an imprint of the Taylor & Francis Group, an Informa Business

Typeset in Times by Garfield Morgan, Swansea, West Glamorgan

Paperback cover design by Sandra Heath

British Library Cataloguing in Publication Data
A catalogue record for this book is available from the British Library

Library of Congress Cataloging-in-Publication Data
Supervision of sandplay therapy / edited by Harriet S. Friedman and Rie
Rogers Mitchell.
        p. ; cm. – (Supervision in the arts therapies)
    Includes bibliographical references and index.
    ISBN 978-0-415-41089-2 (hardback) – ISBN 978-0-415-41090-8 (pbk.) 1.
Sandplay–Therapeutic use–Study and teaching–Supervision. 2. Child
psychotherapists–Training of. I. Friedman, Harriet S., 1930- II. Mitchell, Rie
Rogers, 1940- III. Series.
    [DNLM: 1. Play Therapy–education. 2. Mentors. 3. Play Therapy–
organization & administration. 4. Teaching–methods. WM 18 S9597 2007]
    RC489.S25S87 2007
    616.89'1653–dc22

                                                            2007008415

ISBN: 978-0-415-41089-2 (hbk)
ISBN: 978-0-415-41090-8 (pbk)

This book is dedicated to our sandplay teachers: Dora Kalff, Kay Bradway, our colleagues and friends in STA and ISST, our supervisees, and our clients.

Thank you for all we have learned from you.

Contents

List of illustrations

Notes on contributors

Kate Amatruda, LMFT, CST-T, BCETS, is a licensed marriage and family therapist, board-certified expert in traumatic stress: Diplomate, American Academy of Experts in Traumatic Stress, and a teaching member of the International Society for Sandplay Therapy. She lectures internationally and has taught in the extended education departments at U.C. Berkeley and Sonoma State University. She is the author of *A Field Guide to Disaster Mental Health: The Very Big Wave and the Mean Old Storm* (www.psychceu.com, 2001), *Psyche and Soma: Trauma, Terror and Treatment* (www.psychceu.com, 2005). She is co-author of *Sandplay, the Sacred Healing: A Guide to Symbolic Process* (Trance-Sand-Dance Press, 1997, revised 2007). She practices in Northern California.

Ruth Ammann, Dipl.Arch.Eth., is a Jungian analyst and president of the International Society of Sandplay Therapy. She has traveled and trained sandplay therapists worldwide and, consequently, is highly qualified to address the variety of ways sandplay is supervised internationally. She is the author of *Healing and Transformation in Sandplay: Creative Processes Become Visible* (Open Court Publishing, 1991) and has recently produced a videotape, *Gardens of the Soul: Sandplay Therapy* (Roug Production, 2003). She is also a qualified and still practicing architect.

Kay Bradway, Ph.D., a founding member of the C.G. Jung Institute of San Francisco, is also a founding member of the International Society of Sandplay Therapy, and Sandplay Therapists of America. Kay has been a major figure in the national and international Jungian community for many decades for her leadership contribution and scholarly works. She has written numerous articles and is the co-author of *Sandplay Studies: Origins, Theory and Practice* (San Francisco C.G. Jung Institute, 1981), *Sandplay: Silent Workshop of the Psyche* (Routledge, 1997) and *Sandplay in Three Voices: Images, Relationships, the Numinous* (Routledge, 2005).

Maria Ellen Chiaia, Ph.D., is an analyst and member of the C.G. Jung Institute of San Francisco and a teaching member of the International

Society for Sandplay Therapy (ISST) and Sandplay Therapists of America (STA). She has served as board chair of STA, and member of the board of ISST and STA. She teaches internationally, has published numerous articles and book chapters, and has co-authored *Sandplay in Three Voices: Images, Relationships, the Numinous* (Routledge, 2005).

Lauren Cunningham, LCSW, Jungian analyst in San Francisco, California, is a certified teaching member of the International Society of Sandplay Therapists. She is an associate professor for the expressive arts program at California Institute of Integral Studies. Lauren is founding member of the Sandplay Therapists of America as well as the founding and former editor of the *Journal of Sandplay Therapy*.

Patricia Dunn-Fierstein, LCSW, has been a licensed clinical social worker in private practice in Tampa, Florida for over 20 years. She is a certified teaching member of the International Society for Sandplay Therapy and a certified EMDR therapist. She has studied at the Jung Institute in Switzerland and is a published author in the *Journal of Sandplay Therapy* and *Living the Tides of Uncertainty: Proceedings, Sandplay Therapists of America, National Conference 2004*. Patricia teaches in the Tampa area and nationally.

Harriet S. Friedman, M.A. M.F.T., Jungian analyst, is a certified teaching member of the International Society of Sandplay Therapy. She is a founding member and former president of Sandplay Therapists of America, and served as vice-president of the international board. She is on the teaching faculty of the Jung Institute of Los Angeles, former director of the Hilde Kirsch Children's Center, and co-author of *Sandplay: Past, Present and Future* (Routledge, 1994). For over 25 years, she had led sandplay supervision groups in Los Angeles. Harriet has also published several journal articles and book chapters, and has lectured internationally on integrating sandplay and Jungian psychology.

Gao Lan, Ph.D., is a professor of child psychology and preschool education at South China Normal University in Guangzhou, China. She is currently a consultant for UNICEF as a specialist in children's mental health. She has introduced sandplay into residential and nonresidential preschools throughout China, conducts ongoing supervision of teachers, and publishes widely in this field and others. She is currently working toward certification by the International Society of Sandplay Therapy.

Mariellen Griffith, Ed.D., LMFT, is a teaching member of the International Society of Sandplay Therapy, and also specializes in dream analysis, regressive therapy, play therapy, and hypnosis. She has a private practice in Bloomington, Illinois, and has published articles in various educational journals, including the *Journal of Sandplay Therapy*. She is a registered play therapist and certified as a supervisor by the Association of Play Therapy.

Gretchen Hegeman, MASW, diplomate in clinical social work and candidate member of the North Pacific Institute of Analytic Psychology, practices on Mercer Island, Washington. She is past president of Sandplay Therapists of America and has been STA's representative to the International Society of Sandplay Therapists (ISST). She is images editor of the *Journal of Sandplay Therapy* (JST) and has contributed articles to JST and *Sandspiel-therapie*. She has taught sandplay therapy throughout the United States and in Taiwan.

Betty Jackson, LCSW, has over 30 years of experience working with children and adults in school, mental health, and private practice settings. She is a teaching member of the International Society for Sandplay Therapy and Sandplay Therapists of America. Betty trained in Zurich, Switzerland with Dora M. Kalff, originator of sandplay, is a former board member and vice president of Sandplay Therapists of America, and has authored articles for *The Journal of Sandplay Therapy*. She is currently in private practice in Media, Pennsylvania, offering psychotherapy for children and adults, sandplay training, and clinical supervision of sandplay practice.

Rie Rogers Mitchell, Ph.D., RPT-S, ABPP, professor of educational psychology and counseling at California State University, Northridge, is a certified sandplay therapist and teacher, vice-president of the International Society of Sandplay Therapy, and co-president of Sandplay Therapists of America. Rie is the clinical director and supervisor at her university department's clinic, a nationally certified counselor, and a licensed psychologist in private practice in Calabasas, CA. Rie is co-author of *Sandplay: Past, Present and Future* (Routledge, 1994), and has published numerous book chapters and journal articles in both sandplay and other areas of psychology.

Gita Dorothy Morena, Ph.D., is a transpersonal psychotherapist, a certified sandplay therapist, and an adjunct professor at the University of California, San Diego. She has been in private practice in the San Diego area for over 30 years and is the author of *The Wisdom of Oz: Reflections of a Jungian Sandplay Psychotherapist* (Frog Ltd, 1998).

Denise G. Ramos, Ph.D., is a clinical psychologist, Jungian analyst, and professor at Pontifícia Universidade Católica de Sao Paulo, where she coordinates the Graduate Program in Clinical Psychology. She has discussed analytical psychology on radio and television in various Brazilian cities, and has given papers at conferences throughout Latin America, Europe, and the United States. She was vice-president of the International Association for Analytical Psychology and the director of the Brazilian Society for Analytical Psychology for many years. She is currently editor-in-chief of the journal, *Junguiana*, and has authored the books *A Psique do Coração* (*The Psyche of the Heart*) (Cultrix, 1990) and *The Psyche of the Body* (Brunner-Routledge, 2004), among others.

Sachiko Taki Reece, Ed.D., MFT, is a Jungian analyst in Los Angeles and a certified teaching member of the International Society of Sandplay Therapy. Sachiko has published many sandplay research articles in English and in Japanese. In September 2002, she received the Hayao Kawai Award for her sandplay research articles published in the Archives of Japanese Association of Sandplay Therapy in Japan. She is a board member of Sandplay Therapists of America, and she supervises and teaches sandplay in the United States and Japan.

Heyong Shen, Ph.D., is a professor of analytical psychology at South China Normal University in Guangzhou, China, and originator of the first Chinese Ph.D. program in analytical psychology. He is a Jungian analyst and president of the Guangzhou Institute of Analytical Psychology. Heyong hosted the first Jungian conference held in China in which he included sandplay. He is a member of the International Society of Sandplay Therapy and has published in numerous English and Chinese journals. He is a specialist in the *I Ching*.

Lenore Steinhardt, MA, ATR, is a teaching member of the International Society of Sandplay Therapy. She is founder and director of an art therapy training program and a sandplay training program in the Kibbutz College of Education, Tel Aviv. She is the author of *Foundation and Form in Jungian Sandplay* (Jessica Kingsley, 2000) and *Between Stars and Sand* (Sea Gate, 2005) (Hebrew), and has written many articles on art therapy and sandplay therapy. She has a private practice in Ramat Hasharon, Israel. She is a member of the American Art Therapy Association, the Israeli Creative Expressive Therapies Organization and is an associate member of the Israel Institute of Jungian Psychology.

Rosalind Winter, MSW, is a Jungian analyst and a teaching member of Sandplay Therapists of America and the International Society for Sandplay Therapy. From 2001 to 2006 she directed a training program in Symbol Formation (an adaptation of Sandplay Therapy as a response to trauma) for the counselors of the Ground Zero schools in New York City. Rosalind has served as president of the New York Association of Jungian Analysts and has been a faculty member of the C.G. Jung Institute of New York. She now has a private practice in Portland, Oregon where she is also teaching and consulting in Symbol Formation and Sandplay Therapy.

Judy D. Zappacosta, MFT, is a teaching member of the International Society for Sandplay Therapy (ISST) and Sandplay Therapists of America (STA). She has served as Board Chair for STA and currently serves on the executive board. Judy has published nationally and internationally and has taught sandplay for many years. In addition, she completed the Leadership Program in the Marion Woodman Foundation, integrating sandplay, dreams, and the body. She teaches and maintains a practice in Santa Cruz, California.

Preface to the series and this book

Supervision of Sandplay Therapy is a title in the five-volume series *Supervision in the Arts Therapies*. The series was conceived as a result of collaboration with colleagues from art and music therapy, drama and dance movement therapy as well as Sandplay. This led to creative discourse regarding the similarities and differences between the roles of the different arts media in supervision. It became clear that, although there was a developing body of theory in the field of supervision in the arts therapies, there was relatively little written on the topic. So it was that the idea of a series of books on *Supervision in the Arts Therapies* was conceived and, with the encouragement of Joanne Forshaw at Routledge, the series came into being.

It is a great pleasure to have the opportunity to introduce this, the first book on *Supervision of Sandplay Therapy*, to a readership which it is hoped will include arts therapists, Jungian analysts and child and adult psychotherapists as well as sandplay therapists. The inclusion of sandplay in this series on supervision is innovative because sandplay is not officially one of the "arts therapies." In the UK, the arts therapies, art, music, drama and dance movement therapy, are now state-registered professions. Sandplay comes from a different tradition. Although Jung was a source of inspiration for many arts therapists, sandplay was originally primarily a Jungian practice. Now, however, it has gained widespread popularity among therapists of diverse orientations. It began in Europe and has been disseminated widely in the USA and Japan, and indeed throughout the world. Like the arts therapies, sandplay offers potential for a very different type of experience from other forms of psychotherapy supervision. The common element in practices explored in this series is that an object mediates psychological processes in the context of a therapeutic relationship. Sandplay could be understood to combine aspects of all the others. As miniature worlds are created, sand pictures emerge and, like a theatre, the sand tray is a space where imaginal dramas are enacted; a form of *dance-movement* occurs as the player moves, taking object from shelves and placing them in the sand, sometimes accompanied by natural *musical sounds*. Moreover, in the

supervision of sandplay therapy, pictures of the sand tray are shown, con-
stellating a triangular relationship comprised of therapist, picture, supervisor (or group), which is reminiscent of art psychotherapy supervision.

The editors and contributors to this book are highly experienced sandplay therapists, many of them are also Jungian analysts, and whilst most
are based in the USA, they come from widely diverse international backgrounds. This makes this book an exciting and timely contribution to
the literature in this expanding field. It is anticipated that, along with its
companion volumes in the series, this book will be of interest to a wide
readership: supervisors and supervisees, whether experienced practitioners
or students, from the disciplines of sandplay, analytical psychology, art
psychotherapy, music, dance and drama therapy, as well as child and adult
psychotherapy and integrative arts therapy. All involved in supervision of
the arts therapies, as well as sandplay therapists, will find this book inspiring reading and an essential companion to supervision.

Joy Schaverien
April 2007

Foreword

I was delighted when I was asked to write a foreword for this first book on the supervision of sandplay. The need for this book, I believe, demonstrates how much sandplay has expanded and the growing worldwide interest in it. Because many of the large numbers of clinicians now using sandplay are seeking sandplay supervision, the time has come for a book that addresses this subject.

In reminiscing about my own supervision experiences with sandplay, my earliest memory begins in 1962, at the time Dora Kalff first visited California when she was invited to speak at the joint conference of San Francisco and Los Angeles Jungian Institutes. She stole the show! Because of the impact of her dynamic presentation and the power of seeing the unconscious reveal itself so dramatically in the sand, many analysts signed up for private supervision with her . . . and I was one of them.

Dora Kalff's initial visit was followed by yearly trips to the Northern and Southern California Jung Institutes during the 1960s. In those early years, she gave case presentations and also had private and group supervision sessions. The San Francisco Jung Institute very soon set up a special "Kalff Committee" that was responsible for making an appointment schedule for Dora's individual supervisions. Later, sponsored by the University of California at Santa Cruz, she stayed at a retreat center at Pajaro Dunes in Northern California, where people from far and wide came to study with her. In the afternoon, after her morning sandplay presentation, she provided individual supervision in her suite, delighting us with cookies, tea, and sometimes chocolate.

During the 1970s, her visits became more irregular and shorter because she was also in demand in Japan and throughout Europe. However, most years she continued to come to California for a weekend, sometimes a week or two. In addition to her teaching, she began to provide sandplay supervision for even larger groups of up to 20 clinicians from all over the United States. Often the participants presented their own case material for her input. Frequently, individual supervision hours were arranged for those analysts who asked for them.

These visits were too short to provide time for sandplay processes to be done – at least to be completed. I don't know of anyone who did a complete sandplay process with her at this time. We had to go to Zurich for our processes. Because I wanted to have some individual experience with sandplay, I did a preliminary short sandplay series with Rene Brand, who was Dora Kalff's first American student and a member of the San Francisco Jung Institute. It was 1974 when I did my individual sandplay process with Dora Kalff.

In 1982 I was indeed fortunate to be one of the 11 therapists invited by Dora Kalff to her home in Zollikon, Switzerland. She wrote: "I am happy to inform you that from September 10–17, 1982 I organize a meeting with a few representatives of Sandplay therapists of various parts of the world. This letter is to extend an invitation to you to participate in this meeting in order to share experiences which you have undergone in the field of Sandplay therapy . . . During the meeting there should be ample time for the participants to exchange views among themselves, to discuss case material outside the formal sessions."

Of the 11 invited, happily all but one arrived at Dora Kalff's in September. The therapists invited were: from England, Joel Ryce-Menuhin; from Italy, Paola Carducci and Andreina Navone; from Japan, Kazuhiko Higuchi, Hayao Kawai, and Yasuhiro Yamanaka; from Switzerland, Kaspar Kiepenheuer and Martin Kalff; from the United States, Estelle Weinrib, Chonita Larsen, and me. Dr Higuchi of Japan was the one unable to attend. Cecil Burney joined us the following year, and with his unfortunate and untimely death, Sigrid Loewen-Seifert from Germany was invited by Dora to join the group. The only participant I knew beforehand was Dr Kawai, whom I had contacted when I was in Japan a few years previously.

While we were there most of us stayed at the Sonne Hotel in Kusnacht and went daily to Dora's 15th-century home in Zollikon, where we participated in a full but relaxed schedule that she had planned in advance. Each day from 9:00 to 12:00 noon, two of us presented a case using slides of the sand trays, followed by discussion. From noon to 4:00 we had time for a leisurely lunch, rest, and individual or group pursuits. From 4:00 to 6:30, another participant presented. Dora usually presented the final case, which always was a "wow" case. Sometimes we discussed more general questions such as the history of certain symbols, the handling of negative input from the sandplayer, or responding to a sandplayer's "What does it mean?" question after completing a tray. Some place in this schedule there was time for business. I don't remember exactly when this was, but we were working on establishing an international sandplay association. Dora had not referred to this in her invitation, but it soon became clear that this was on her agenda. We continue to meet annually.

To give us pleasure and renew both body and spirit, Dora planned a special surprise for us for afternoon or evening. The first year she took us to

Jung's tower in Bollingen, where she invited us to enter our names in the guest book under her heading "the first international meeting of sandplay." This was quite impressive to us – in this place most important to Carl Jung.

Another year she asked Al Huang, the tai chi master, to give a performance for us. Another year we were privileged to go to Jung's house in Kusnacht and explore his library, with tea served by his grandson, Heinz.

The time with these very special people, enjoying the hospitality of Dora, and the combination of intellectual challenges and relaxing entertainment was "heavenly."

It was out of this incredibly rich experience that the International Society for Sandplay Therapy (ISST) was officially founded at the end of our fourth meeting in 1985.

In 1988, when I retired from individual practice, I started my own consultation/supervision groups. I always preferred calling what I did in this capacity "consulting" rather than "supervising." This was especially true after I had inactivated my state license at the time I had retired from individual practice.

I limited these groups to four members. It felt like the right number for members to bond. One group, at their request, consisted of only two members. I had one all-male group.

When I first started the groups, I asked the prospective members to fill out a one-page, ten-item questionnaire that I had developed. I asked such questions as "What individual supervision of your sandplay work with clients have you had?"; "Is your focus mostly on children, adults, or both?"; "In what aspects do you wish training would include or emphasize?" I do not recall anyone objecting to filling it out, but I soon abandoned it. Perhaps I felt that relevant information could be obtained in a less formal way.

The groups met on Thursday or Friday for two hours. We met monthly, with three months off in the summer. Each group had an option of dividing a two-hour fee among the four of them, regardless of attendance, or to divide the fee just among those present. Most groups chose the former. Just a single case was presented at each meeting. Who would present was always decided at a previous meeting.

One of my main purposes was to make the bonding among the members easy and long-lasting. To begin each meeting I served tea and cookies around our dining table and invited members to tell about any events that were happening in their lives that were particularly important to them. I think this initial check-in time together provided a baseline for the kind of self-revelation that is required in sharing the intimacies of the therapy that one does. It has always seemed to me that exposing to others how we have "handled" situations in therapy is a very delicate matter. I did come to feel that the members of each group were at ease at disclosing therapeutic situations to each other.

When members of the group traveled it became quite usual to bring back something they had seen in their travels that they wanted to share as gifts to each of us. Sometimes members brought reprints of pertinent articles that they wanted to share.

After the check-in the presenting member summarized the case history of the client to be presented. I did not encourage the kind of detailed history that is sometimes given. It seemed to me that quantities of details encouraged looking at a tray with a conscious point of view: "that item is his brother"; "that figure is her aunt." I thought it was more important that we attended to what the unconscious was revealing in the trays.

After the presentation of the case history, we went downstairs to the room in our home where the slide projector and screen are always set up. By this time each member seemed to feel at ease in presenting, questioning, throwing out ideas, disagreeing, or whatever. Sometimes the members wanted to see the whole case without too much interruption and then return and discuss each tray as it related to the whole.

I thought it was important to emphasize the nature of the relationship between therapist and sandplayer. There are many ways in which this relationship is shown, for example: the sandplayer's praise or criticism of the items offered; the placement of guns or paths in the tray in relation to where the therapist was sitting; the relation between certain items in the tray showing negative or positive feelings between the figures. There were times when a tray would be shown and one of the members or I would say, "What happened? Had you been on a vacation and the sandplayer was mad at you?" I think these observations occurred more frequently as we continued our meetings. They led to general discussions of the co-transference.

In these groups I tried to respond and adapt to the individual differences of the members. I wanted them to feel that I respected what they were doing and how they were doing it, even though I might make suggestions for it being done other ways. I wanted to establish a general atmosphere of respect for individual differences in their clients, as well as in themselves and each other. I think a vital ingredient in these groups is relationship: between therapist and sandplayer, between member and member, and between member and leader.

I "retired" from my consultation groups in the year 2000. The groups meant so much to me as I know they did to the members. Retiring from individual practice was very difficult. I knew the time had come but I also knew it would leave a large part of my life "vacant."

Kay Bradway
Sausalito, CA
February 2006

Acknowledgements

Most books are birthed because of a growing idea from the author(s). In contrast, this book is a result of the work and care of many minds and hearts.

Our deepest thanks go to Joy Schaverien for the initial idea of writing this book and for her kind invitation to write one of five books she is editing on supervision in the arts therapies. She graciously asked us to edit the volume on supervision of sandplay. Our heartfelt gratitude goes to Joy for this challenge and for what we have learned in the process of editing this book.

Always an edited book is only as good as its contributors. We are especially thankful to the superb writers and experienced sandplay therapists who responded to our call for papers from the membership of Sandplay Therapists of America and others.

Thanks to our partners and all our children, grandchildren, and families for their patience, understanding, and support during the reclusive time necessary for the writing and editing of this book: Richard Friedman; Andy, Jimmy and Rebecca Friedman and Jodi Carlson; Ellen Friedman and Louis, Lucy and Jacob Blumberg; Julie Friedman and Robert, Jacob and Aaron Kagon; and Rex and Scott Mitchell, Richard and Frances Rogers, and Robert and Annette Rogers.

We are also grateful to the following persons for their support at various phases in the development of the book: Claire Alphin, Irene Baron, Joanne Culbert-Koehn, Harriet Roth, Eva Silver, and for the colleagues and friends in the C.G. Jung Institute, Los Angeles, and in the Department of Educational Psychology and Counseling at California State University, Northridge.

Our deepest appreciation goes to the many researchers, writers, and clinicians who have contributed to the sandplay literature over the past many decades.

A big thank you to our angel editor Margaret Ryan who has made these creative, inspired chapters even better. Thanks also to Betsy Caprio for her editorial help.

Thank you to Cecil Burney's brother, Frank Burney, who allowed Gita Morena to use Cecil's poem.

We also acknowledge our indebtedness to Joanne Forshaw, senior editor, Claire Lipscomb, senior editorial assistant, Kathryn Russel, senior production editor, and others at Routledge.

Introduction

Harriet S. Friedman and Rie Rogers Mitchell

This very first book on supervision of sandplay therapy began for us as an unexpected event when Joy Schaverien invited us to be part of her dream. Her vision was to publish a series of books on supervision in the arts therapies. She wanted us to edit the fifth book of this collection on sandplay supervision.

The initial effect of her dream on us was similar to an unplanned pregnancy. We felt both excited and apprehensive. Eventually, through nurturance and care, the book became our own "divine child," bringing light and pleasure to us, as if it were our own idea. With this came new levels of consciousness and it expanded our ways of thinking about supervision of sandplay therapy.

What is sandplay?

Sandplay, as developed by Dora Kalff, is a Jungian-oriented, non-verbal form of therapy that facilitates the psyche's natural capacity for healing. In a "free and protected" space provided by the therapist, a child or adult creates a concrete manifestation of his or her inner imaginal world using sand, water, and miniature objects. Thus, sandplay illuminates the client's internal symbolic world and provides a place for its expression within a safe container, the sand tray. This sandplay experience provides a balance to the extraverted, verbal, and outer-focused everyday world and leads to a more open, balanced, and integrated way of life.

In 1982, Dora Kalff officially founded the International Society of Sandplay Therapy (ISST). Since that early period, sandplay has spread worldwide with official branches in England, France, Germany, Italy, Japan, Switzerland, and the United States. In order to be a certified member, candidates must successfully complete educational requirements, write papers, involve themselves in their own personal sandplay process, and participate in group and individual supervision. To become a certified teaching member, and thus be certified to supervise others, additional requirements must be met, such as co-teaching with a certified teacher and presenting cases before an evaluative audience. From the outset of this organization, it was understood, and included in the by-laws of the organization, that those who were certified as ISST teaching members could also provide supervision in sandplay.

Implicit in the assumption that any certified sandplay teacher could supervise is the assumption that supervision is merely an extension of didactic teaching and clinical practice. Given this assumption, supervision itself received scant attention from sandplay writers, although supervision was recognized as an essential component in becoming a sandplay practitioner.

Now, with this book on supervision, the situation has changed. Supervisors have taken the opportunity to explore their experiences and insights about supervision with more conscious awareness. This new awareness brings the realization that supervision calls for highly developed abilities that integrate the intuitive and feeling capacities with thinking, cognitive, and verbal skills. The writers of these chapters have successfully assimilated these skills and translated their insights into engaging and sometimes deeply moving accounts of their own supervision experiences.

With this book, sandplay supervision moves through a rite of passage to become a serious field of study.

Historical roots of sandplay supervision

Although clinical supervision has always been an integral part of learning sandplay, the historical roots in the larger psychological profession are quite different. Freud, Jung, and their immediate contemporaries had no supervisors, nor did they officially supervise other's clinical work. However, from time to time, colleagues did consult with Freud and Jung by letter, in personal meetings, and at professional congresses (Weiner, Mizen, & Duckham, 2003).

Jung was the first analyst to propose that trainee analysts should undergo a personal analysis (Mattoon, 1995). And, in their own personal analysis, future analysts received supervision as they discussed their own clients during personal sessions and, subsequently, often modeled their own clinical work on their individual analytic experience. Opportunity for supervision did not formally occur until 1948, when the Jung Institute in Zurich included supervision in its curriculum.

Dora Kalff's approach to supervision appeared to be modeled after C.G. Jung's teaching/therapy supervision style. Kalff taught small groups in a formal didactic style, did extensive sandplay therapy with professionals who traveled from all over the world to work with her, and lectured to large groups both nationally and internationally. She was also frequently videotaped while making public presentations where she spoke about sandplay theory and illustrated her own work with slides from her cases. However, differing from Jung, who was a prolific writer, Kalff's written contributions were limited to one book and a few journal articles. To represent her work and move it further out into the world, she selected specific people from Europe, Asia, and North and South America whom she had taught personally. These colleagues shared her deep appreciation for the healing powers of sandplay and were respected clinicians in their own right. They not only brought sandplay to their countries, but also became the leading supervisors of many of the current certified sandplay therapists worldwide. Kay Bradway's foreword to this book refers to her own experience of being included in Kalff's early group and her practice as a supervisor.

The supervisor's role

From our perspective, a thoughtful supervisor is a teacher and a mentor (not a personal analyst or therapist), who is able to establish a collaborative relationship in a free and protected environment. The goal of supervision is to activate the supervisee's own potential and individual connection to the Self, and help facilitate the supervisee's growth as an ethical and effective professional in a manner that best reflects his or her gifts, abilities, temperament, spiritual, and temporal values. At the heart of supervision is a focus on the supervisee's feelings, reactions, thoughts, and fantasies that emerge as a result of his or her relationship to the client and to the entire clinical matrix. The task of the supervisor is to bring all of his or her cognitive knowledge, experience, feeling and intuitive capacities, and communication and relational skills, along with a generosity of spirit, to the supervision sessions.

We, as supervisors, are mindful that supervisees may identify with us and incorporate our supervisory role in their psyche as a reference model. This model or internal guide becomes an essential part of the supervisees' own developing identity and frequently stays with them over their professional career, developing and changing as they grow and change as therapists. Thus, the supervisor is much more than a temporary teacher, who is with a supervisee for only a few months or years. The supervisor, as an archetype, can be a powerful influence, both consciously and unconsciously, throughout a therapist's lifetime.

Jungian theory and supervision

While acknowledging the value of the current literature on supervision, it is time for us to characterize a specific Jungian approach to sandplay training, which requires that we discern the workings of the Self and its archetypal constituents in the process.

In working with a client, a Jungian-oriented therapist is always alert for newly-emerging potentials for future healing and unification of the personality (e.g., in dreams, sandplays, behaviors, creative impulses, ideas, fantasies) rather than to just looking backward and dwelling on old events and wounds. This is what Jung refers only as a *prospective attitude*. The prospective attitude is a result of Jung's observation that the psyche has a natural tendency to heal itself, given the proper conditions. Similar to how our physical wounds heal under certain conditions, the psyche also has an instinctual wisdom if left free to operate naturally in a safe and protected environment.

According to Jungian theory, the *Self* is located in the unconscious – the place of wisdom – and is the central ordering principle of the entire personality. The conscious part of the psyche is called the *ego*, but it is less than the whole personality. When the ego and Self are in relationship and communication, then the individual is living closest to his or her own most actualized state, thus feeling more balanced and alive. Sandplay can be an effective means of evoking and nurturing the vital bridge between the Self and the ego.

Jungian theory also offers us a language to both observe and identify the movement of the deeper level of the personality. In sandplay, the symbolic use of miniatures, water, and sand are viewed through a Jungian lens. The understanding of these symbols is greatly enriched by exploring their many meanings using myths, alchemy, history, religion, other cultures, animal behavior, etc. It is through understanding symbols that the language of the unconscious comes alive and leads us to an understanding of the archetypal and collective levels.

Supervising sandplay from a Jungian point of view is, in fact, supervision of the unconscious process and the creative imagination. The unfolding of a series of sand creations also allows us to view the vastness and complexity of the unconscious. Through study of sand pictures, we are able to identify the development of the relationship between the ego and the Self, the journey toward individuation, bridging and integration of unresolved issues (i.e., the tension of the opposites), emergence of new creative energies, and movement towards wholeness.

Jungian theory, along with the prospective attitude, enlarges our understanding of the language of the unconscious and provides the largest map available to understand and supervise the workings of the psyche. Also, when the supervisor highlights the supervisee's unique emotional and intuitive responses then the supervisee's own approach emerges. In this safe environment, therapists' individual gifts and talents are validated and allowed to flourish.

Goals of the book

Because of the important role that supervision plays in the teaching of sandplay, many certified sandplay therapists have had wide experience as both supervisees and as supervisors. Until now, however, their vast knowledge and experience have not been organized into a usable source for others. One of the several goals for this book is to provide a collection of articles written by seasoned sandplay supervisors that describes the state of the art of sandplay supervision. With this volume, supervisors will be better equipped to help their supervisees understand the complexities of this technique and its use in treatment.

This book provides a contemporary Jungian-oriented approach to sandplay supervision that is integrated with the current broader field of clinical supervision. Sandplay calls for a unique supervisory approach, as do the other expressive arts therapies, in which language skills are less necessary. Supervision in this field is supervision of what emerges from the imagination and the symbolic movement of the psyche with a focus on the inner responses of the therapist. This book acknowledges the importance of the dynamics of transference/countertransference not only within the interactive field but also as expressed in the sand creations as well. We hope this book will appeal to readers from various schools who feel the need to create a depth-oriented approach to supervision.

It is our desire to place this technique firmly within the domains of expressive art therapies, play therapy, EMDR, and the larger arena of contemporary psychotherapy that recognizes the importance of both verbal and non-verbal approaches. All of these non-verbal, expressive therapies also appreciate and incorporate imagination, creativity, fantasy, metaphors, and/or symbols in bringing about the healing process.

Supervision of expressive arts therapies includes similar challenges and rewards. In academic training, verbal cognitive approaches are primarily emphasized; therefore, one of the major challenges is to help therapists appreciate and integrate the non-verbal, more unconscious, right-brain approaches in therapy. Because of the ephemeral and intuitive nature of this work, even experienced therapists sometimes need to reach out to supervisors to help them translate the unconscious processes that guide the therapy.

In the early beginnings of sandplay, most supervision was conducted on a one-to-one basis. Now, with so many more therapists and supervisors, an organized and documented perspective is necessary for us to move forward. We must be able to articulate as well as write about both the questions and the answers that supervisees need to know. Learning the ability to communicate the intuitive experience is an essential component for sandplay supervisors if we are to support, sustain, and disseminate this valuable, non-verbal technique.

With these many goals in mind, we contacted all certified members of Sandplay Therapists of America and other sandplay therapists worldwide with a long history in sandplay supervision. We were surprised and delighted to receive so many papers, including some from Switzerland, China, Brazil, Israel, as well as North America, all with so many different points of view. From a list of supervision issues, each author was invited to choose a particular aspect of supervision, paying attention to his or her own supervision experiences or training interests. Given that all the authors come from a similar theoretical view, it was an amazing experience for us to see the range of styles and approaches they presented, and we felt it was a testament to the many ways that sandplay can be supervised.

As you read this book, we believe that you will find that the contributors have been able to translate their intuitive, feeling responses to their work into clearly expressed statements of what was actually going on in sandplay supervision. To further clarify and illustrate their work, case studies and real life experiences are often used. Names and identifying information have been changed to protect the identity of their supervisees and clients.

Kay Bradway's Foreword

Kay Bradway was our clear and natural choice to author the foreword. Kay was one of Dora Kalff's earliest supervisees, and had a lifelong, ongoing relationship with her. For many decades now, Kay has been the leader and mother of sandplay in the United States. She facilitated many of Dora Kalff's visits to the United States, inspired the founding of the national organization, Sandplay Therapists of America (STA), with Estelle Weinrib, and sponsored training and supervision in the United States for sandplay clinicians who were unable to go to Switzerland to study with Dora Kalff.

Kay directly supervised many of the current certified sandplay therapists, teachers, and supervisors. Clinicians throughout the western part of the United States regularly attended her monthly supervision groups, and the majority of these fulfilled the certification requirements and became leaders in STA. Gretchen Hegeman's chapter speaks to the unique experience of attending Kay's supervision groups, and in Lauren Cunningham and Kay's article, Kay discusses her thoughts about the organization and group process.

We are so appreciative of Kay's generosity in graciously writing the foreword and reminiscing about her experiences of supervision with Dora, sharing her wisdom, knowledge, and long experience in supervising sandplay. Her foreword adds a sense of the long history of sandplay supervision, placing it in the mainstream with other psychologies that have also stressed the importance of supervision.

Overview of the book

The first part, "Creating original supervision models," moves from Kay Bradway's foreword describing Dora Kalff's historical model of supervision to Lauren Cunningham and Kay Bradway joining together to share their own visionary models of supervision in leading sandplay case consultation groups in the United States. Gretchen Hegeman writes of her own enriching experience in Kay Bradway's group as a participant for over ten years. Harriet Friedman tells the compelling story of her odyssey in creating and developing her many supervision groups over the past 25 years.

In the second part, "Designing contemporary supervision models," Patricia Dunn-Fierstein explores the primary ingredients necessary for excellence in supervision of sandplay therapy. Mariellen Griffith proposes a collaborative model for supervision of sandplay therapy covering five vital principles. Betty Jackson follows with a creative model, based on Joseph Campbell's hero's journey, for helping supervisees understand the unfolding of sandplay process.

The third part, "Meeting special challenges in supervision," addresses a variety of issues that practicing sandplay therapists may experience in the course of their practice. Gretchen Hegeman discusses significant ethical issues and challenges that certified sandplay therapists face in the relatively small world of sandplay. Kate Amatruda delights us with her dilemma in working with an inexperienced and defensive trainee using sandplay. Denise Ramos reflects on the important issues arising in transference and counter-transference that occur between supervisee and supervisor. Maria Ellen Chiaia focuses on the unique aspects of sandplay therapy that impact the interactive field between supervisor, therapist, and client.

In the fourth part, "Moving into the cross-cultural world," Ruth Ammann speaks of her travels in Europe, the United States, Australia, and Asia including many of the developing nations, where she has both super-vised as well as taught sandplay therapy. She thoughtfully shares her special adventures and reflections about her experiences. Sachiko Taki Reece vividly describes how she uses the sand tray as a supervision tool to help supervisees better understand their ethnically diverse, low socioeconomic clients. Gao Lan describes her ground-breaking approach of supervising and using sandplay in residential preschools and kindergartens in China in order to create a free and protected space in the schools themselves.

In the first chapter of the fifth part, "Supervising special groups," Rie Rogers Mitchell addresses the unique topic of mentoring supervisors and helping them deal with problems that sometime arise in supervision. Then we are immediately drawn into post 9/11 New York City schools, where Rosalind Winter both teaches and supervises counselors in using sand tray as they work with traumatized children and adults. Next, Heyong Shen and Gao Lan write about their bridging of the western and eastern experience when training and supervising Chinese graduate students. What often manifests is a unique Chinese meaning of sandplay that encompasses the archetypal and symbolic meanings in the *I Ching* and other Chinese philo-sophies. Then, Judy Zappacosta invites the beginning clinician to develop and refine the ability to observe, listen, and relate to young children in a meaningful way.

The final part, "Making connections with other expressive therapies," begins with Gita Morena exploring the distinctive advantages of using sandplay therapy and other expressive arts for the supervision of clinical material. Lenore Steinhardt discusses her approach to sandplay supervision using the lens of two diverse and valid approaches: sandplay informed by Jungian theory and, secondly, the connection between an art therapy based approach and sandplay.

Readers may choose to start at the beginning of the book and progress to the end, or may select chapters that attract their particular interest. Although some chapters overlap in what interests the writer, each discusses the subject in his or her own unique way.

About our terms

We would like to add a clarification regarding the word *supervision*, as used in this book. In the world of psychotherapy, supervision has evolved from its historical meaning of overseeing and controlling the supervisee into a cooperative activity between supervisor and supervising therapist. Another development is that supervision now encompasses two activities: supervision and consultation. *Supervision* applies to the relationship between a licensed therapist/supervisor and a pre-licensed trainee or intern who is working under the license of that supervisor. Or, a therapist who is in a system that requires evaluation of therapists even though they are licensed. *Consultation* applies to a relationship between two licensed individuals in which a licensed individual chooses to consult with a more experienced therapist. However, for the purpose of this book, we use the word *supervision* in a generic way that encompasses both supervision and consultation. For the sake of consistency, we have asked all authors to refer to the people with whom they supervise as *supervisees*, regardless of their developmental stage (i.e., student, pre-licensed, or licensed).

The term *cotransference*, developed by Kay Bradway, is often used in this book. Cotransference refers to the relationship between therapist and client that embraces a "feeling with (*co*), rather than a feeling against (*counter*). I use the term co-transference to designate the therapeutic feeling relationship between therapist and patient. These inter-feelings seem to take place almost simultaneously, rather than sequentially as the composite term transference-countertransference suggests" (Bradway & McCoard, 1997, p. 34).

The term *sandplay* therapy refers to a Jungian/Kalffian approach in which a tray, sand, and miniatures are used. As a non-directive, depth approach, sandplay accesses and activates the internal healing energies of the individual psyche.

The term *sand tray* refers to any other use of tray, sand, and miniatures; for example, using it with groups, couples, and families or as a research or assessment instrument, or if the play is directed by the therapist.

Sand play is uniquely different from sand tray as it emphasizes the importance of using and understanding the symbolic language of the unconscious as well as the value of silence.

Conclusion

This book provides a specifically Jungian approach to supervision, written by experienced teachers and supervisors worldwide, using their own voices from the depth of their experience. Our desire is that this book will provide information about the current state of the art in sandplay supervision for psychotherapists, practitioners, counselors, Jungian analysts, supervisors, researchers, teachers of supervisors in various settings, and sandplayers around the world. We hope that the many voices speaking together in this book will enhance your professional skills, stimulate your imagination about supervision, enrich your own sandplay work, and open doors to new consciousness.

References

Bradway, K., & McCoard, B. (1997) *Sandplay: Silent workshop of the psyche*. New York: Routledge.

Mattoon, M.A. (1995) Historical notes. In P. Kugler (Ed.), *Jungian perspectives on clinical supervision*. Einsiedeln, Switzerland: Daimon.

Weiner, J., Mizen, R., & Duckham, J. (Eds.) (2003) *Supervising and being supervised*. New York: Palgrave Macmillan.

Part I

Creating original supervision models

Chapter 1

Group sandplay supervision: synergy at play

Lauren Cunningham and Kay Bradway

This chapter emerges from participating in and leading sandplay supervision groups for more than 20 years. Our experience has been with groups of four or five members that have stayed together for 3–10 years. Normally participation in a group includes a yearly commitment of monthly meetings, each two hours to two and a half hours long, from September to June. New members are introduced into a group infrequently and then only at the beginning of a year. This chapter reviews practicalities in leading a supervision group, including the group culture, the group development, limitations and challenges, and confidentiality issues of conducting sandplay supervision groups. The first four sections are from Lauren's pen; Kay contributed the last section on confidentiality issues.

Practicalities

Forming a group that bonds and meshes is part luck and part skill. I always meet individually with potential members to assess whether there is a fit with me as well as with the group. Dual relationships among the members have to be considered and the members have to be prepared for a new person joining. I try not to change the group's membership during a yearly cycle, only adding a new member, if need be, in the fall.

Over the years varying presentation formats have been tried. Generally members want to present as often as possible, but the groups have found that too many presentations in one meeting flood the members with clinical and symbolic material, which makes it more difficult to deepen the group process. My recent groups have settled on having a main presenter who uses the majority of time, with a secondary presenter introducing a vignette or issue for about a half hour at the end. The following month the secondary presenter then becomes the main presenter. Although participants may present two different cases or themes, they also have the opportunity to extend and elaborate the previous month's discussion. It's interesting to notice the synchronicity of interweaving themes in the two presentations in a given month.

Participants generally have an opportunity to present four to six times during the year. Projections of slides or digital images are preferred; sometimes Polaroid photos are shown or the tray is reconstructed with figures that the presenters bring from their collections. Most participants present ongoing cases that are challenging. Some prefer to bring in trays relating to themes around a particular image, such as the mermaid, or a specific clinical issue, such as latency-age boys with absent fathers. I encourage presenters to bring questions about the case that will focus the group discussion. Research about a symbol that will be used in papers for application to STA/ISST membership sometimes makes its debut in the group. Optimally participants support each other in reading, writing and deepening their sandplay training.

The presenter is asked to set up the projector and screen for slides or digital images (with some coaching as needed), so that they can become familiar with the equipment. As an intuitive-feeling type, I remember how stressed I became when I had to set up my screen and projector before making sandplay presentations. The sensation function needs to be worked on as part of our individuation process! It's interesting how some members of the group want to "help" the others by setting up the equipment for them rather than watching an awkward struggle with the levers, buttons, and plugs. This can become a model of tolerating uncertainty as another masters a task.

Group culture

A relaxed, accepting atmosphere is nurtured so that the members are willing to become more candid and open about difficulties in their work. Kay claims that one feels more vulnerable divulging what one does as a therapist than in giving sensitive material about oneself. It can help establish group rapport by having participants check in with each other before presenting case material. I encourage people to speak freely about their associations or feeling reactions before circling in closer to the possible meanings in the clinical and symbolic material. Play, intuition, and curiosity are encouraged. The supervisor becomes a model for developing the symbolic attitude. Students new to sandplay sometimes attempt to reduce their anxiety by hurrying to "this means this" in a concrete and reductive way.

Usually the group is able to move deeper together when there is stability in the membership and regularity in attendance over the year. Members feel safer and more open to sharing their feelings around confusing or uncomfortable moments with their clients. The group culture often promotes this process when seasoned members relate their "mistakes" in a session with a client. This example helps less experienced members become more candid about their work.

Experiencing trays as a group promotes a back-and-forth movement between *abaissement de niveau* and a development of consciousness, or deintegration and integration. Archetypal and clinical impressions depend on the orientation of individual therapists. The group ethos fosters a movement toward integration of perspectives while respecting and honoring the mystery of "not knowing."

As a case is held by the group, various aspects of the client's, the therapist's and the group's psyches (including personal, family, cultural, relational/cotransferential, and archetypal elements) tumble forth. Group supervision involves both an immersion in and reflection of this mix. The collaboration and sharing of impressions and knowledge can have a synergistic effect on participants' capacity to think symbolically and to hold the tension of the opposites. There can also be a tension between "moving through" a case in order to see the flow of process and settling into deeply experiencing and being with the images of a particular tray. There can be a play between the symbolic content of specific images or themes that run through a series of trays, on the one hand, and the clinical material that focuses more on the cotransference and analytic process, on the other. The presenter may feel anxious for a variety of reasons and offer more material than the group can digest. The supervisor needs to stay attuned to the group's anxiety level and capacity to tolerate the chaos and distress that may be manifesting in the sandplay images as well as in the presenter to help the group slow down, reflect more and re-integrate. The group learns to comment on parallel processes happening in the case and occurring in the present moment of the group.

Participants learn how to give and receive feedback with each other in a way that can be metabolized and built on. Many will become sandplay supervisors themselves. The supervision models supportive commentary that enlarges the container rather than constricting it – more of a "yes and" attitude than a "yes but." Before I became a supervisor, I was a supervisee in one of Kay's groups. Our teachers influence us. Kay set an accepting, receptive atmosphere. We learn how to learn and teach from our best teachers.

Inevitably students are at different levels and have different presenting styles and typologies. For the most part I support the presenters in finding and developing their own style rather than imposing a strict format. The leader needs to stay aware of group process and make sure that runaway competition or exclusion isn't happening, especially with newer or less experienced members.

Group development

Students start with varying skills and at different levels. It is important that group members have both enough in common as well as sufficient differences to enhance the mix. In a working group the more seasoned sandplay therapists become mentors for the less seasoned therapists. Expressive arts, art therapy, bodywork, EMDR, and teaching backgrounds may be part of the therapists' repertoire of working with their patients. Cross-learning happens by listening and discussion; we become familiar with each other's collections, clients, and ways of working with sandplay. Some therapists use a multimodal expressive arts approach; others use sandplay more exclusively, which they integrate with an analytic, verbal approach.

Strong connections are made among members as well as with the leader. Members appreciate having a group roster with their contact information. As the group and individuals mature, more fluidity develops in the leadership. A member might present something that he or she has thought about and studied, using the group as an opportunity to practice teaching in a small seminar setting. Members often hand out copies of relevant articles.

I offer group members something equivalent to a teacher's "office hours" a half hour before the group meeting for individuals to discuss specific training questions or where they are in terms of their development as a sandplay therapist. Students are often in different stages, and this pre-meeting period is an opportunity to open conversations that would not necessarily be addressed in the group but that can affect group process.

Over time the symbolic function of the group is enhanced as members are steeped in the unconscious material of a variety of sandplay trays over many hours. As the group matures, members become more comfortable with the tension of not knowing and sitting in uncertainty. There is less need to jump to conclusions. Fewer words may be spoken, but more is said. There is a felt experience in the room that we are circumambulating the mystery of the living psyche.

Limitations and challenge

Group supervision is rich but cannot replace individual supervision. The number of times each group participant can present in a year is limited. In individual consultation there is more opportunity to meet more frequently and to follow a single case closely over a longer period of time. The intimacy co-created in the group psyche is quite different from the one in individual consultation. In group supervision, complex family dynamics may come into play and there are certainly more psyches in the mix than in individual supervision. There is always the psychic mix of the consultant, of individual group members, of the whole group, of the patient, and of the sandplay itself. As an introvert, I have found that when a complex gets activated between a member and myself, it is easier to work through it in a one-to-one supervisory relationship than in the group. In such an occurrence, it may be helpful to have an individual meeting. From time to time, the group as a whole may need to discuss its own process to revitalize and tweak the format or emphasis. This is part of the group's maturation.

Confidentiality issues

In supervision groups we must not forget that the hallmark of Kalffian sandplay is the "free and protected space." The "protected" includes protection from exposure to the eyes of people other than the therapist. This means that therapists have to be very careful in sharing case material under any conditions. We weigh the benefit of the group's suggestions and understanding of the material as being helpful in the therapy against the breaking of strict confidentiality. This is the reason that we limit the number of persons in a supervision group. In the years that I led supervision groups, I limited the number in my group to four. The STA guidelines recommend up to six. We watch the comfort level in a group and new members are seldom added. The group is a cohesive unit that can represent an extended container or *temenos*.

The protection of identity is of prime concern. Of course the true name is never used. When I recognized I would be seeing a sandplayer for more than one or two sessions, I found it helpful to immediately assign a code name that I used for all my notes, photos, and labeling of relevant folders. There were often times when I forgot the true names of sandplayers because I was so used to thinking of them in the code names.

The question of amount and nature of identifying data to include is important. In some instances age and gender are sufficient. We have experimented with giving only age and gender and found that the presentation did not seem to be damaged. In fact, it allowed the viewers – the other members of the supervision group – to see the images in the tray at a less personal level. The images immediately became more archetypal in nature.

Such data as marital status, constellation of family, occupation or profession, and reason for referral may be important. The therapist, of course, has to make the decision as to what data are necessary in order for the therapist to feel satisfied about the presentation.

The effect on the ongoing therapy of sharing sandtrays with even this small number of persons is a question. Does it adversely affect the co-transference? Actually, neither Lauren nor I can recall an instance in which the presenter told us that the relationship was adversely affected. Presenters often report at the group meeting, following the meeting at which they presented a case, that at the next session with the sandplayer, the sandplayer had seemingly improved.

Of course, ongoing or "live" cases are presented in the supervision groups and this is the reason for such care with regard to confidentiality.

The "rules" for presenting a case to a larger group or for publication are well known, or should be. No "live" cases are presented outside a supervision group. The case has to have been closed for several years. For any presentation to a group outside a teaching group or for publication, therapists must obtain written permission from the sandplayer. STA has a form for obtaining such permission. It is considered good practice to let the sandplayers read and pass on any article about themselves before it is published.

Conclusion

We are grateful for the learning we have received from our students, who have brought their varied experiences to bear and have contributed to our development as group sandplay supervisors and consultants. In a sandplay supervision group we are continually reminded of the vastness of the psyche and the need for honoring the "free and protected space" just as we do for a single psyche.

Chapter 2

Memories of Kay Bradway's supervision group

Gretchen Hegeman

For most sandplayers the time arrives when a strong urge emerges to teach sandplay. We want to share with others what sandplay is all about. We are smitten. Something as powerful and fascinating as sandplay calls upon us to do this. But how do we become good teachers? How do we learn to communicate the complexities of sandplay – the theoretical, the numinous and the practical? How do we teach creating a "free and protected" space?

Sometimes the prompting comes from outside. We're asked to speak publicly about sandplay at a conference or to an agency. There might be an article to write for a professional journal. These possibilities require us to use our thinking and sensate functions to pull our ideas together coherently. Sandplayers' personality types notoriously tend toward intuition and feeling, so this can be a struggle. How do we learn to be good teachers? How do we find our way?

I'd like to share a personal experience with you that reflects how I found my way. Over many years, I was a member of one of Kay Bradway's supervision groups. The group met once a month for two hours at Kay's home in Sausalito, California. Kay and Kay's home were welcoming. I traveled from Seattle to San Francisco for the group meetings, and my traveling was always acknowledged. Kay's front door was usually ajar when we arrived, conveying the feeling that we were expected. The view from Kay's living room, looking onto San Francisco Bay and across to Tiburon, reminded me of the beauty and power of the natural world. It helped us all relax and enter into our work together.

We were a group of four plus Kay. Her two-hour format was simple. For the first hour we sat together at Kay's dining table and talked while having tea and something sweet. Sometimes one of us would bring something, and sometimes Kay surprised us with a fresh baked treat. I particularly remember mini-muffins that were just an inch in diameter. Kay often had a new book for us to look at or an article that she thought was helpful. Sometimes we learned of an interesting conference or talk on sandplay. Other times there was news from a sandplay colleague. On rare occasions an international sandplay visitor joined us.

We took turns "reporting in," sharing something about our work, updating the group on a case recently presented, or raising a question about a troublesome case or a symbol. This informal time was very important. I had the feeling that I was cared about by Kay and the group, and that Kay was thinking about us during the time that we weren't together.

During the last 15 minutes of the first hour, the presenter gave us introductory information about the case he or she was presenting. If the presenter had a specific concern or question, it was voiced at this time.

At the end of the first hour, we would leave our payment for the group on Kay's table. Our fee was Kay's hourly fee divided between the four of us. We then proceeded downstairs to a darkened room that was set up with a screen, slide projector and pointer. I loved that we went downstairs to look at "the work." Along the walls of the stairwell were photographs and art images of the ancient worlds. They felt like guides as we literally went down into the dark unconscious.

So much of sandplay's history is associated with Kay. When we entered the consultation room, we knew that Dora Kalff had been there as well as other founding members of ISST. Their wisdom and energy were available to us in this room.

We settled in and the presenter began. The time in this darkened room was always too short. And, it was always rich. An aspect that stood out to me was that Kay did not take over the case discussion. She did not impose her opinions on us. This was the presenter's time and material. Our learning came through discussion. A great sense of trust developed between us within this environment – it was a free and protected space. Over time, we presented more and more troublesome, scary material. We felt safe enough to share incidents that were shameful to us personally, especially situations in which we felt we had not done our best. It was so helpful to know that colleagues struggled with similar issues and that we could talk about these issues in a caring and supportive way.

I'm grateful that Kay's mentoring and supportive role in the group relieved me of the belief that I'd had that I needed to know all the answers. The attitude that there is no right or wrong answers held forth here and reinforced the principle that psyche finds its way when there is a safe container for it to do its work. We pondered and shared together, caught up in the richness of the work and the respect and wonder at the psyche and how it revealed itself.

Time was up. We went back upstairs into the light. We gathered up our things and headed out into the day, looking forward to the next time we would meet.

How did these experiences help me find my way? (1) The group was a constant in my life. We met every month for nine months. The summers were off. (2) The group membership remained the same so that we really learned to trust one another, accept feedback and give feedback in a respectful way. (3) The process of the meeting was consistent. (4) I felt welcomed and respected. (5) My ideas and professional contributions were acknowledged. (6) I learned that I didn't have to have all the answers. (7) I accepted Kay's mentorship.

Corbett (1995) writes: "I hope that the model of the mentor will stand in useful contrast to those attitudes found in some analytic institutes, which consciously or unconsciously promote a parental attitude to trainees which is either one of Apollonian remoteness or narcissistic parenting" (p. 60). He continues, quoting Burton (1979), "The mentor is a personality model 'that can stand in a special creative relationship to us – not as father, mother, friend or lover . . . but as peer and self-possibility'" (p. 62). Corbett also quotes Levinson (1978): "In his usage, a mentor is a teacher, advisor and sponsor, a host and guide to the world his or her protégée wishes to enter, an exemplar who provides counsel and moral support" (p. 63).

Certainly Kay Bradway has mentored more than one generation of sandplayers, blessing and believing in their dreams of self-possibility. Mentoring seems harmonious with sandplay and its major tenet, of providing a "free and protected space."

Reference

Corbett, L. (1995). Supervision and the mentoring archetype. In P. Kugler (Ed.), *Jungian perspectives on clinical supervision* (pp. 59–77). Einsiedeln, Switzerland: Daimon.

Chapter 3

Becoming a group sandplay supervisor: my personal odyssey

Harriet S. Friedman

As I reflect over my personal odyssey as a group supervisor and where it has taken me, I feel so grateful when I think of the clients we have considered together, and the meaningful and rich associations I have had with the gifted and creative therapists in my groups who have been part of my journey. Here is the story of how it all began and how it has evolved over the past 25 years.

As I attempt to recall the long-ago beginnings of these groups that have become an ongoing part of my professional life, and write down this personal memoir of how the whole enterprise of supervising sandplay groups was initially birthed, I am amazed at how my journey of becoming a sandplay supervisor has unfolded.

I had recently returned from working with Dora Kalff, in Zollikon, Switzerland, having experienced my own personal sandplay process, as well as having had the opportunity to participate in her ongoing sandplay study groups. This time of study with her had been a huge experience for me, and it was to have many life-altering consequences. One was the feeling of gratitude for all that I had received, both personally as well as professionally.

Little did I know that the task of integrating this legacy into my personal and professional life would continue to reverberate within me over the following decades and have a profound impact on determining how I wanted to proceed in my own professional work.

However, the current reality was that I was back home in Los Angeles, accompanied by a strong and growing desire to gather together with others to talk about sandplay cases. It was clear to me that I wanted to create more collegial dialogue about sandplay in my own professional world here at home. I was clearly committed to this technique, drawn to deepen my understanding about how this window into the psyche operated, and also eager to learn even more. I was hoping to create a place where I could share with colleagues our experiences, thoughts, and feelings about this therapeutic modality and understand more about what was to be discovered in the sand creations from this level of the psyche. I was curious to know what others were doing and thinking about their own sandplay experiences. I started by asking a few colleagues I knew who used the sand tray from time to time, but any plans to get together with them never materialized. It was clear that here at home in Los Angeles there was hardly anyone to talk to about this rich and evocative part of my clinical work that I personally found so enlivening.

I pondered this dilemma and then one day impulsively decided to put out a flier into the larger therapeutic community, announcing the beginning of a sandplay supervision group. I wondered if perhaps such a group might interest others and if it would possibly be a way to satisfy my own need. It only dimly crossed my mind that perhaps others might benefit from this experience as well.

I didn't have to wait long after the flier went out for a response. Quite soon I began to get inquiries from other clinicians, some licensed, some not. In the first group that gathered in my office, several of the members were primarily interested in Jung's work and looking for an opportunity to learn from a Jungian analyst. Others were hardly aware of my Jungian orientation, but were intrigued by this new sandplay technique. Some were already using the tray in their practices; others had only heard of sandplay and wanted to learn more, perhaps even include it in their therapeutic work.

The first gathering started out with seven people and included a spiritual director, a married couple who were both family therapists and worked together with couples using the tray, a group therapist, an artist, a school teacher who used cooking with young children (and also provided us with delicious and beautifully prepared snacks) and a priest/therapist.

We began by introducing ourselves and voicing our hopes and desires for what we wanted from the group. Right away, I felt at home and was relieved from the feeling of isolation, delighted to find myself with a group of colleagues with whom I could share my deep interest. It was only later that I came to realize that, essentially, this was sandplay/supervision . . . and I was the leader.

Beginning in those early years of the group (which later became two groups: one eventually got named the "first Friday group" and the other the "second Friday group"), my awareness grew that I was learning to supervise as issues and challenges of leading the groups began to present themselves. Eventually, it dawned on me that I was indeed developing the skills necessary for being a group leader and/or supervisor.

Yes, over the years, I did get the sandplay companions that I desired, and a whole lot more. I also have benefited greatly by learning the many skills that go along with being a supervisor: how best to help groups organize the time spent together, how to screen applicants and consider how potential members might fit together in the group, where personalities might clash, how to address confidentiality, how to deal with conflicts within the existing groups, how to identify and then deal with the issue of envy between group members, how to help members adjust to the sometime painfully exposing process of presenting cases. These are only a sampling of the issues that arise in the group supervision setting that I have learned to identify and address. Over these many years it has been an important learning opportunity from which I have greatly benefited.

Looking back at these supervision groups and comparing them to the ones in which I participated with Frau Kalff, I see how very different they are. Her groups were more formal and structured, with less discussion and more teaching coming directly from her. Essentially she presented her own cases, or those of her supervisees, showing us slides and for the most part teaching extensively from the picture on the slide. After her presentation and a brief discussion, the group would end. Sometimes afterwards, several of us would go to lunch at a typical Swiss café near Lake Zürich, and there we would spontaneously discuss what we had seen and learned together and share our own cases. In the formal morning sessions there had been very little opportunity to dialogue or question Frau Kalff about what was going on in her client's trays.

Current group sessions

Nowadays, the current sessions generally begin with a quick "check in" as we all sit together in my main consulting room when each participant brings us up to date as to what is going on in his or her life. When my turn comes, I often bring attention to an upcoming sandplay workshop or some news about what's happening in the national organization, Sandplay Therapists of America. I might mention a particular article in our *Sandplay Therapists of America Journal* that might have relevance to some group members' interest. When visitors from the International Society of Sandplay Therapists are in Los Angeles, we also take the opportunity to include them as participants.

Following our beginning "check-in" ritual, the previous month's presenter updates us on his or her client whose trays we studied together. Often, it is at this point that subsequent thoughts and reactions to the past presentation emerge and are considered and discussed. This "after-thought" component, we discovered, gives the past month's presenter the time and distance to continue reflecting on the issues relevant to the case in an ongoing way. With the schedule of presenters having been decided upon earlier, it is now the moment for the current presenter to display one or two trays (sometimes a series of trays) created by his or her client. The presenter may choose to share the trays with us in a variety of ways. Some presenters use slides, others who have mastered PowerPoint use that method, others bring photographs of the tray, some recreate their client's tray with their own miniatures and set them in the sand tray in my sandplay room, as they were originally created.

The presenter may choose to offer clinical background at this time, or reserve that information until the viewing of the sand creation has taken its effect.

When the presenter chooses to recreate a client tray, we all proceed into my sandtray room, adjacent to my office. It contains two sand trays and has miniatures lining three walls. There is room enough here for all to stand or sit on stools or on the floor around the tray with the unseen client's sand creation. In this contained space, we first let the tray speak to each of us in silence, and then begin to verbally respond to the tray. How alive that tray becomes for the group! This process invites so many ideas, questions, reactions, associations, and feelings. Very quickly, peer supervision has begun. As the group leader, I see my task as providing the free and protected space so vital in helping group members find their own individual voices. These voices begin emerging here as we all join together in this endeavor. At the end of what is usually a lively and creative discussion, I generally summarize, and then for the last few moments we return to the larger consulting room for any final thoughts about the case.

The fruits of our work together expands

Over the many years of being together and presenting our cases to each other, the fruits of our sandplay group began overflowing into the larger community. For example, after a public workshop we gave, we decided to publish each of our presentations in a book on sandplay. To make this possible, Betsy Caprio, one of our fearless members, took on the job of editing for us. We were able to support this project financially from the funds raised from this previous public presentation. In 1997, with additional funds contributed by the Los Angeles C.G. Jung Library and Bookstore, the book was published as *Sandplay: Coming of Age*. It was published by the members of the founding group of the Los Angeles Sandplay Association in association with the C.G. Jung Bookstore. The contributors included Gloria Avrech, Joyce Burt, Betsy Caprio, Faye Campbell, Thomas M. Hedberg, Rie Rogers Mitchell, Ozma Mantele, Amy Padnick, and Sachiko Taki Reece.[1]

In subsequent years other public presentations and workshops followed. A group member in the second Friday group suggested that we give a presentation, entitled "A Picture Worth a Thousand Words: Sandplay – a Nonverbal Approach", for a conference sponsored by the California Association of Marriage and Family Therapists. All the group members were enthusiastic about this idea, and we spent a great deal of our time that year preparing for the conference. We each wrote a paper, read and gave feedback to each other in the group, and prepared for the public presentation. We all learned a lot from this experience and became more polished and comfortable public speakers, with the added benefit of pride and a sense of accomplishment. This event proved to be a growing as well as an initiation experience, as most of the members were presenters for the first time. We were also very proud of having brought sandplay into a larger clinical community and enjoyed the audience's enthusiastic response. The presenters included Patricia Absey, Cynthia Belzer, Terry Dabrowski, Carol Fahy, Debbie Mego, Audrey Sagerman, and Rae Thrasher.

Because this presentation was also videotaped, we had the additional experience and pleasure (and sometimes agony) of learning by watching ourselves.

Benefits of group supervision

Through these many years of discussions with these groups, I have had some of the most enlivening, challenging, playful, and profound experiences of my professional career. I always find myself looking forward to the next session and the surprising insights that come out of these group discussions.

Clearly, these discussions open the door to the psyche to let in all kinds of ideas, experiences, and archetypal energies. I have come to realize that what enlivens the group process and makes this possible is an atmosphere that encourages engagement with our own clinical material, free from judgment about right or wrong, and with a sense of curiosity about what is being presented in the trays. This sort of environment also allows for an opening into the unconscious and an opportunity to observe how it comes alive in the sand creations.

The group has the potential of bringing together a wide variety of perspectives and emotional responses to bear on what is being presented, each perspective opening up different and important insights into what may be present in the unfolding sandplay process.

I believe that it is my fundamental job as the group leader to cultivate the mutually supportive and open-ended environment where we can all experiment with ideas, explore possible approaches, and become more conscious of what we already know, as well as learning how to "imagine into" what is yet unknown.

The shadow side of group supervision

Group supervision, with all its benefits, also has a shadow side. The experience of presenting can be a painful, exposing one that triggers very vulnerable feelings. When I asked one group for feedback about the experience of presenting in our sandplay group, as compared to other kinds of supervision they'd had, I was quite moved by the comments:

"There is even more exposure here in this group as I show my client's trays, as opposed to just telling my client's ongoing case history in one-to-one supervision; I feel much more 'out there' showing the trays."

"It feels as though I'm exposing my most vulnerable self to you all as I show my own client's trays."

"I feel as though everyone will see what is so obvious in the tray that I haven't seen myself."

"It's such a humbling experience for me and I worry that all your eyes will see what I hadn't seen myself, but it's also worth it in the long run as I'm grateful to be able to look at the tray from so many different ways, so many different perspectives."

"Besides all the other things that you can see about me, I am also exposing my countertransference as I tell you all about the tray and I feel everyone will know more about me than I really want you all to know."

Two comments voiced about group experience as contrasted to individual supervision were: (1) "One on one supervision is harder because there is only one person in the know, here in the group there is a variety of perspectives from which I can see things and I feel freer to choose what fits for me." (2) "I like the group setting better because of the inequality I feel in the one-on-one setting."

These are all brave souls willing to show their vulnerabilities in this way, session after session. I have great admiration for them and their courage to expose themselves as they respond to other group members while presenting their own cases.

My awareness of all these feelings that get evoked elicits a protective and respectful feeling within me for the group members as they both present and give feedback in the group. The actual performance in the group may appear to be going well, with members contributing and responding according to pre-arranged group norms, however when I solicit feedback about how the presentation, just given, has been experienced, I am often reminded of another scenario . . . of the unseen vulnerability.

As the group process proceeds, it is also important for me to be aware of possible divisions in the group and to respond, when necessary, to a group member without being rejecting or punishing, particularly when one group member may possibly be confronting another member. My continuing awareness of other potentially problematic behaviors includes "radar" for periods of frustration, when there has been insufficient time for in-depth exploration of all the client material; rivalry and competitiveness within the group; my *not* relying on one supervisee more than others for necessary interventions; and *not* using the group members to confront other members when it's my job. I keep in mind that if I'm not aware of these dynamics, I could remain ostensibly benevolent and uncritical when interventions are necessary. As the group leader it is my responsibility to contain the tension and mediate disruptions when they occur. I am aware that denial or avoidance on my part of these kinds of situations may leave group members feeling unsafe and unprotected.

What I've learned

I have also have learned much about myself within these group dynamics, and I continue to learn how to meet new challenges. An example of how my own lack of consciousness can make itself known is when a group member forgets that I have asked all presenters to use pseudonyms for his or her client. I personally have strong feelings about maintaining confidentiality and not using the client's names or revealing any personal information that may identify them. This issue of confidentiality is one of my own pet peeves. I have gotten feedback from group members that when I respond to a group member who uses a client's actual name, I tend to have a sharp tone in my voice that can feel painful to the presenter.

In the work on editing this book, I have become aware that many supervisors are almost never trained and tend to be chosen without having demonstrated any ability to supervise. Historically, formal guidelines for supervision have not been available. Similar to many other supervisors, I have also learned on the job.

Supervising in a group context seems to suit my more extraverted side, even though, over the years, I have realized that supervision in a group setting is more complicated in many ways than individual supervision where the complexity of all these dynamics is not present.

Now so many years later, my commitment to this group supervision has only grown, and it is my favorite way of "teaching" sandplay. It remains a special part of my ongoing professional week's activities, for it challenges me and keeps me thinking about the many issues that are discussed in these sessions. I always find myself looking forward to what the next month's discussions will bring.

I am aware now that I love supervising sandplay in a group, and I feel a deep sense of gratitude for the special privilege of helping therapists realize their own unique therapeutic gifts. It also gives me a great deal of satisfaction to know that the faceless, anonymous clients we have discussed are being benefited by this non-verbal approach that facilitates the natural healing process – this amazing modality of sandplay!

Note

1 This book can be ordered from the C.G. Jung Bookstore, 10349 W. Pico Blvd., Los Angeles, CA 90064, U.S.A. Telephone number: (310) 556-1196.

Further reading

Clarkson, P. (Ed.) (1998). *Supervision, psychoanalytic and Jungian perspectives.* London: Whurr Publishers Ltd.
Hawkins, P., & Shohet, R. (2000). *Supervision in the helping professions.* New York: Open University Press, McGraw-Hill Education.

Kugler, P. (Ed.) (1995). *Jungian perspectives on clinical supervision*. Einsiedeln, Switzerland: Daimon

Wiener, J., Mizen, R., & Duckham, J. (2003). *Supervising and being supervised: A practice in search of a theory*. New York: Palgrave Macmillan.

Part II

Designing contemporary supervision models

Chapter 4

The complex responsibilities of the sandplay supervisor

Patricia Dunn-Fierstein

Good supervision of sandplay therapists is a complex matter. Because supervisors are presented with countless intriguing sandplay scenes to explore, they run the risk of intellectualization and premature interpretation. In addition, the alluring sandplay pictures can lull supervisors into focusing primarily on the symbolic image, to the detriment of other aspects of supervisees' development as fully functioning therapists.

The ingredients of sandplay supervision must be in synch with the ingredients necessary for a good sandplay process. Just as clients are held safely in the alchemical vessel, supervisees must be contained in their supervision and supervisors must create a safe *temenos* for their growth as a container for others. This involves modeling how to hold a symbolic process by helping therapists develop their own spacious intuitive stance so that the deeper meaning in the trays can unfold in a way that actually mirrors the process itself. The supervisory process also involves exploring the internal process of the therapists, and all parts of the therapist–client relationships. This aspect demands more from supervisors, who must consider factors other than those observed superficially in the rich images that are presented. Sandplay supervision requires an integration of many facets of therapeutic knowledge. With a greater understanding of these facets, the consultation room may be entered with the kind of humility, openness, and preparation that ultimately enhance the growth of the supervisees, and foster healing for the client.

A snapshot of a seasoned sandplay therapist

It does not seem prudent to discuss what is unique about the tasks of the sandplay supervisor without briefly considering the goals of sandplay supervision. Goals can often best be identified by studying successful professionals in their field of expertise, such as seasoned sandplay therapists. What do seasoned sandplay therapists "look like"? That is, what skills and knowledge do they have? What capacities are integrated or developing? What character traits are beneficial? What behaviors are critical?

The seasoned sandplay therapist, first and perhaps foremost, has completed a deep sandplay process so that his or her clients' journey is personally known, in its most essential form, from the inside out. Bradway and McCoard (1997) refer to the necessity of being empathically connected to the client by "feeling into" (p. 29) his or her experience. The supervisee's ability to perform this primary function will be affected by the depth of his or her own sandplay process.

The experienced sandplay therapist possesses keen self-awareness with access to his or her emotions, intuitions, bodily sensations, and thoughts. He or she is aware of personal complexes, prejudices, and limitations of other kinds. The seasoned sandplay therapist has a sharp ability to observe others and the environment. These kinds of perceptual capacities enhance the therapist's ability to observe both subjective and objective levels of experience, which makes him or her a more useable container in the transference field.

A seasoned sandplay therapist recognizes the critical element of containment to the process as a whole. He or she can "assimilate the feeling and atmosphere of the process, as well as the individual pictures . . . The therapist participates empathically in the act of creation, thus establishing a profound and wordless rapport" (Weinrib, 2004, pp. 32, 33). This rapport is critical to the creation of the alchemical vessel that is necessary for healing to occur. There is a larger understanding of the significance of the office space, the sand tray and miniatures, and the use of self to the creation of this vessel for the client's development.

Finally, an experienced sandplay therapist has knowledge of relevant theories and the sandplay process as a whole. That awareness is used to hold the "big picture" of the client's process. As the client senses that the therapist accurately perceives his or her being, defenses are lifted and self-trust is gained to enter the more harrowing or shame-filled corners of the psyche. Healing does not occur without this trust.

Although this is not a complete profile of the abilities and characteristics of a seasoned sandplay therapist, it does provide an overview of what the sandplay supervisor is trying to accomplish when the job of supervision is assumed. To summarize, the seasoned sandplay therapist has achieved the following:

1   A personal experience of a deep sandplay process (knowledge from the inside-out).
2   Skill at observing self and others.
3   An integrated capacity to contain.
4   An integrated knowledge of critical theories (knowledge from the outside-in).

Sandplay supervision may be a daunting task at times; supervisors should be aware of the complexities, but not overwhelmed by them. Above all, they should remember the comparative admonishment of Winnicott (1992). Supervisors may strive to help supervisees achieve as much as possible, but being "good enough" (p. 214) psychotherapists is quite sufficient – and may help supervisors sleep better at night.

The slippery slopes of supervising the symbolic process

Supervision in sandplay therapy is typically focused on understanding the images created and what they might be communicating about the client. Much of case consultation is spent examining photographs or slides of miniature worlds, and, like an archeologist piecing together an artifact, attempting to put these pictures together with snippets of story from the client's life to create meaning in relation to his or her development. The more skilled the supervisor is at assessing the pictures, the easier it is to fall into the traps of intellectualization and premature interpretation. We have all taken a spill on these slippery slopes at times. Consider Dora Kalff's warning in a presentation given at Harvard University in 1988 (Johnson, 1990):

> Again, however, I emphasize that the client's work is an inner, uncon-scious process *not to be disturbed or even influenced by the therapist's speculations* [italics mine] . . . Therefore it is vital not to disturb nascent images, because one never knows to what uses they may be put or what meanings they may be required to carry.
>
> (p. 105)

Ideally, the sandplay supervisor helps the therapist understand the client without making the kinds of speculations that could disturb the client's process. This spacious position can be achieved if the importance of the symbolic process is recognized. Jung (1971) states this significance clearly:

> The symbol is always a product of an extremely complex nature, since data from every psychic function have gone into its making. It is, therefore, neither *rational* nor *irrational* . . . The profundity and preg-nant significance of the symbol appeal just as strongly to *thinking* as to *feeling*, while its peculiar plastic imagery, when shaped into sensuous form, stimulates *sensation* as much as *intuition*.
>
> (p. 478)

Operating from the premise that the symbol is a significant healing agent demands that we impart to supervisees the proper attitude to hold toward the symbol. Jung (1971) states, "whether a thing is a symbol or not depends chiefly on the *attitude* of the observing consciousness" (p. 475), which Jung refers to simply as the "*symbolic attitude*" (p. 476). It is of utmost importance that the supervisor's attitude supports the life of the symbol; according to Jung "the symbol is alive only so long as it is pregnant with meaning" (p. 474). Conveying theoretical premises such as these to the supervisee helps him or her achieve the fourth goal outlined earlier: possessing knowledge of critical theories.

An approach I have found that enhances the life of the symbol is to enter a field of play with the images by initially exploring the scenes with the three functions of sensation, feeling, and intuition. This play of functions mirrors the sandplay process itself and helps us engage in case consultation with the necessary respect. After this play is done, the thinking function can be brought in with greater assurance that it will not run roughshod over the process in a manner that could diminish its vitality. It is, in fact, a common mistake that students learning about sandplay will first approach the images with their thinking function. I remember myself as a beginner at workshops, eagerly attempting to understand this enigmatic process – deliberating over each picture and being aware of a sense of competition among the participants to produce the most cogent response. By the end of the presentation most of us had headaches. In our attempts to comprehend, we squeezed the very life out of the healing we were witnessing.

Now I prefer to offer a structure for supervisees to approach the image so that they will be discouraged from their natural inclination – to *think about it!* In this activity the supervisor encourages the supervisee to exercise the skills needed to achieve the second goal of the sandplay therapist: that of being skilled at observing self and others. Casement (1991) supports this idea of play in the supervisory experience and states that "it is through this that the therapist can share in the patient's creativity. It is also here that he can discover a balance between what he knows of the nature of the unconscious and the pitfalls of premature assumption" (p. 35).

As we supervise, the questions are more important than the answers because these will be the invitation to enter the fearless play of imagination that is necessary to keep the symbols alive. I like to invite supervisees to attune to the feeling tone of the image first.

Questions such as these may be helpful:

- What emotions come up in you when you look at this scene – or a part of a scene?
- What do you think the client was feeling when it was created?

Next I ask therapists to consider their bodily response:

- How does your body respond to this scene?
- What sensations do you experience viscerally?

The responses may tell us something about the trauma and emotions stored in the client's physiology if they have not been processed. These additional statements and questions may help supervisees explore further in the area of the senses:

- Let yourself take in the big picture as a sensory experience. Imagine physically feeling the sand. Imagine being in the tray. What is this like?
- Do your senses become aware of anything that seems significant, such as texture, temperature, moisture or lack of it, color, shapes, use of space, repetitions?

After exploring the image with the feeling and sensation functions, supervisees can enter the play with intuition. The supervisor might suggest:

- Allow the unconscious to speak to you. What intuitive flashes come forth?
- Be open to the fact that these flashes may come in the form of memories, images, physical experiences, thoughts, or feelings.

From this sequence of questioning, it is natural to move into exploration with the thinking function; in this fourth position, it is far less likely to dominate or harm the life of the client's process.

This technique can be especially useful in group consultation in which the presenter displays the images, initially sharing little or no information about the client. The rest of the group participates in the reflections noted above. This method, in itself, can be quite helpful to the presenting therapist. After fully exploring the images through the functions of feeling, sensation, and intuition, more information may be revealed about the client, such as age, sex, presenting problem, and what may have been said. Then additional feelings and thoughts may be elicited about the scenes and the case as a whole.

I have observed that some remarkable things happen when the process is done in this way. There is less pressure to perform and less of a sense of competition because everyone has entered the field of play. Respect and empathy flourish because the supervisees have had a chance to "feel *into*" (Bradway & McCoard, 1997, p. 29) the images and therefore into the client's situation or frame of mind as well. Of most benefit: when the supervisees then begin to explore the process with their thinking function, it is filtered through the lenses of the other three functions so that it is much less likely to destroy the symbolic process. In fact I have found that when this technique is used, even very novice sandplay therapists produce remarkable insights about the scenes being studied. I have also witnessed the opposite happen. When we clamor through the exploration of images with an overbearing thinking function, even very seasoned sandplay therapists (myself included) tend to display a lack of empathy and insight, and generally murder the symbolic process along the way.

A word of caution regarding these exercises: emphasize the importance of spaciousness in observations and awarenesses that may come forth. Supervisees must be reminded that they bring their own projections into the client's field, and there is always a danger of contamination. This process must be done with the attitude of a brainstorming in which no idea is condemned or grasped tenaciously. Ultimately, what the client has to say about his or her own image holds the greatest insight for the process.

One of the reasons supervision is so challenging in the field of sandplay therapy is that there is a great deal to attend to and so much information to be transmitted. In regard to the symbolic process, there are not only images to comprehend but metaphorical language to consider. The language of metaphor becomes more complex when the client population is younger, more mentally disabled, or when there are language differences.

I remember one of the first times I experienced the importance of this; I was 23 and working as a psychiatric technician at a remarkable psychiatric hospital, Chestnut Lodge. An adult female (I'll call her Julie), diagnosed with schizophrenia, was expecting a visit from her parents later in the evening; they were from out of town. In the morning she began to act out in many ways – demanding attention, screaming, crying, and generally behaving in a much more regressed state than usual. I tried to help her reflect on what was happening, to no avail. Finally, after significant time had passed, and she seemed to be decompensating, I spoke firmly to her: "Julie, if you keep this up, you're going to ruin your family visit later today! You need to pull yourself together and stop this!" She got quite angry with me and stormed off to her room. At lunchtime I walked her and another patient to the cafeteria. Julie complained to this patient: "Do you know that Patricia woke me up this morning? I was in a very comfortable sleep and she woke me up!" I did not understand what she was talking about and initially responded to her, "I didn't wake you up, Julie. You were awake when I got on the unit this morning." She grew more emphatic, "Yes you did! You woke me up out of a dead sleep!" Suddenly it hit me. In my limit-setting with her, I had awakened her from her regressed state and "dead sleep" frame of mind. Once I understood her meaning, I was able to respond in a way that was helpful: "I'm sorry I had to wake you up Julie. I didn't mean to upset you." With that response and further conversation that remained at the metaphorical level, I was able to empathically enter her world, which enabled her to feel mirrored, contained, and less anxious so that she could have a successful visit with her family.

Teaching the importance of the language of metaphor is no small task yet it is critical to the third goal of the sandplay therapist: possessing an integrated capacity to contain. When the therapist shows the client he or she understands the unconscious communication, the client feels held empathically in a safe *temenos*. This understanding can be conveyed to the supervisee in much the same way that the pictures are reflected upon. The most important point seems to be to encourage therapists to keep the language alive in the same way the image is kept alive. They need to learn to "listen with the third ear" (Reik, 1948, p. 144) for the communication that is beyond the story and the words they actually hear – for the myths and metaphors that are being divulged, ever so cautiously. The primary concept to convey is the importance of understanding that much more is shared than initially realized, and that the same respectful, empathic, and open approach must be brought to the language as it is to the image. In this way the therapist learns the importance of the use of self for containment.

Supervising the dynamics in the therapeutic process

Sandplay images contain a compelling quality, so it is a common oversight to focus exclusively on the pictures to the potential neglect of other dynamics that are present in the therapeutic process. In addition to understanding the sandplay process itself, attention must be given to what is occurring in the sessions before and after trays are made, and on the sessions when no trays are created. The supervisor needs to convey the importance of attuning to what is going on within the therapist as well as in the field between the therapist and the client. Supervisors must be aware that these dynamics may even get played out in a parallel process in the supervisory relationship. It takes time and a consistent relationship for a supervisee to gain the kind of insight that will help him or her to become a seasoned sandplay therapist.

Hawkins and Shohet (2000) have developed a model for supervising psychotherapists that has come to be called the "seven-eyed model of supervision." This model offers a useful framework to bring to bear when considering supervision of the therapeutic process beyond the content in the trays. It is not the scope of this piece to outline the entire model. Briefly, the seven modes of supervision include the content, the strategies and interventions, the therapy relationship, the therapist's own process, the supervisory relationship, the supervisor's own process, and the wider context (e.g., governing organizations, agencies, and employers). As the authors point out, "good supervision must inevitably involve movement between modes" (p. 71). By exploring these modes individually, supervisors can gain a better understanding of their preferred supervisory style and areas they might be "avoiding out of habit or lack of familiarity and practice" (p. 71). It is just this avoidance that has limited the effectiveness of sandplay consultation. For the purposes of this piece, I focus on the first four modes of supervision.

Mode one: content of the therapy session

In the first mode the focus is on the content of the therapy session. It is my premise that content often becomes the primary focus in sandplay supervision because the images are so alluring. A great deal of time is spent encouraging supervisees to witness the sandplay process, but there is more to contend with in the therapy session than these images. In this mode of consultation, the supervisor needs to hear about the client's appearance, what was said, what emotions came up, whether a tray was created or not and how it was approached, the aspects of his/her life that were focused on, and how all of these factors relate to prior sessions. This mode encourages the development of the supervisee's observational skills, as stated in the second goal of the sandplay therapist.

This is where supervisees are taught how to *be* with the process, which is much more difficult than it seems. During the sandplay process therapists are taught the role of the silent witness – respectfully "holding" the client as the tray is being created. The concept of the witness must go beyond the trays, however. Shainberg (1985) states that true understanding comes from being able to "observe and describe what is going on in the present in accurate, concrete, and complete detail. This witnessing is different from wanting to change or get rid of or compare or assume a fixed meaning about what is happening" (p. 164).

Emphasizing the importance of close observation will focus the supervisee on a primary need of the client – to be seen. Shainberg points out that although the experience of the other will never be completely known, "it is in the mutual participation of discovering the essential quality of the patient that the healing takes place" (p. 164). In part, supervisees must learn how to "sit with" the anxiety of not "knowing," which means that the supervisor must be familiar and comfortable with this nebulous space first. Without this basic level of comfort, there is an increased risk of premature interpretation and incorrect assumptions about the client.

Supervisors must expect therapists to be eager to understand their clients; in addition, they must be careful not to heighten the supervisees' anxiety with their own. As Hawkins and Shohet (2000) point out, supervisors' anxiety often comes from a "need to be potent and have answers for their therapists" (p. 72). This need is especially true in a symbolic process such as sandplay, where therapists look to their supervisors for meaning. The supervisory role demands the ability to sit with the unknown observed elements of the sessions. It is the task of supervisors to contain their supervisees as they experience their fears and conflicts, so that they will have the security of the "free and sheltered" space to support them as they enter the painful places within themselves and with their clients, and ultimately begin to know and trust themselves as therapists.

Mode two: interventions and strategies

The supervisor can also help the therapist develop self-trust as he or she moves into the second mode of supervision, in which therapeutic interventions are explored. Here the supervisor wants to know how the therapist

responded to a client, what limits were set, and what suggestions or decisions were made. In sandplay supervision, this phase includes exploration of
a wide array of issues specifically related to sandplay therapy. The supervisee must consider a variety of options available, such as when and how to
introduce sandplay, whether to encourage the use of the sand, when and
how to help if it is needed (e.g., finding a miniature, constructing something
difficult), how to handle the interest and intrusions of caregivers who may
be present or nearby, and much more. In this mode of work supervisees
exercise the skills needed to achieve the second and third goals of the
sandplay therapist: They will be working on observation of the client as well
as containment strategies.

The danger for the supervisor here is that he or she will impinge on the
supervisee's natural development as a therapist by intervening too narrowly
or too quickly. According to Casement (1991), such impingement "can
mislead students into learning by a false process, borrowing too directly
from a supervisor's way of working rather than developing their own"
(p. 25). In the end, the therapist may feel that the therapy has been appro-
priated by the supervisor.

Although there are some critical precepts in sandplay therapy, the
primary job of the supervisor focused on the intervention mode is to help
the supervisee increase "choices and skills in intervention" (Hawkins &
Shohet, 2000, p. 70). This step can be accomplished by brainstorming a
variety of reasonable options and considering the potential outcome of each
one. The supervisor needs to encourage the therapist to attune to the
relationship with the client in order to decide which option to implement. In
this way the therapist is helped to acquire his or her "own capacity for
spontaneous reflection within the session" so that the "internal supervisor
can begin to operate" (Casement, 1991, p. 32).

Modes three and four: the therapy relationship and the therapist's process

According to Hawkins and Shohet (2000), in mode three "the supervisor
focuses on the conscious and unconscious interaction between therapist and
client" (p. 75), and in mode four the focus is on "the internal processes of
the therapist and how these are affecting the therapy that is being explored"
(p. 78). I do not believe that these can be entirely separated in the field
of sandplay supervision because we view ourselves as working in a field of
mutuality in which the client and therapist are both impacted by the
relationship. In addition, it is through the therapist's internal process that
much is learned about the therapeutic relationship and what is needed
for healing.

The sandplay supervisor has a challenging job in these areas, and yet this
is where the work can get quite interesting as he or she listens and looks for

the subtle ways in which the client's unconscious informs the therapist, as well as how the therapist responds. This phase demands that the supervisor achieve a deep level of internal attunement to the metaphors, images, intuitions, and feelings that come from within as the case is being presented. Attention must be given to the therapist's approach. Is he or she racing through the case? Is there anxiety, hesitation, over-intellectualization, affectation, or countertransference displayed? These behaviors may speak to the supervisee's relationship with the client. By helping the therapist gain self-awareness as well as attunement to his or her client, the supervisor encourages progress toward goal two stated earlier: gaining skill at observing self and others.

The transference–countertransference relationship, which Bradway refers to as "co-transference" (Bradway & McCoard, 1997, p. 8), is always present. Navigating the mercurial quality of the therapeutic alliance is a formidable task for new therapists. They are often unprepared for the emotional vicissitudes that they must weather with their clients. It is the job of the supervisor to prepare supervisees for variations in the feeling tone of the sessions, which can range from hope to hopelessness, love to hate, equanimity to frustration, and so on. When supervisees see "progress" being made, they feel more confident in their ability to help, but few new therapists grasp the critical feature of any process: "they do not see the being together as a centrally important fact of the treatment," but this is "when patients learn they can be with another person and be respected for who they are, as is" (Shainberg, 1985, pp. 171, 172). Teaching the supervisee this crucial tenet, as well as how to ride the waves of the co-transference, are essential tasks of the sandplay supervisor and necessary to the fulfillment of the third goal of the sandplay therapist: an integrated capacity to contain.

These tasks are facilitated as the supervisee develops attunement to the internal process. The sandplay supervisor can help in this regard by encouraging the "therapist to explore all forms of countertransference in order to have greater space to *respond to* rather than *react to* the patient" (Hawkins & Shohet, 2000, p. 78). I once supervised a sandplay therapist who presented images and case material of an adult woman that clearly pointed to some significant early trauma. The supervisee had avoided asking much about the client's childhood and assumed it was uneventful. It was apparent to me that the client was repeatedly displaying material in the trays that she would eventually need her therapist to help her digest. As I explored these issues with my supervisee, she said that she did not see any trauma in the scenes, but admitted to being afraid of her client's affect. She resisted delving into her past for fear of dredging up more than either one of them could handle, but she did not understand why. Further exploration revealed the countertransference and the ways in which her client was triggering her own issues. As this therapist repressed her own material, she colluded in repressing her client's. It was fortunate that this supervisee had a therapist of her own to whom to take this significant issue. As she worked on this area in herself, she was able to meet her client where she needed to be met and to listen as her client spoke about some of the deep wounds of her past that needed to be voiced and heard.

It is not uncommon for supervisees to feel apprehensive about this aspect of the supervision. Attending to the complexes that arise within themselves often provokes anxiety. The supervisor needs to aid the therapist in this process so that he or she can be "available enough to be affected by the patient but not in an abusive, impinging way" (Solomon, 1997, p. 131). The supervisor must be able to recognize if the supervisee is so triggered emotionally by a client's process that the supervision is moving perilously close to therapy. At these times it is appropriate to require that the supervisee consult with a therapist to work through unresolved personal issues that interfere with the ability to relate to his or her clients. Through the exploration of his or her complexes, the supervisee makes progress in the area of the second goal of the sandplay therapist and gains greater self-awareness.

Conclusion

It is critical for the supervisor of sandplay therapists to remember that sandplay supervision has a myriad of nuances, all of which must be attended to at some point in the supervision process. Because this kind of depth study requires significant time and trust, it is of great value for a supervisee to receive supervision from one supervisor over an extended period. The supervisor must be able to hold the therapist in a *temenos* of compassionate inquiry so that the therapist feels safe to express ambiguity as he or she struggles to comprehend what is truly incomprehensible. The supervisee will bring the supervisor enticing scenes and stories, which will be used to gain awareness of the symbolic process of the client. It is critical that the consultant attend to all aspects of the therapy and therapeutic relationship, either reflected in the sandplay scenes or beyond what is identified in the trays.

Conclusions that are drawn from a deep inquiry, such as the ones outlined above, are of tremendous value. It is a "form of art which skillfully combines a totality of approaches in a balanced manner" (Kalff, 1993, p. 19). Estelle Weinrib (2004) speaks to this totality when she notes that "a concrete representation of a visual image carries an immediacy of shared experience between patient and therapist that words may dilute" (p. 89). The supervisor must allow the words to enter the images slowly. A fertile field must be created for symbolic understanding to mature and for all aspects of the therapeutic relationship to be explored. In this way, the environment will nurture the supervisees as they develop into therapists who have the necessary understanding and respect for the healing that is possible in sandplay therapy.

References

Bradway, K., & McCoard, B. (1997). *Sandplay: Silent workshop of the psyche.* London: Routledge.

Casement, P.J. (1991). *Learning from the patient.* New York: Guilford Press.

Hawkins, P., & Shohet, R. (2000). *Supervision in the helping professions.* Buckingham: Open University Press.

Johnson, F.C. (1990). In memoriam: Dora Kalff (1904–1990), *Quadrant, XXIII(1),* 103–113.

Jung, C.G. (1971). *Psychological types: Vol. 6. The collected works of C.G. Jung.* Princeton, NJ: Princeton University Press.

Kalff, M. (1993). Twenty points to be considered in the interpretation of a sandplay, *Journal of Sandplay Therapy, II(2),* 17–35.

Reik, T. (1948). *Listening with the third ear.* New York: Farrar, Straus.

Shainberg, D. (1985). Teaching therapists how to be with their clients. In J. Welwood (Ed.), *Awakening the heart* (pp. 163–175). Boston, MA: Shambala.

Solomon, H.M. (1997). The developmental school. In P. Young-Eisendrath & T. Dawson (Eds.), *The Cambridge companion to Jung* (pp. 119–140). Cambridge: Cambridge University Press.

Weinrib, E.L. (2004). *The sandplay therapy process: Images of the self.* Cloverdale, CA: Temenos Press.

Winnicott, D.W. (1992). *Through paediatrics to psycho-analysis: Collected papers.* London: Brunner-Routledge.

Chapter 5

A collaborative model of clinical supervision in sandplay therapy

Mariellen Griffith

Clinical supervisors in sandplay therapy are dedicated professionals who have obtained the educational experiences required to become certified supervisors of sandplay therapy and have had extensive personal and professional experience in sandplay. As supervisors they serve as mentors who are able to support and nurture their supervisees' strengths and resources, and provide a free and protected learning environment in sandplay training. Primarily these supervisors work from a Jungian (1954) and Kalffian (1980) orientation, yet are able to use a variety of theoretical approaches in their own practices.

The collaborative model of clinical supervision

The model of clinical supervision that is most appealing to me is a collaborative one. Fordham (1978) suggests that having a model is important in integrating a client's material, and it must be one that relates to the supervisor's own personal experience either in life, personal training, analysis, or in experience with clients. In short, the model needs to become personal and owned by the supervisor.

From my experiences as a professor and supervisor of students working on a master's degree in counseling and marriage and family therapy, a collaborative model is different from the familiar hierarchical and dualistic teacher–student relationships and learning processes the supervisees may have experienced. Anderson (1998) suggests that in this collaborative model there is a sharing of knowledge that is both personal and collective. This sharing involves trusting the supervisee and the collaborative learning process. Bordin (1983) refers to this collaboration between the supervisor and supervisee as a working alliance. This supervisory-related working alliance is based on mutual agreement on the goals and tasks of supervision and a strong bond of caring, trust, and respect.

Another perspective of the collaboration process, from the Jungian and sandplay literature, is one of a mythic or archetypal journey by the hero/ heroine, who meets a wise person or guide who shares wisdom and knowledge. Corbett (1955) suggests that tasks of the mythic journey are carried out during the supervision process and goals are met at the end of supervision. Not only do supervisees experience a supervision–supervisee journey, but they are also witnesses to the personal journey of their clients in sandplay.

There are five principles in my collaborative model:

1   Connect with the supervisee and work together in a free and protected space.
2   Value each supervisee's perspective.
3   Convey to supervisees that they are responsibile for their learning.
4   Hold the view that relationships and processes spontaneously emerge out of the experience itself rather than through lecturing.
5   Develop an ongoing, evaluative process during each session of supervision.

Connect to the supervisee and work together in a free and protected space

As in sandplay therapy, the therapist and the supervisor first need to create a free and protected space, as suggested by Dora Kalff (1980). In this space the supervisee feels completely free, accepted, and protected by the supervisor, who must recognize the challenges and resources of the supervisee. That first connection with the supervisee needs to be friendly, open, and trusting. Often supervisees, from prior supervisory experiences in graduate school, feel intimidated, dependent, or anxious about the supervisory process. A discussion of past supervisory experiences and an explanation of the collaboration supervisory model will help the supervisee feel less anxious and become a co-creator of the collaborative experience. Also, a discussion of the similarities between the archetypal journey of the hero/ heroine and the therapeutic process of the client can be helpful and insightful. The supervisor assists the supervisee in becoming aware of the two simultaneous processes of the archetypal journey: the first between the client and the therapist, and the second, between the therapist/supervisee and the supervisor.

Value each supervisee's perspective

I personally have found it helpful to respect, invite, and value each supervisee's voice within the individual supervisory session or the group supervisory session. By promoting a non-judgmental environment that is supportive of all contributions, each person feels freer to reveal his or her unique personal experiences in life and perspective on the symbols and case presented. The more supervisees feel accepted and heard, the more information they will share.

It is important for the supervisor to use and model supportive interventions such as active listening skills (e.g., attending, paraphrasing, summarizing, reflection of feelings, perception checking, restatement, clarifying feelings or thoughts), encouragement, agreement, reinforcement, empathetic responding, self-disclosure, and open-ended questions (Borders *et al.*, 1991; Eagan, 1998). By modeling these skills, the supervisee will become familiar with them and will find them easier to use in the therapeutic session with the client.

Also, treat each person as an individual and be spontaneous and creative in doing what the occasion calls for in the present moment.

Supervisees are responsible for their learning

Guiding supervisees in learning the collaborative process involves helping them take responsibility for their own learning, being able to identify, elaborate, and produce their unique competencies. The supervisor works as a guide during this archetypal supervisory journey, trusting supervisees' level of knowledge, their practice, and personal development. The supervisor can use process questions to elicit responses that reveal supervisees' degree of learning.

"What is your feeling response to the sandplay scene? How does that make you feel?"

"What thoughts come to you as you view the scene?"

"What was it like for you watching the tray being made?"

"What comments were made about the sandplay process?"

"What feelings were evoked in the client by creating the tray?"

The supervisor works with the supervisee not as a superior therapist or expert but as one who guides, facilitates the learning experience, and shares knowledge and wisdom. This non-hierarchical role allows the supervisee to feel free to speak up, comment, and make contributions to the ongoing process.

Often supervisees exhibit a degree of dependence during the early stages of the supervisory process and may not be willing to take responsibility for their own learning. The supervisor needs to stop giving out answers and interpretations of symbols. Instead, the supervisor can use brainstorming or problem-solving techniques to assist a supervisee find the most reasonable answer or interpretation. For example, when a symbol appears in the sand scene and the supervisee has no idea what it might mean, first I ask the supervisee, "What is happening in the present life of the client that may relate to the symbol?" Followed by a second question, "What has happened in the past of the client that may relate to the symbol?" Then I suggest that the supervisee think of as many interpretations as possible for that particular symbol, from his or her personal experiences. The last step is to ask the supervisee to select one or more interpretations of the symbol that best explain the sandplay scene.

Relationships and processes spontaneously emerge out of the experience

It is important for the supervisor to remember not to have certain expectations for the outcome of each supervisory experience. Being free and open allows spontaneous learning to emerge. Supervisees will develop and change within their own unique way or style of learning. The supervisor needs to be aware of individual differences and experiences and to allow changes to occur naturally.

Develop an ongoing, evaluative process

As a supervisor, I provide an ongoing assessment of supervisees' knowledge and clinical and personal readiness for integrating theory and practice throughout each session of the supervisory experience.

The goal of supervision is to understand what is actually happening between therapist and client, because it is assumed that real understanding will lead to effective and responsible therapeutic behavior. The supervisor checks to see if supervisees follow the lead of their clients. Are they attending and listening to their clients as well as being aware of their own imagery and somatic reactions (Corbett, 1995)?

Questions that I often raise during the sandplay supervisory sessions are:

1   Has a free and protected space been established?
2   Is the client–therapist relationship non-judgmental and based on trust?
3   Can the supervisee identify the client's internal resources in the sandplay scene?
4   Are transference, countertransference and cotransference issues represented in the tray?
5   How does the symbolic language enhance the communication in the tray?
     What symbols in the sandplay scene suggest shadow material?
     What symbols in the sandplay scene suggest archetypes?
     What transcendence-related symbols can be seen in the sandplay scene?
     What symbols represent healing?
     What symbols represent transformation?
     What is a numinous experience?
     What symbols illustrate "coming home" or the return journey?

Mechanics of the supervisory process

Although sandplay supervision sessions generally follow an organic unfolding, I have found it helpful initially to establish the mechanics of the
process. These mechanics include developing a contract that lists goals,
time, fees, place, and procedures, written and signed by the supervisor and
supervisee, with a copy going to the supervisee.

The overall goal is to learn how to use sandplay in therapy. Other goals
of the supervisory working alliance, as described by Bordin (1983), are:

- Mastering of specific skills.
- Enlarging one's understanding of clients.
- Expanding awareness of process issues: that is, being alert to the how,
  what, when, and where of therapy sessions.
- Increasing self-awareness, exploring the impact of self on the clinical
  process, and sensitizing the supervisee to his or her own feelings, which
  may have an impact on the client.
- Overcoming personal and intellectual obstacles that impede learning.
- Deepening understanding of concepts and theory.
- Maintaining standards of service.
- Fostering an awareness and observance of ethical guidelines.

Methods of clinical supervision of sandplay

Methods of clinical supervision include individual (in person or on the
telephone) and group supervision and the use of case material, photos,
and slides.

In individual supervision the clinical supervisor works alone with the
supervisee in a one-on-one relationship. If supervisees live in the same city,
supervision can be conducted on a weekly or bi-weekly basis. If supervisees
live out of town or in another state, monthly supervision can be scheduled.
The primary method used in individual supervision is to review photos or
slides of individual cases. Sometimes the supervisee has access to video-
taping. Before viewing the photos or slides, supervisees are asked to fill out
a supervision form on which they define the problem and present a family
history.

Group supervision consists of one clinical supervisor and two to six
supervisees. My supervision groups meet for a minimum of two hours.
Supervisees are asked to present cases for 20 to 45 minutes, followed by
group discussion and feedback. Methods include photos, case presentation,
slides, or video tapes. Photos and a completed supervision form are mailed
to the supervisor for supervision by telephone.

The process of clinical supervision

The process of clinical supervision moves along a continuum that is similar to the archetypal journey. The supervisee begins the journey by seeking out the supervisor or guide to assist in the supervisory process. There are three stages: (1) establishing a relationship between the supervisor and supervisee; (2) exhibiting decreasing dependence and increasing autonomy; and (3) stabilizing growth within the supervisee.

Stage one

At each stage of the supervisory process the tasks of the supervisees (hero/heroine) are viewed as expanding their competence, knowledge, and skills as they grow professionally. During this first stage, supervisees may have a concern about their competence or performance when presenting. They may struggle with dependence versus autonomy and ask many questions. Some of these questions are: What is the meaning of this figure? How do we know when healing has occurred? What does cotransference mean? The supervisor has to be careful not to respond as the expert. I use process questions (how, what, when, who) to help supervisees begin to trust themselves and draw upon their own personal experiences. Judith Hubback (1995) suggests that the supervisor should enable and facilitate supervisees. *Enabling* includes empowering, strengthening, and assisting supervisees to improve their individual analytic abilities. *Facilitating* includes lowering supervisees' anxiety, which occurs as supervisees improve their understanding of the art, the craft, and the method of therapy.

Stage two

During the second stage of the supervisory process, supervisees tend to exhibit less dependence and more autonomous behaviors. There appears to be some integration of their fears and anxieties with feelings of confidence. They may experience more freedom in sharing information. They may exhibit more excitement about the supervisory process and value the ongoing collaborative relationship. They read and do more research on symbol interpretation and bring that knowledge into the session.

Stage three

In the final stage of development supervisees are more self-aware, self-confident, and feel more like a colleague. There is a desire for mutual sharing. They have completed the many tasks of becoming a competent sandplay therapist. They are able to follow their clients for extended periods of time and become aware of the dynamics of the relationship and developmental stages of the sandplay process. They can recognize transference and cotransference with their clients as well as with the clinical supervisor and members of the supervision group. They learn to understand what is going on between their clients and themselves as a sandplay therapist.

Evaluation and closure

Typically, evaluation and closure of the clinical supervision process occurs at the end of the supervisory experience. However, many supervisees want to experience other sandplay supervisors, which I encourage them to do so that they may have a wide range of experiences with methods and perspectives. In fact, they may complete their process with another supervisor. However, if they complete the process with me, we spend the last 30 minutes of the final supervisory session summarizing and evaluating our collaborative endeavor of supervision, using symbols of the archetypal journey. Questions asked are: "What did we experience? What did we gain from this supervisory process? What new skills or methods did we learn?" I ask the supervisee to fill out a supervision consultation evaluation form and together we review the completed form for additional comments.

Conclusion

Clinical supervision is similar to the mythic and archetypal journey that all of us experience on our own personal paths in life. In the sandplay process supervisees are witnesses to the journeys of their clients as sandplay scenes are created. Supervisees become aware of the developmental process that occurs in sandplay over the months of sandplay therapy as well as the personal relationship that develops between themselves and their clients. During the final session of clinical supervision, supervisees are asked to discuss the archetypal supervisory journey that they have experienced in an individual or group session, and they are asked to articulate their insights regarding the collaborative process of supervision.

References

Anderson, H. (1998). Collaborative learning communities. In S. McNamee & K.J. Gergen (Eds.), *Relational responsibility: Sources for sustainable dialogue* (pp. 65–70). Thousand Oaks, CA: Sage.

Borders, L.D., Bernard, J.M., Dye, H.A., Fong, M.L., Henderson, P., & Nance, D.W. (1991). Curriculum guide for training counseling supervisors: rationale, development, and implementation, *Counselor Education and Supervision, 31*, 61–78.

Bordin, E.S. (1983). A working alliance based model of supervision, *The Counseling Psychologist*, *11*, 35–42.

Corbett, L. (1995). Supervision and mentor archetype. In P. Kugler (Ed.), *Jungian perspectives on clinical supervision* (pp. 96–98). Einsiedeln, Switzerland: Daimon.

Eagan, G. (1998). *The skilled helper*. Pacific Grove, CA: Brooks/Cole.

Fordham, M. (1978). *Jungian psychotherapy: A study in analytical psychology*. Chichester: Wiley.

Hubback, J. (1995). Styles of supervision. In P. Kugler (Ed.), *Jungian perspectives on clinical supervision*. Einsiedeln, Switzerland: Daimon.

Jung, C.G. (1954). *The practice of psychotherapy. Vol. 16. The collected works of C.G. Jung*, R.F.C. Hull, trans. Princeton, NJ: Princeton University Press.

Kalff, D. (1980). *Sandplay: A psychotherapeutic approach to the psyche*. Boston, MA: Sigo Press.

Chapter 6

Mapping the cycle of sandplay process

Betty Jackson

When I first began supervising sandplay trainees in the early 1990s, I found that most arrived at this stage of training with a fairly good grasp of the meaning of individual sand trays. As a rule, they brought to the supervisory process a cogent understanding of symbolism and perceptive insight regarding the meaning and placement of figures in relationship to one another. Aside from the occasional amplification of certain figures unfamiliar to the trainee, my role as a supervisor regarding the understanding of individual sand trays tended to be more affirmative than instructive.

Where I found trainees most in need of supervisory guidance was in the area of appreciating the movement and flow of the process as a whole. I found that they needed more instruction, elucidation, and clarification of the stages of sandplay process. Although most trainees were astute at reading the symbolic statement made by the visual imagery of a given sand tray, their understanding of where that sand tray fitted within the overarching "story" was more elusive, their grasp of the unfolding process amorphous. Help was needed in orienting trainees as to how a progression of sand trays meaningfully relates to the structure of the whole. Such understanding is critical to appreciating whether or not the process was (1) moving forward, (2) experiencing a regression, (3) disrupted, or (4) vulnerable to premature termination.

At the risk of imposing preconceived notions about the natural sequential flow of sandplay, I responded to my trainees' need for a more comprehensive understanding of process by developing a conceptual map, outlining the stages of the sandplay process as analogous to the stages of the archetypal hero or heroine's journey. In particular, I drew from the work of Joseph Campbell (1949) in *The Hero with a Thousand Faces*. When I first read this book, after having practiced sandplay for at least ten years, I experienced an immediate and profound sense of recognition. Page after page, as Campbell described the type of imagery or symbolism associated with the stages of the hero's journey in myth and fairytale, I realized I had literally seen what he was describing, over and over again, in the sandplay work of my clients. For me, Campbell's description of the stages of the

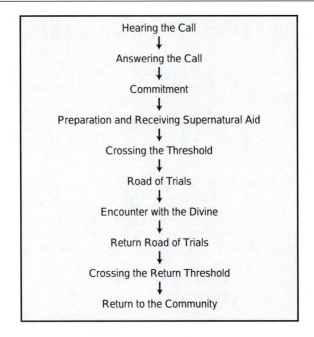

Figure 6.1 Stages of the archetypal journey

archetypal journey (Figure 6.1) was illuminating, providing clear descriptions of themes, motifs, and symbols corresponding to the stages of the sandplay process. There was a clear and surprisingly precise resonance, especially so because these stages were not described as unfolding in perfect linear fashion; rather, the circuitous thread of connection was traced in all its rich diversity of color, texture, and weight.

The fundamental difference between an ordinary journey and an archetypal one involves intention or purpose. Whereas the purpose of the former may be social, recreational, or educational, that of the latter is transformative. The archetypal journey takes the hero or heroine through the arduous passage of psychological and spiritual death and rebirth, a process that may be constellated around a series of external adventures, confrontations, discoveries, or achievements. Essentially, it is a serious, challenging odyssey, both internally and externally, undertaken not only for the benefit of the individual but for the greater community.

To envision these stages diagrammed on a circular template begins to more accurately reflect the movement of sandplay process by suggesting ongoing cyclical movement, rather than a one-time, fixed, linear achievement. Movement through this continuous round of process, analogous to the progressive spiraling rounds of a helix, is akin to the ongoing lifework of individuation, of becoming conscious.

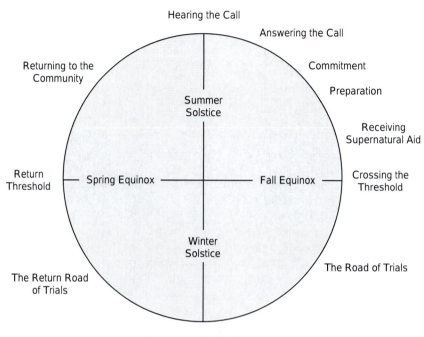

Hearing the Call

Answering the Call

Returning to the
Community

Commitment

Preparation

Summer
Solstice

Receiving
Supernatural Aid

Return
Threshold

Spring Equinox

Fall Equinox

Crossing the
Threshold

Winter
Solstice

The Return Road
of Trials

The Road of Trials

Encounter with the Divine

Figure 6.2 Cyclical stages of the archetypal journey

Additionally, the circular template suggests "above" and "below" phases of the process, congruent with the depth psychological understanding of the necessity to make a descent into the unconscious – the archetypal pattern of the hero "questing" into unknown, unexplored territory. This, too, is analogous to the movement of energy through the cycle of the seasons; retracting inward and downward through fall and winter before emerging upward and outward through spring and summer in response to the waning and waxing of the sun's warmth and light.

Another advantage of a circular diagram (Figure 6.2) is that it visually reflects the fact that it is in the "below" phase of the cycle that the bulk of sandplay process happens. As a rule, most people enter therapy or begin sandplay when their psyche is pulled toward the unconscious, or when they have been abruptly thrust into it by trauma or loss. The "below" or most inward phase of the cycle can be likened to the movement into, through, and back out of the labyrinth, a kind of labyrinthine underbelly, if you will. As a general rule, when the psyche is pulled back toward consciousness after having experienced psychological death and rebirth, people tend to initiate talking about termination. So it is in the depth phase of the cycle, represented by the lower half of the diagram, where the most substantive, transformative work, so graphically mirrored through sandplay, happens.

Reviewing the cycle of sandplay process

Hearing the call

Psychologically, "hearing the call" refers to the moment when it registers in awareness that something beckons. An idea, urge, or impulse, usually associated with something new – a departure from the norm – captures one's attention and demands consideration. Often (but not necessarily) associated with pain, loss, or general malaise, the external particulars of the call may be vague, clear, or anything in between, but what is unmistakable is the sure and certain sense of being drawn to something.

With respect to sandplay process, hearing the call usually manifests as the awareness of the need to seek therapy, or once in therapy as the need for a different approach. Perhaps the individual feels that the benefit of traditional talk therapy has been exhausted or has not been helpful. Regardless, the pull of the psyche toward engagement with the sand and miniatures is felt or articulated.

Answering the call

Once a call has been heard, the individual is faced with whether or not to answer. A decision to act, or not, is the next task – one that may be willingly embraced, a clear given, or one met with considerable avoidance or resistance. I recall an experience with a therapist who came to see me with the clearly stated intention of doing a sandplay process as a first step in training. In spite of her stated intention, session after session she sat and talked while the sand tray stood untouched across the room.

I noted this pattern, along with the mounting tension in her voice and body, but did not bring it to her awareness. Finally, there came a session where she burst into tears and cried, "I don't know when I'm going to be able to go over there. I'm so scared!" Together we sat and gazed at the empty sand tray, the distance between it and where we sat. It was as if the empty, untouched sand tray was the first picture. For her, as is the case for many people wounded in their primary mother relationship, to touch the sand was frightening. On a symbolic level to touch and move the sand is to touch and move the earth element, as in "Mother Earth," quintessential symbol for mother. If an individual carries difficult unresolved material regarding the personal mother, tactile contact with the sand can be threatening. For my client to finally name her dilemma (and to have developed an initial positive transference) diffused the tension so that by the next session she began actively doing sandplay.

Whether or not the individual proceeds eagerly with apparent ease or struggles with resistance, answering the call means taking that first step to engage, to create an image. The first picture or series created, referred to as "initial trays" (Friedman & Mitchell, 2005) provides insight into the issues and challenges facing the individual as well as his or her resources and strengths. Sometimes the initial tray gives an indication of prognosis or of what is needed in order for the individual to make a descent into the unconscious.

Commitment

Earlier in my career as a clinician and sandplay therapist, one of the things I needed to learn (and later convey to supervisees) was the need to check my enthusiasm for clients to embrace sandplay. Rather, I had to learn to embody complete neutrality in order to offer a truly free space for clients, free of any desire, hope, or agenda on my part that they do sandplay. I needed to learn to respect resistance and to accept that it is sometimes unwise for certain individuals to commit to a depth process, that for the too-fragile ego, it is sometimes unsafe.

I recall the example of another professional who came to see me with the stated intention of training in sandplay, understanding that completing a process was required. In her first sand tray, in the center she placed a group of figures representing family members, all almost completely buried in dry sand. Included in the near left corner, facing outward, was the "see no evil, hear no evil, speak no evil" figure of the three monkeys. Had this figure been placed closer, facing the buried grouping, it might have indicated a workable resistance, but in this case she clearly showed that she could not face this material; could not look at it, hear about it, or speak of it. Indeed, she did not return. Rather than looking at a decision not to commit to therapy as a failure, it can be understood as the psyche intuitively recognizing that to proceed would be too overwhelming or dangerous. Ego strengthening is usually called for at this juncture.

For the individual with a "strong enough" ego, evidence of deepening commitment to the process is almost always reflected through the hands. Because we use our hands to make contact and to work, commitment to depth psychological work can be reflected by the level of tactile engagement of the hands at this stage of the process. In general, increasing tactile contact with the sand – touching, molding, digging, shaping, sculpting, in particular, in damp or wet sand – reflects increasing engagement in, and commitment to, the process.

This is one of the stages in which clients sometimes leave the image of their handprints in the sand. It is as if they are making a statement, "I am really here . . . my work here will leave a lasting impression."

Preparation and receiving supernatural aid

Many things are required in preparation for a journey; with respect to depth psychology, trust in the therapeutic relationship is crucial. In my professional work, I have seen that in order for a client to make a meaningful or fruitful descent into the unconscious, the securing of a positive, supportive transference is absolutely necessary.

As individuals approach the brink of descent in sandplay process, it is often the case that symbols of transference appear. Some of the most frequently used symbols from my practice include Glenda, the good witch from *The Wonderful Wizard of Oz*, angels, or goddess figures. Often they are placed in such a way as to give them the advantage of height; on top of a pedestal or blocks, on the edge of the sand tray, even suspended over the tray from a string tacked into the ceiling – some type of placement suggesting watchful guardianship. Also related to these symbols would be the appearance of special jewels, crystals, or stones clients associate with having the properties of protective amulets or talismans.

Crossing the threshold

At this stage of the process, there is usually the sense that things are really beginning to move, and clients generally image this development by placing figures suggesting a point of demarcation, movement from one realm to another. One of the most common ways this is depicted is through the increased use or representation of water. Clients may shift from using the dry sand tray to the wet one or may create pictures showing larger and larger pools or streams of water. Entry into water is often symbolized at this stage of the process by the appearance of swimmers, divers, fishermen, or figures setting out in canoes or boats.

Also common during this stage is the placement of figures depicting openings such as doorways, windows, arches, or gates. The sense of descent is heightened by images symbolizing entry into the earth, such as the mouth of the cave or holes in the ground. These openings are sometimes attended by archetypal figures associated with protective watchful presence or guidance in the underworld. Just as often they may appear unprotected and vulnerable, suggesting falling into the water or earth. For the child, the gateway into the unconscious is often symbolically played out as being devoured by, or consumed in, the mouth of the monster.

Another fascinating symbol that frequently appears in association with crossing the threshold is the in-turning spiral, either placed as a symbol or scribed in the sand. A related figure is that of the labyrinth, suggesting circuitous movement toward the center. Regardless of the particular imagery, the unifying thread or theme throughout images conveying the crossing of the threshold is the sense of passage from the known, familiar realm to another that is less clear, hidden, unknown.

Road of trials

Descent into the unconscious inevitably involves encounters along what Campbell called "the road of trials." This part of the process is usually experienced as arduous, daunting, and painful. It is a time of going into the wounding, where real work and struggle are experienced. Psychologically, a number of crucial developments occur during this phase. Denial and defensive structures begin to be penetrated, shadow material is encountered, and complexes are revealed.

In sandplay, people frequently create images relating to the theme of movement. Flowing movement or energy is often reflected by images of roads, paths, or rivers, whereas blocked or impeded movement may be shown by the placement of obstacles, barriers, or walls. Chaos, disorder, and conflict may be predominant themes, as the old familiar form or way of being falls away. Consequently, images of vulnerability, darkness, destruction, and despair are common during this phase, reminiscent of Parsifal's travel through the wasted and dying land.

Another frequently imaged theme during this stage reflects the tension of opposites. As complexes are identified, awareness of the tension between opposing impulses or feelings is heightened. Ambivalence, indecision, or feelings of being stuck and the internal sense of being split are often depicted visually. I recall one client who had suffered greatly as a child at the hands of a borderline mother prone to unpredictable rages. As a young adult, she was caught between wanting, on the one hand, to appease her mother through compassionate understanding and, on the other, to express her own rage at having been so unreasonably treated. Over and over again in her sand trays she depicted a stand-off between Kuan Yin, the Buddhist goddess of compassion, and Kali, the Hindu mother goddess in her destructive aspects.

The road of trials phase of sandplay process can go on for a long period, challenging both client and therapist to endure the sobering weight and intensity of the energies during this time. It is not uncommon for clients to fall into despair or to express anger and frustration at the relentless round of trials, conflicts, or obstacles they experience. It can seem to go on forever, with picture after picture reflecting the struggle, but just as the energies of deepest winter move toward the light at winter solstice, so too does a successful process reach a turning point. Sometimes gradually, sometimes suddenly, the dark and heavy energies give way, and something different appears. It could be symbolized by anything: a candle, a jewel, an egg, a bit of greenery. We recognize it not so much because of what specific figures are used to represent it but because it is new, something not seen before, something with a felt sense of being positive, of conveying hope.

Encounter with the divine

The archetypal experience of encountering the divine, referred to analytically as the constellation of the Self, is a profound milestone that is essential for achieving the wholeness necessary for living an authentic life. When encountered, the palpable presence of the numinous renders the experience unmistakable. Although a gradual increase in imagery associated with centering – use of circular or spherical objects, circular or concentric configurations, or attention to symmetry – may herald the constellation of the Self in sandplay, in my experience it is usually accompanied by an element of amazement and surprise. I liken it to the experience of arriving at the center of the labyrinth where it is not given to see too far ahead around the next turn, where the path seems to approach and then recede from the center, then suddenly, a corner is turned, and one is there.

Encountering the Self is a truly restorative experience of the sacred. It is a return to our original creative source, to our rootedness or groundedness in God. It is a true reconnection, accompanied by a sense of reverence, mystery, and awe. What has always amazed me is that this numinosity is experienced by everyone: the very young child, the child whose family is not religious and who has never been to church, the child who has no familiarity with concepts such as "sacred" or "holy," who has never heard the word "mandala," nevertheless sits in wonderment at a spontaneously but carefully constructed image of the Self.

What is remarkable in sandplay is how clearly and literally the experience of the Self is spontaneously visualized. Typically, images of the Self in sandplay are more intentionally symmetrical, circular, or mandala-like configurations marked by a heightened sense beauty or artistry. They frequently include religious figures, lit candles, and precious objects such as jewels, crystals, or polished stones.

Birth, particularly birth of the divine child, is another common theme depicted at this time, and one that highlights the paradoxical vulnerability of this stage of sandplay process. Jungian analyst Estelle Weinrib (1990), author of *Images of the Self* (1983), described this achievement as analogous to the miracle of a human birth, when the celebratory energies and feelings constellated around the event run high. But, just as the newly-born infant cannot survive on its own and needs careful, ongoing tending, so too does the newly restored connection to the Self. I find this to be one of the most misunderstood and resisted truths in sandplay: that the stage reflecting the constellation of the Self, although it feels like an ultimate achievement, a culmination, the reaching of a final destination, is actually a mid-point, not an end-point, in sandplay process.

Psychologically, the vulnerability at this juncture is that the ego can claim and absorb the achievement, so that what takes root and grows is inflation rather than wholeness. Such vulnerability is not exclusive to the client but may extend to the therapist, who becomes overly identified as the archetypal guide "responsible" for the client's development. The inclination toward premature termination must sometimes be addressed at this point, with the paradox being that this stage of encountering the divine, of experiencing the constellation of the Self, is simultaneously a time for joyous celebration and wakeful caution.

Return road of trials

It is often the case that the return road of trials appears similar to what came before and therefore can feel like a loss of forward momentum – a frustrating and disheartening regression. There is, understandably, the naïve hope that the ecstatic high or deep sense of peace associated with the constellation of the Self can be sustained indefinitely, but this hope is neither realistic nor beneficial. Having struggled hard to obtain the treasure, the archetypal hero or heroine has more trials to face, more work to do. What is different now is that these trials can be met and overcome in a new, more constructive way precisely because of having encountered the divine. Psychologically, the shift that emerges at this stage reflects the difference between living and acting out of the Self versus living and acting out of a fractured or wounded ego.

When the personal ego can avoid succumbing to inflation and stay grounded in the newly restored Self, a development Dora Kalff (1988) referred to as the "relativization of the ego," significant growth and change is possible. One development frequently noted at this stage of sandplay process is a more effective working through of complexes. Whereas along the preceding road of trials complexes were encountered and gradually brought into awareness, during this later phase effective working through can take place.

A second related development, often seen during the return road of trials, is the reconciliation of opposites, typically symbolized by the placement of bridges, the bridal couple, or other significant pairings. The previously referenced young woman who placed Quan Yin and Kali in a stand-off, at this stage of her process had them standing side by side in support of one another. The trial of dealing with a borderline mother was still with her, but she had gained an ability to integrate both of the energies and was much more able to discern which would be most constructive to call forth to meet any given situation.

Crossing the return threshold

Just as the earlier stage of crossing the threshold is associated with descent, movement in and down, crossing the return threshold is associated with ascent, movement up and out of deep unconscious work. Many clients at this stage create images depicting a sense of freedom born out of the discipline of hard work. The ability to move forward, "take flight," or "take off" is frequently shown through the use of figures such as the eagle, the winged goddess, airplanes, or boats. One of the most revealing figures I have seen used in my practice to reflect the arrival at this threshold is that of the dancer or ballerina. As performers, these figures symbolically capture the achievement of crossing from inner to outer, private to public, practice to performance and service.

At this point in the cycle most clients can safely initiate termination with the grounded confidence that having weathered the trials of depth work, their restored connection to the Self and hard-won consciousness will take root. It is common at this stage to hear clients initiate termination or a reduction in the frequency of sessions, a now appropriate "leaving of the nest."

Return to the community

Dora Kalff (1988) stressed over and over the importance of the return to daily life after a period of immersion in depth work – not just a return to individual daily life, but to daily life in the context of relationship, to the family, circle of friends, or community of which one is a part. Over and over again in myth and fairytale we see that the hero or heroine bringing the wisdom treasure home, offering it to the community, gifting it to the king or queen responsible for the people, or taking his or her seat in a position of leadership and service, emphasizing that the ultimate beneficiary of the work is not self but other.

As I think back over the adult clients whose work I have had the privilege of witnessing, and those whose work has been shared with me in supervision, not one who has authentically progressed through the complete cycle of sandplay process has "returned" without being inspired to share what he or she has learned or gained with others. This offering could be anything, the simple everyday extension of increased kindness and understanding to one's children or spouse, the contribution of help and service to those in need, the sharing of one's creative talents for the enrichment of others. Regardless of the specific nature of the offering, the unifying theme is one of relationship. However articulated – whether as moving through the stages of the archetypal journey, progressing along the path of individuation, or "completing" a sandplay process – coming full circle in the cycle of depth work brings the individual into more authentic and meaningful relationship to the community, small or large, intimate or social.

It is curious that in sandplay practice, pictures reflecting the return to daily life are seen less often in the work of adults. This is not because adults fail to engage in integrating what they have learned into daily life, but because they tend to *live into* this phase of the cycle after termination. Where this phase is marvelously seen is in the work of children whose work has been allowed to play out in a natural and organic way. Many culminate their sandplay process by creating touching scenes of everyday life, such as towns, farms, or homes.

Conclusion

In coming full circle with this description, I have endeavored to convey the flow of the sandplay process, implying continuous movement by deliberately identifying it as a cycle rather than a set of stages with an end. From this perspective, sandplay process is ongoing, and what is meant by a "complete" process is simply coming full circle through one round of the cycle. This is no small achievement; indeed, it is a significant imprinting analogous to the first planting of perennials in a garden, which, once established through the first cycle of seasons, return again and again. In practice, it is as if a certain kind of knowing, or awareness, gets seeded, catalyzing ongoing growth.

At the beginning of this chapter I spoke of the risk of imposing pre-conceived notions about the natural flow of the sandplay process. One of my favorite quotes comes from *The One Woman Jewish Theater Company* in San Francisco, CA, and follows:

> Nothing interesting or important ever happened in a straight line. In fact, it's the quickest way to the wrong place. And don't pretend you know where you're going. Because if you know where you are going, that means you've been there, and you're going to end up right back where you started from.

Nevertheless, I have presumed to share something about how and where a complete sandplay process might go, what it might look like. If not in a straight line, I've mapped it out along a perfectly uniform circle. But in real life, it is never so neat and clear, and in offering this conceptual map I don't mean to imply that it should be or even could be. Rather, I offer this conceptual map in the spirit of Ariadne's thread, the ball of flax she gives to Theseus so that he can unwind it as he makes his way into the labyrinth, with all its confusing twists and turns and doubling back and forth. I offer it as the thread of archetypal pattern that can be traced underneath the intricate, seemingly convoluted, path a given individual's process may take. My hope is just as a map can be a helpful tool to get and keep one's bearings, this model can aid in tracking the course and contributing to safe passage through the strange and exotic territory of the unconscious.

References

Campbell, J. (1949). *The hero with a thousand faces*. Princeton, NJ: Princeton University Press.

Friedman, H., & Mitchell, R.R. (2005, July). Initial trays in sandplay. Jung on the Hudson: the wonder and mystery of sandplay. N.Y. Center for Jungian Studies, Rhinebeck, NY.

Kalff, D. (1988, July–August). Sandplay in Switzerland: intensive training. Zolliken, Switzerland.

Weinrib, E. (1983). *Images of the self: The sandplay therapy process*. Boston, MA: Sigo Press.

Weinrib, E. (1990, May). Sandplay and Jungian theory. Workshop presented Colorado Sandplay Therapy Association, Boulder, CO.

Meeting special challenges in supervision

Ethical dilemmas in sandplay supervision

Gretchen Hegeman

The *American Heritage Dictionary of the English Language* (2000) describes a boundary as "something that indicates a border or limit." As modern-day clinicians we are constantly aware of boundaries. Our lives are filled with terms such as "dual or multiple relationships," "boundary violation," "inappropriate self-disclosure," "fuzzy boundaries," "ethical behavior," "standards of behavior," "conflict of interest," and so on.

How does a therapist maintain an open and trusting relationship with clients when there is this collective concern about boundary violation? How can a safe container be maintained?

I frequently receive course offerings in the mail that focus on the boundaries arena. An intense level of self-scrutiny is becoming the norm. The clinician must always be on his or her toes. One could become paranoid. What happens to the "free and protected space" in this environment?

The sandplay world is small. In 2006 approximately 200 clinicians were certified members of the International Society of Sandplay Therapy (ISST). A hundred of these are in the United States. Except for people living in a few major cities (i.e., Los Angeles, New York, San Francisco, Minneapolis, and Seattle), most parts of the United States may only have one certified member within reach for personal work or supervision. Because of this scarcity, "dual" relationships are common as members are asked to perform more than one task. Initially, a certified member might provide a sandplay process and then later be asked to provide supervision of sandplay cases.

The history of psychotherapy includes many examples of dual and multiple relationships. This boundary overlap is a result, in part, of the fact that psychotherapy and analysis are just barely 100 years of age, and the founders were pioneers without maps. Many of the founding members of ISST and senior sandplayers had multiple relationships with their sandplay students and supervisees. For example, they might start out as a therapist, then become a case consultant, followed later as a colleague sitting on the same sandplay board or committee. Additionally, many social situations arise that need to be to navigated.

The cost of acquiring sandplay training has been of constant concern. It is part of both the Jungian and sandplay tradition to travel long distances to study with a teacher. Mrs Kalff, like C.G. Jung, had students and analysands who came from all parts of the world. Many of these people – for example, Professor Hayao Kawai, who introduced sandplay to Japan – sent their students to Switzerland to study. Trainees were encouraged to travel so that they would be exposed to a variety of sandplay therapists. On a practical level, this need to travel doesn't work for most people. Therapists who work in the public sector have notoriously low incomes. Many clinicians just cannot make such a huge time, energy, and financial commitment to travel for training. Unfortunately, these issues also encouraged the claim that sandplay is elitist and "only for wealthy people."

It is important to understand this history and how "unprofessional" the entire profession of psychology, including sandplay and analytical psychology, was at the beginning. Feeling comfortable with multiple relationships is light years away for those of us who learned of sandplay at a clinic, university, hospital, or through public lectures and conferences.

Boundary dilemmas occur when ISST members emulate our pioneer forefathers and foremothers by settling in some virgin territory and beginning "a colony." In these situations, there are few or no therapists with whom to interact. Boundary issues emerge when community members want to learn sandplay, first as clients and then as practitioners. In a small community, a therapist cannot remain anonymous even if he or she is quite introverted.

Wondering how boundaries and dual relationships are addressed in sandplay, I read, with interest, the Sandplay Therapists of America (STA) *Code of Ethics* (1993) and then, with a sigh of relief, I realized that these issues had been addressed thoughtfully in this document. For example, in "Section A, Principle I (b). Responsibility of the Sandplay Therapist (A.3)," the code states: "As practitioners, Sandplay Therapists act with care and responsibility because their recommendations and professional actions affect the lives of others. Sandplay therapists avoid personal, social and financial situations and pressures that might lead to misuse of their influence" (p. 1).

"Section A. Principle I (c)" continues:

> It is recognized that in some cases members of STA may assume dual roles in the training of Sandplay Therapists, if the personal psychotherapeutic process required of every candidate for membership in STA and case supervision is undertaken by the same individual. Special consideration must be taken to preserve the boundaries between the personal psychotherapeutic process and the supervision and training of a candidate. In such special situations, Sandplay Therapists avoid conflicts of interest tending to interfere with their dual functions.
>
> (p. 1)

In discussing the issue of dual roles with a Jungian analyst colleague, I learned that this issue is much debated in that community. Current thinking is that it takes three to five years for the transference-countertransference to dissolve, or at least dissolve as much as it can. "Section A, Principle V. Confidentiality" touches areas that are relevant to the problem of dual relationships: "Case material of identifiable clients shall not be presented at case seminars or professional meetings, but shall be confined to the supervisory relationship" (p. 5).

The predominant view is that the client must sign a written release for his or her material to be presented and must be informed regarding the materials used and venue.

"Section A, Principle VI (b). Welfare of the Client" states:

> Aware of their own needs, and of their influential position vis-à-vis those in their care, Sandplay Therapists shall make every reasonable effort to avoid dual relationships, such as in the treatment of close friends and relatives that could impair their professional judgment. Special caution is exercised in regard to the dual relationships involving those who are clients as well as students or supervisees. When possible, dual roles that increase the risk of exploitation, such as those of Sandplay therapist and supervisor, are to be avoided.
>
> (p. 6)

What is most comforting about these stated principles is that the problem of dual relationships is addressed and acknowledged as being inevitable in certain situations. The welfare of the client is uppermost, but the difficulty of being in a dual relationship is also acknowledged.

To become a certified sandplay therapist, a person must have an advanced professional degree. Professions represented in STA include social work, clinical psychology, counseling, psychiatry, marriage and family therapy, art therapy, and pastoral counseling, among others.

Each professional organization has its own code of ethics and, as state licensees, therapists are bound to observe ethics-related precepts of state statutes and state regulations. In most cases, sandplay therapists uphold three codes of ethics, which may contradict each other: state regulations, professional affiliation codes of ethics, and STA's code of ethics.

Because sandplay therapists are bound by several codes of ethical behavior, I was curious to see what the ethical codes of two of the largest professional associations – those in counseling and social work – had to say about dual relationships.

The American Counseling Association (ACA) *Code of Ethics* (2005) is very thorough and speaks to issues of concern to sandplay therapists. Its guidelines are up to date and, in their clarity and caution, reflect the litigious culture in which we live. Counselors are asked to document in writing any changes in their relationships with their clients. For example, "Section A.5.e. Role Changes in the Professional Relationship" states:

> When a counselor changes role from the original or most recent con-tracted relationship, he or she obtains informed consent from the client and explains the right of the client to refuse services related to the change. Examples of role changes include:
>
> 1   changing from individual to relationship or family counseling, or *vice versa*;
> 2   changing from a nonforensic evaluative role to a therapeutic role, or *vice versa*;
> 3   changing from a counselor to a researcher role (i.e., enlisting clients as research participants), or *vice versa*;
> 4   changing from a counselor to a mediator role, or *vice versa*.
>
> (p. 5)

"Section A 6. Clients Informed" continues with informed consent: "Clients must be fully informed of any anticipated consequences (e.g., financial, legal, personal or therapeutic) of counselor role changes" (p. 5).

According to the ACA *Code of Ethics*, client information and records must remain confidential, unless the client grants permission for sessions to be recorded and allows the therapist to review recorded material with others, such as supervisors and peers. Since sandplay supervision requires case material, including photos or slides of sandplays, this section (B.6.a–c.) is particularly pertinent.

Although some clinicians state that they are consulting with other pro-fessionals in their personal disclosure statements, some do not inform their clients that they are using their client material in their own training.

Some clinicians ask permission when showing material publicly, whereas others do not. Two examples demonstrate difficulties that can occur if permission has not been sought:

> A well-known analyst walked into a large public presentation given by her sandplay therapist and found her trays being presented. She had not been asked for her permission, and the information given was explicit enough to identify her to many people in the room. She was horrified and lost a great deal of respect for the therapist.

> A case was being presented at a small local training of therapists using sandplay. The presenter gave such explicit information about her client (who was married to a male celebrity) that many people could identify the client. There was a great deal of discomfort among the attendees, and she was asked to stop her presentation.

These two examples are extreme; however, they demonstrate the painful consequences of not asking permission when sharing cases publicly.

Section F.3.a. of the ACA *Code of Ethics* covers "Relationship Boundaries with Supervisees":

> Counseling supervisors clearly define and maintain ethical professional, personal, and social relationships with their supervisees. Counseling supervisors avoid nonprofessional relationships with current supervisees. If supervisors must assume other professional roles (e.g., clinical and administrative supervisor, instructor) with supervisees, they work to minimize potential conflicts and explain to supervisees the expectations and responsibilities associated with each role. They do not engage in any form of nonprofessional interaction that may compromise the supervisory relationship.
>
> (p. 14)

Developing a friendship with a supervisee may be easy, especially if both are living in a small community with few therapists. However, the power differential can be problematic. For example, the supervisor/therapist might find it difficult to let go of his or her power position and become intimate. Consequently, supervisees may not feel safe to share deeply and intimately and become genuine themselves.

In my role as a teacher of sandplay, I have visited small sandplay groups across the country. In each instance, people worked together to create a meaningful learning community. However, they often knew more about their therapist/supervisor than would be ideal or expected. The same situation held for the supervisor/therapist, who knew more about his or her clients and supervisees than if they lived in a more anonymous big city environment. In a way, the experience of the founding members was being recreated, because only a few people were available to fill critical roles.

The *Code of Ethics* for the National Association of Social Workers (1996) speaks to the issue of conflict of interest under "Ethical Standard, 1. Social Worker's Ethical Responsibilities to Clients, 1":

> Social workers should not engage in dual or multiple relationships with clients or former clients in which there is a risk of exploitation or potential harm to the client. In instances when dual or multiple relationships are unavoidable, social workers should take steps to protect clients and are responsible for setting clear, appropriate, and culturally sensitive boundaries. (Dual or multiple relationships occur when social workers relate to clients in more than one relationship, whether professional, social, or business. Dual or multiple relationships can occur simultaneously or consecutively.)

The Ethics Code of the American Board of Examiners (ABE) in Clinical Social Work (undated) states under "Principles, 1. Responsibility to Clients, 5":

> Clinical social workers do not use clients for self-interest, do not socialize with clients in a manner detrimental to treatment, and do not exploit clients or engage in sexual harassment or sexual relationships with supervisees, students, employees, research subjects, or current and former clients. The clinician carries the burden of determining that a relationship is appropriate, not detrimental and does not violate boundaries.

It is reassuring that boundary issues are being addressed and guidelines suggested by many professional organizations. What is crucial for us to remember is that we are dealing with real-life situations and real people. We cannot merely adhere to rules but must look at the situation in its reality, not abstractly. In a recent visit to Seattle, Murray Stein (2006) stated that the problem with ethics is that you can never see the whole picture, so that ethics issues can break down to the bottom line question, "Did you break this rule?" He further stated that this attitude is legal, not psychological. Ethics are related to community, not to the individual. It is the community's sense of "right behavior." Keeping the "free and protected space" is not always easy when living in a fragile and litigious world. Hopefully, we can keep "soul," compassion, and understanding alive in our work and emphasize the psychological, not the legal, aspects.

References

ABE (American Board of Examiners in Clinical Social Work) *Ethics Code* (no date or publishing information available).

American Counseling Association. (2005). *ACA Code of Ethics*. Alexander, VA: American Counseling Association.

American Heritage Dictionary of the English Language (2000). Fourth edition. New York: Houghton Mifflin.

National Association of Social Workers (1996). *Code of ethics*. Washington, DC: NASW.

Sandplay Therapists of America (1993). *Code of ethics of sandplay therapists of America*. Walnut Creek, CA: Sandplay Therapists of America.

Stein, M. (2006). Presentation to analytic candidate members of the North Pacific Institute for Analytical Psychology, April 9, 2006, Seattle, WA.

Chapter 8

Reflections on sandplay supervision: as above, so below, as inside, so outside

Kate Amatruda

Glancing at me through wire-rimmed glasses, not really making eye contact, my new intern came into the consultation room. Daniel (as I will call him) had been assigned to me by the Counseling Center, and this was our first meeting. My agenda was to begin to get to know him, to put him at ease, and to review the legal and ethical implications of being an intern. He looked scared; no doubt concerned that I would judge him, finding him inexperienced, incompetent, and whatever else his self-doubt could throw at him. This is his first placement. I remember, when I first started seeing clients in my first internship, I felt so scared! I knew I didn't know anything, although I would have never admitted it to my supervisor.

I hope Daniel is in therapy; unfortunately, the Counseling Center cannot require therapy for its interns, nor could I even ask him if he is in therapy. In California, by law, if I had been hiring him, I could not ask his age, marital status, ethnic background, religion, if he has children, whether he has any disabilities or health problems, etc. – basically anything that could be considered discriminatory if I did not hire him. Counseling Center ethical standards were very clear that supervisors were not to do therapy with interns, including sandplay. Supervisors were precluded from contact outside of the supervisory hour, including having coffee or lunch with a supervisee, bartering in exchange for services or products, working with an intern in more than one capacity, and most certainly, having a sexual relationship with a supervisee.

Not knowing anything about an intern makes it arduous to explore the terrain between us and to see how it parallels the field between the intern and his or her clients. There is a synchronicity in the work, in which the archetype of "As above, so below, as inside, so outside" becomes activated. The resonance in the field between supervisee and supervisor mirrors that between intern and client, establishing a "parallel process":

> The concept of parallel process has its origin in the psychoanalytic concepts of transference and countertransference. The transference occurs when the counselor recreates the presenting problem and

emotions of the therapeutic relationship within the supervisory relationship. Countertransference occurs when the supervisor responds to the counselor in the same manner that the counselor responds to the client. Thus, the supervisory interaction replays, or is parallel with, the counseling interaction.

(Sumerel, 1994, p. 1)

I wanted to model for Daniel the feeling of an initial session, because he would soon be starting to see clients. Initial sessions in supervision involve discussion regarding responsibilities, law and ethics, paperwork as well as the most important part – beginning to get a sense of the person. In some ways this is akin to an initial therapy session, particularly in a clinic setting where there are intake forms, releases to be signed, notification of intern status, etc.

I also wanted to get to know Daniel a bit, and for him to get a sense of who I was, because we would be spending one hour a week for the next nine months together, unless something drastic happened. Whenever I consider this timetable, my thoughts go to the other nine months in our lives, the time in the womb. My job was to create the "free and protected place," as Dora Kalff used to say, for a therapist to develop.

My first supervisor had been brutal; supervision with her was the opposite of the "free and protected place." When I reported to her after my first session as an intern, she told me that it was the "worst session she had ever supervised." It did not help that all my friends had raved about her as a professor. Only years later did I realize that none had had her as a supervisor. Teaching, doing therapy, and supervision are quite different skills. The person who creates the unconditional safe space of therapy may, in fact, be a lousy supervisor, unwilling to confront the supervisee. Similarly, the professor with many publications, who is his or her own harshest critic, may also be a poor supervisor. Such was the case with Dr M and me. Her blunt style and high expectations were a poor match for a feeling type, brand new baby therapist. I never wanted to hurt anyone I supervised the way Dr M had hurt me.

Years later, with the help of the most wonderful consultant I ever had, Kay Bradway, I realized that those who have been initiated cruelly tend to be cruel in their initiation of others. She taught me that "it is the wounded who wound," unless they find within themselves the archetype of the wounded healer. Having been hurt by my first supervisor, I knew to be careful, to not repeat history. In fact, I tell my students and interns, "It is a 'practice' that we do, not a perfect!"

I introduced myself to Daniel and asked him to tell me about himself. Daniel responded by saying that he felt quite ready to see clients. I asked him what part of seeing clients excited him, and he said that actually he was not very excited about seeing children, that he had no experience with children and had never done a "sandbox" or any kind of play therapy. This placement had been his second choice. He had applied to a psychoanalytic center, but they turned him down, saying he needed more experience before he could be accepted there.

Great! Just what I need – a person who doesn't want to be here! But then I got a little *bing* in my brain, and realized in some ways this was perfect, because many of the children and adolescents Daniel would be seeing would not want to go to therapy; rather, it was imposed on them from outside sources: school or parents.

I asked Daniel how it felt to be here when he really did not want to be here. I knew I had to be careful here, because I did not want to cross the boundary between supervisor and therapist. I tried the old open-ended question, and Daniel stammered a bit and was clearly uncomfortable with my question about how he felt. I tried again, asking, "Daniel, can you please tell me something about yourself?" He bent down to his briefcase and pulled out his résumé. It stated that he was 33 years old and had graduated with honors from a very prestigious school with a major in engineering. There were references listed, all in his former field. He stated on the résumé that he was single, with no children. There was nothing in his résumé at all related to psychotherapy. I had no idea how he had gotten from engineering to psychology. I was wary, however, in the process of what had occurred – not red-flag alarmed; more like a yellow warning sign. It seemed as if he were being very open and self-disclosing by offering his résumé; in fact, it told me nothing. This was my first indication that my intuitions about him as being frightened, inexperienced, incompetent, and concerned about my judgment of him were all projections.

After seeing Daniel's résumé, I had no recourse but to fall back on trusting the process. By and large, whatever needs to be revealed, will be revealed. If Daniel's issues regarding changing fields were to become a factor in his work, I trusted that I would know about them when I needed to. I also tuned into my own process as Daniel and I were talking and realized that all my images concerned my own scientific and technical ineptness. I know that I am a feeling type, and Daniel was certainly presenting like a thinking type. This would explain the blank expression he had when I asked how he *felt* about being here.

So, taking a deep breath, I tried a different tactic.

"Daniel, what do you *think* about being here?"

Suddenly, Daniel began talking about being at the counseling center and all that he had done to prepare for his internship. Time and time again, when I reflexively asked him how he felt, he drew a blank. When I asked about the exact same issue but instead remembered to ask him what he *thought*, then he would address the issue at hand. "Typological diversity" often is overlooked; yet, in some ways typology seems to be "hardwired" into how we process information. We leave the comfort zone of a shared way of being in the world when we supervise a person who has different typology. It can be frustrating; it can be maddening; and it can ultimately be rewarding.

I asked Daniel if he had any other thoughts or concerns about becoming a therapist. "No," he said. "I feel ready. In fact, I have the first session mapped out." The red warning light went on in my brain. I was psychically starting to hyperventilate, as feeling types do. I pulled myself back from the edge of hysteria. I cannot imagine how someone could have a treatment plan without having seen the client, without knowing anything about him or her!

Fortunately, my training stood me in good stead, as I assumed the "poker face" of the therapist or supervisor who has been taken off guard. "Hmmm . . ." I said to Daniel. No response. Therefore, I tried again. "Hmmm . . . can you say more about that?"

Daniel again bent down to his briefcase, pulling out a bibliography of many pages. "You see," he said, "I made a quantitative analysis of initial sessions and have figured out exactly what has the best chance of success. First, you need a complete developmental history, and here is the diagram that you need to figure out the core issue. It is an equation with .333 given to the symptom, .333 to the family history or family of origin, and .333 to how the client behaves while in the session. Then you find out what these issues have in common, and when that is isolated, you have the 'core' issue. From there, everything you say or do relates to the core issue."

"Hmmm . . ." I said. "Daniel, have you given any *thought* to how this will apply with a 7-year-old? Or a teenager?"

"Well," he said, "that was my reason for wanting to work with adults at the psychoanalytic institute. But I have prepared this form to get an accurate history." He handed me a copy of his 20-page developmental history form. "I think with young children, I will send home the developmental history form for the parents to fill out. Latency-age children might need some assistance, but they could do it primarily by themselves. I know I could have, when I was that age. Adolescents would certainly have the capacity to complete the questionnaire on their own."

Now, many of the children he would be seeing in the school had parents who had recently immigrated and spoke little or no English. When I looked over the form, mentally filling it out regarding my son, I realized that there was no way that my son could do it, and I was doubtful that I could complete it either. I could not imagine why it would be relevant to know at what age his third tooth came in. I wondered what trickster had assigned Daniel to me. I actually feared asking Daniel why that was on his developmental history, not wanting another bibliography to come out of his briefcase.

Daniel knew that his first client in the school was an 8-year-old Hispanic girl; I'll call her "Maria." Maria had been referred to the school counselor because of acting-out behavior and suspected diagnoses of attention deficit hyperactivity disorder (ADHD) and oppositional defiant disorder (ODD). Her mother had recently given birth to a boy, after a tenuous pregnancy that involved almost five months of bedrest. Maria's brother, born prematurely, was fine now.

I suggested to Daniel that he could ask Maria why she thought she was seeing a counselor and what she wanted to do. If Daniel could hear what Maria said, he would learn not only how to work with her, but also he would get clues to Maria's transference. I asked Daniel what projections he thought he might carry, and he answered that he might have "father or big brother" transference from his clients. He started to take out his printouts regarding ADHD and ODD, but I stopped him. I asked him what he *thought* about play.

He looked a bit confused and again reached for the briefcase. "Daniel," I said (trying really hard not to be impatient), "Play? What was your favorite thing to do as a child?"

"Umm, well, I guess I played a lot of video games. I had my picture in the Lego magazine when I was an adolescent, for a Lego ship that I built. Games? I don't really remember much about my childhood. Let's see, I was very good at chess and was always in the chess club at school. Play? That's about it really. I was the only child of two professors, who were quite old when I was born, so I did not really play with many other children. I was always in the accelerated learning courses. On weekends I would do my homework, read, and then play chess with my father or play video games alone."

He ended the session by asking, "What does play have to do with me seeing a child in therapy?"

After he left, my head was pounding. My dilemma was clear. My task was to supervise a brand new intern in sandplay therapy . . .

- Who did not want to be there
- Who was a typological mismatch with me (thinking vs. feeling)
- Who didn't seem to value play or even know how to play
- Who had never done sandplay
- With whom I couldn't do a sandplay

How could I possibly succeed?

Daniel sees Maria

Daniel came into our next session looking somewhat dejected. "I saw Maria, and I don't think it went very well. She didn't seem to know why she was there and didn't understand about confidentiality and Tarasoff.[1] She could not even read my developmental history form and kept wiggling all around when I tried to do the paperwork with her. She covered her ears when I asked her if she had been breastfed. She struck me as extraordinarily immature for an 8-year-old.

"I tried to explain about being an intern and that I would be discussing the work with my supervisor. I reviewed with Maria the reasons I would have to break confidentiality and then asked her if she had any questions. All she said was, 'No, who cares, blah blah blah!' and then she laughed and asked if she could play.

"All she wanted to do was play. And the worst thing was, when I suggested chess, she laughed at me, again! I can see exactly why she is considered defiant.

"And all she wanted to do was play Candyland![2] Then she put the Candyland figures and little dolls eating candy and desserts in the sand tray. She refused do a house-tree-person drawing or play with something that had some symbolic content to it, like dollhouse play or sandplay, which I have read extensively about. No, all she wanted to do was play Candyland! I don't think putting those little dolls eating candy in the sand tray right after playing Candyland counts as anything symbolic; it is just copying."

I asked Daniel what he did.

"You said to 'follow the psyche of the child' and I tried, but her psyche wasn't really there. She resisted my suggestions to do anything meaningful, so I played Candyland. For 30 minutes, I played Candyland, and then she did the same thing in the sandbox. The galling thing is, there is no strategy to Candyland, no skill, no logic. I can see why my parents never let me play Candyland. I do not think it should be in the playroom; it has no educational value whatsoever. I did not take a picture of her Candyland sandbox because it was just copying from the game. It wasn't from the depths of her unconscious."

Daniel did not know how to play, and he seemed quite judgmental with regard to what had value: chess does; Candyland does not; certain sand trays do; others do not. He was still mirroring his parents' belief system.

This is an issue in supervision that comes up again and again. Where is the line between supervision and therapy? How much does a supervisor need to know about an intern in order to be an effective supervisor? Rather than immediately focus on Daniel's issues so early in our work together, and perhaps meet resistance, I decided to address Maria's desire to play Candyland. I asked Daniel what he *thought* about it.

He said that he had been thinking of Candyland in the psychoanalytic tradition, and that it seemed to be about the earliest stages of development: the oral stage. He said that is why he wanted to know if Maria were breastfed, and if so, for how long.

I asked Daniel if perhaps he thought Maria was drawn to Candyland because she was feeling somewhat deprived. She had lost her mother's attention for a long time, during her bedrest and preoccupation with her difficult pregnancy. The birth of a premature baby, such as Maria's new brother, can be very disruptive to the older child in the family. Did Maria miss her parents? Did Maria fear that the new baby would die? Did she, at some level, want the new baby to die? Could Candyland be comforting to her? Could it represent "yummy" times? Could it counter a feeling of deprivation? (I doubt that many children would play a game called "Vegetableland" in which the goal was to attain a big salad or a plate of broccoli.) Did Maria need to regress? Was she going back to a time when she had more of her parents' attention? Did the randomness of Candyland help her feel a sense of mastery despite how out of control her life had become?

Daniel looked at me as if I were nuts! His unspoken question was, "How could a stupid game like Candyland reveal all of this?" He crossed his arms over his chest. "No thanks," his body language seemed to say, "I am sticking with my theory, not yours!" He asked me for documentation and a bibliography regarding what I had suggested. He looked at me with disdain when I told him I did not have any.

I knew I had to address how he had dismissed Maria's sandplay so cavalierly. It would be hard to do this in a gentle way because I felt fiercely protective of sandplay. I took a deep breath. "Daniel, can you tell me anything else about the toys Maria put in the sand?"

"No," he responded, "she only used the stupid Candy kids from the game. I won, you know, did I tell you that? She got frustrated and threw the cards in the box too. Then she went to the toy shelves – which, by the way, are very disorganized – and found a doll that had long dark hair like her hair. And she copied Candyland. She put in only unhealthy food: soda, cake, and candy. That is all. I had to make her clean it up, because she had thrown in all the Candyland cards, so it was a big mess. That is why there is no picture. However, when she was cleaning up, I saw there was a baby thrown in a corner. That's all. Not a real tray. Just a copying from the game and a mess."

I took a deep breath and tried not to invoke Kali, protector of the sacred, with her necklace of skulls. I needed another deep breath. "Daniel" . . . (*It's funny, when I just typed his name, it came out "Damniel" . . . there really is an unconscious! I do take protecting this sacred space very seriously.*) "Daniel, I don't remember a baby in the Candyland game . . ." Daniel responded with silence. I think he got it.

As he was leaving the session, he said, "Oh! I wanted to tell you. The baby's name is 'Daniel' but they call him 'Danny'." I must have looked puzzled, wondering if Daniel were talking about the baby in the sandplay or Maria's new brother, because he looked at me as if I were very stupid and said, "The new baby; Maria's brother."

It never ceases to amaze me how often a client or intern will "drop the bomb" at the end of the session. I wondered if Daniel realized the significance of the fact that Maria's little brother had the same name as he. How would that play out? What did this mean, coming at the end of the session?

When I felt withered by Daniel's scorn at my confusion about to which baby he was referring, was my response "objective" or "subjective"? Did his voice really hold the contempt that I experienced at a feeling level, or was it my old stuff, feeling stupid and inadequate around an analytic thinking type? Why did he want to become a therapist anyway? Guys like him should stick to engineering! As I became conscious of that thought, I knew my countertransference was activated. All I wanted to do after Daniel left was go home and read murder mysteries and eat chocolate bonbons. Did I need to examine the drive to read murder mysteries as a covert urge to murder Daniel? Did I need to discuss Tarasoff with myself? And what did it mean, coming at the end of the session?

Over the next few weeks, Daniel continued in his work, slowly adding new clients, while I struggled with my countertransference. While he remained very frustrated with Maria, I remained very frustrated with Daniel. He kept saying, "All she wants to do is play that stupid game, Candyland. There is no learning involved – no thinking at all, no method, no tactics. Then she goes to the sandtray and does the same things repeatedly in the tray; the little black-haired girl, the pile of junk food, and the buried baby. It gets boring. So I did take pictures like you said, but when I entered the data into a program I wrote analyzing the content of the trays, it never varied."

I asked Daniel if his data showed any change to the sandplay process. He looked confused, asking me what I meant. I explained that the same ten sandplay figures used by ten different people (or one person in ten different sessions) could indicate very different things depending upon the client's associations, where the figures were placed in the tray, their relationship to one another, etc. Daniel said that he had not really thought about it but that he would work on a program this weekend to factor in the process. I was feeling so frustrated! I really wish I could have insisted that Daniel be in sandplay therapy. He just didn't get it!

There were times when I dreaded seeing Daniel. I remained very frustrated with him, feeling that all he wanted to do was control everything. There was no emotion involved, no playing at all, no spontaneity in his work. He came to supervision and did the same things again and again. It was exhausting to feel pressure to document my every suggestion with copious amounts of research. I often felt that, no matter what I told Daniel, it was not good enough. I felt devalued by Daniel's style, and knew that I needed to work on my issues and past experiences as my negative countertransference appeared.

We were stuck, with Daniel feeling that Maria did the same thing repeatedly, while I was feeling the same about Daniel. Our stalemate broke with the scandal: It came to be known as "CandylandGATE," named after the infamous Watergate scandal.

Another intern came in to supervision upset because Candyland was missing from the playroom. Now, every child therapist knows that toys do get up and walk away, so money was requisitioned for another set of Candyland. Then the first set mysteriously reappeared, then the following week both sets were gone, and then both were back again!

Playing detective, I realized that the intern who had discovered the loss of Candyland used the playroom directly after Daniel did. So I asked Daniel about it, and he sheepishly admitted that he so despised Candyland that he would remove it from the playroom before he saw children there. "I figured if it wasn't there, Maria wouldn't play it. I tried to teach her chess, but she kept calling the "castle" the Candy Castle, and kept trying to get the knights, which she called "horsies," to go to the castle. I wonder if she is learning disabled. And she still did the Candyland sandtray. I am so frustrated that nothing is happening in therapy with her."

I gently explained to him that the toys had to stay in the playroom . . . all of them! I ever so sweetly suggested that the time had come for him to make peace with Candyland. Daniel just did not get it. No matter how much he read, he could not quite understand how game playing, especially Candyland, could actually be therapeutic. Engaging in an *act of desperation as a desperate supervisor*, I pulled out the game of Candyland. Daniel looked surprised, to say the least; horrified might be more accurate.

"OK, Daniel, let's play!"

So, we played Candyland. At first, Daniel did not like the one rule of Candyland, which was that the youngest goes first. Even though this was to his advantage, being almost a generation younger than I am, he didn't think it was "fair." For those of you who have forgotten (or never played), the game is played by choosing cards and moving to that place on the board. There are obstacles to overcome, dangers along the way, and serendipitous cards that can advance your journey. The winner is the first one who gets to the Candy King's castle at the end.

Daniel was very intense as he played, and kept getting flustered by "Plumpy." Plumpy is the card in the deck that sends you back almost to the beginning. No one likes Plumpy; I think of the Candyland game as a highly evolved, spiritual game. It lets us know what we can control (taking turns, not cheating) and what we cannot control (like love, or birth or death, or tsunamis, or earthquakes, or hurricanes).

So, when a Candyland player is going along just fine, then is suddenly swept up to the Queen Frostine card or cast down to the little plum, Plumpy, that is a lesson in things we cannot control. Much of the lives of children involve things over which they have no control: where they live, who their teachers are, whether their parents get divorced or stay together, etc. Candyland mirrors this state very well. I love Candyland; it reminds me of profound truths about life.

However, Daniel did not. At one point he was scowling so much I feared that I had made a huge mistake, having him play. Then I feared perhaps he was diabetic, and candy had been forbidden to him, or that his parents had been dentistry professors. I worried that perhaps he had an eating disorder . . .

As we played, though, he began to open up. After he got a particularly good card (Princess Lolly), while I was stuck in the Molasses Swamp, he actually laughed. Daniel started to talk about never playing games as a child, because there were never any children around. He said his one game was chess, which he had learned to please his father. His parents were very intellectual and serious about their "miracle," late-in-life child, Daniel. As a result, he was not allowed to play rough-and-tumble games. He was allowed to eat only the same number of pieces of candy as his age on Halloween, having to throw out the rest. "I remember really wanting to be 50, so I could eat 50 pieces of candy. It never occurred to me that 50-year-olds don't trick or treat!" My heart went out to him when he told me this; it was my first glimmer of the little deprived boy in him.

He suddenly sat up, as if startled. "I am remembering something else . . . when I was in preschool, I played Candyland! When Mother came to pick me up, she told the teacher that I couldn't play Candyland anymore. I think she thought it wasn't educational enough, or maybe it would make me want to eat candy." He then said that in his three-sessions-a-week psychoanalysis he had never been able to remember much about his childhood. He would see his analyst later in the day, and tell him about his "breakthrough." (*Aha! The Candyland disclosure – I finally found out that Daniel was in therapy!*)

He continued to talk about himself, saying that he had experienced a series of panic attacks when he was designing a bridge; he feared the bridge would fail and people would plunge into the water. His anxiety became so overwhelming that he started going to therapy, which led him to analysis and a career change.

He said that it was easier to talk when he didn't have to concentrate so much, and that playing this game might actually not be a bad thing. Then he said, "I think I have perhaps been a little too controlling with Maria in our sessions."

The best "Aha!" is the one you don't make!

So it went, Daniel learning how to play, with little Maria leading the way. I kept thinking about what Winnicott (1974) wrote:

Psychotherapy takes place in the overlap of two areas of playing, that of the patient and that of the therapist. Psychotherapy has to do with two people playing together. The corollary of this is that where playing is not possible the work done by the therapist is directed towards bringing the patient from a state of not being able to play into a state of being able to play. (p. 38) . . . Furthermore: It is in playing and only in playing that the individual child or adult is able to be creative and to use the whole personality, it is only in being creative that the individual discovers Self.

(p. 54)

The paradox here was that Maria was teaching Daniel to play! If Winnicott had been there, he would have said, "The corollary of this is that where playing is not possible the work done by the *child* is directed towards bringing the *therapist* from a state of not being able to play into a state of being able to play." Repeatedly, I am struck by how our patients are our teachers. I often feel that it is never an accident who comes to us for therapy (and supervision). I wondered what Daniel was teaching me.

Then the oddest thing happened. Daniel came in to our next session. "I am disappointed. I actually wanted to play Candyland with Maria this week, but she didn't want to. She said it was a 'baby game.' She just wanted to do sand trays." And Daniel pulled out his laptop and began to show me Maria's sand trays.

Did Maria stop playing Candyland in part because Daniel was able to name his resistance? I am struck by how frequently a client or intern spontaneously "gives up" a behavior or activity that causes me pain immediately after I do my own work on why it disturbs me so much. This is one of the *reverberations in the invisible energetic field* between two people. Is the offending behavior given up because something has changed in the client or intern, unrelated to me? Or does the person sense that I have let go of my disapproval?

The best explanation I have is that once I "get it," my unconscious reaction somehow changes and the client no longer needs to pursue the behavior. Perhaps to illustrate this point, imagine that there are energetic waves, unheard and unseen, traveling between two people. Imagine ripples in a pond. When one person sends out something (perhaps a feeling, thought, behavior, or memory), it is as if a stone dropped into the water. If the receiver, or witness, is neutral, these ripples hit the opposite shore and are reflected back to the sender. This is therapy or supervision (or any relationship) in its most dispassionate. There is rarely anyone who can truly reflect the emanations back without it sparking some of his or her own issues. Imagine then that the receiver also drops a stone in reaction to the sender's stone. Now there are two circles of ripples in the pond, meeting each other. If healing is to occur for both sender and receiver, these ripples must be made conscious in at least one person. Often it is the therapist, in his or her own person, who becomes conscious of the dynamic. When healing happens, therapist and client, supervisor and supervisee, are healed.

If one person changes the vibration of the waves emanating from him or herself, then the other person will, sensing the change, send back slightly altered waves. This is why a person who is in touch with his or her own self – who has done deep inner work – is soothing to be around, because the unconscious energetic field is much clearer. It is not that people who have done depth work on themselves do not transmit energy, it is that it is more imbued with awareness. There are fewer projections in the field, and more sense of personal awareness and responsibility. This is why it is vital for anyone doing therapy to have done his or her own work. Lewis, Lannon, & Amini (2001) explain the "aura of limbic tones" that underlies our communication:

> Every person broadcasts information about his inner world. As a collection of dense matter betrays its presence through electromagnetic transmissions, a person's emotional Attractors manifest themselves in a radiant aura of limbic tones. If a listener quiets his neocortical chatter and allows limbic sensing to range free, melodies begin to penetrate the static of anonymity . . . As the listener's resonance grows, he will catch sight of what the other sees inside that personal world, start to sense what it feels like to live there.
>
> (p. 169)

Over the course of the school year, Maria went back to Candyland at times, alternating with sandplay. Daniel and I made it a habit to play Candyland periodically, and even used metaphors from Candyland to describe how the work was going. He would confess to a "Plumpy" session, in which nothing seemed to go right, or when he felt stuck, he described it as being "Gloppy," caught in the Molasses Swamp. He began to value her sand trays when he realized the discarded baby could be Maria, rather than her brother. He said he was so amazed by this insight that he asked his analyst if he could do a series of sandplays. The analyst reluctantly agreed, referring Daniel to a sandplay therapist. Daniel said that through sandplay he was getting in touch with how anxious and perfectionistic he had been as a child. He told me, "Even my analyst is coming around. He said this 'sandbox stuff' might have something to it." I tried to suppress my smile of glee.

Maria continued to be Daniel's teacher. She periodically got angry with him and threw sand around the office. And Daniel periodically got angry with me. (No, he did not throw sand around the office . . . even parallel process has its limits!) At one point, as he criticized my lack of documentation and research regarding a suggestion that I had made, I suddenly got it! Daniel was temperamentally like Dr M. Once I realized that, I saw how working with Daniel was healing the wound I had incurred with my first supervisor. Right after I had that realization, Daniel was much more accepting of my ideas and seemed to stop asking for bibliographic references. (However, it may be that it was my perception had changed . . .)

As Daniel learned to stay present to Maria's feelings, her episodes of sand throwing diminished. Daniel had realized that Maria's learning style was more "emotional" than cognitive, and with that, he actually started lightening up on others who also were less analytically inclined. As his personal sandplay process continued, he became more appreciative of everything Maria put in the sand tray. He gave up trying to quantify sandplay therapy. He began to relax and be less controlling, and he started to value his own feelings.

As Maria's anxiety lessened and baby Danny started sleeping through the night, Maria's ADHD-like symptoms and acting-out behavior decreased. An active, impulsive child, she did not meet any criteria for ADHD or ODD by the time the school year was ending.

As Maria started talking about teaching "her baby Danny" to speak, she also began to teach Daniel some Spanish. By the end of his internship, Daniel knew all the names for the Candyland cards, the dollhouse furniture, and the colors of the Candyland cards, in Spanish. He told me that she was quite smart and perhaps should be considered for the GATE (Gifted and Talented Education) program.

By the year's end, Maria had done a lovely sandplay process that, come to *think* of it, replicated the journey of the Candy kids in Candyland; getting stuck in the muck of the Molasses Swamp, of the great leaps forward (Queen Frostine) and regressive periods (Plumpy), all the while progressing toward the goals of mastering the change in her family due to Danny's birth, feeling her mother's love again, and meeting the challenges of third grade. As surely as the Candy kids got to the King's castle at the end of Candyland, so Daniel's journey in supervision replicated this process. Perhaps my journey did as well. I feel that I met the Candy King when I started to appreciate Daniel's thinking, and react less defensively to him.

In their final session, Daniel said Maria told him she wished her new brother, Danny, would hurry up and grow up, so that he could play with her. She said, "I wish he was Daniel, not Danny, and big like you. Then he could play Candyland with me." Daniel said he almost cried when she said that, finally realizing how important those endless hours of Candyland were to Maria.

Notes

1 Daniel was trying to explain the limits of confidentiality to Maria by telling her about a court case (i.e., Tarasoff v. Regents of the University of California, 1976)

in which the Supreme Court of California held that mental health professionals have a duty to protect individuals who are threatened with bodily harm by a patient. The professional may discharge the duty in several ways, including notifying police, warning the intended victim, and/or taking other reasonable steps to protect the threatened individual.

2 Candyland is a colorful and popular racing board game that is a cultural icon in the United States. It is often a child's first game, because it requires no ability to read or count.

References

Lewis, T., Lannon, R., & Amini, F. (2001). *A general theory of love*. New York: Vintage Books.

Sumerel, M.B. (1994). *Parallel process in supervision*. ERIC Digest ED372347. Greensboro, NC: Eric Clearinghouse on Counseling and Student Services.

Winnicott, D.W. (1974). *Playing and reality*. London: Routledge.

Chapter 9

Transference and countertransference in the supervision process

Denise G. Ramos

Without question, supervising sandplay is a unique experience, because it allows part of the therapeutic process to be visible to supervisors. Supervisors not only have verbal reports of the therapeutic process but are also affected by images made and shared by the clients in supervision. Depending on the moment in their individuation process, they (both supervisor and supervisee) can see, feel, and analyze the same scenes in different ways, yet these situations resound in the psyches of both, sometimes resulting in a very creative process.

As all supervision is also "therapy" for the supervisees, their capacity to interact with the work of the clients underscores their own maturity and awareness levels during the process. The difficulty or impossibility of seeing certain angles of the situation highlights those particular shadow points for supervisees and supervisors. It is also possible for supervisors to disregard significant aspects of the situation which are even due to their countertransference with the supervisee.

In this chapter, I reflect on the transference and countertransference processes that occur between supervisee and supervisor when analyzing sessions with clients.

Learning process or analytical process?

Supervision always brings up an old argument: is it a learning process or is it part of the candidate's analytical process? Is supervision the learning of a technique and teaching of a psychotherapeutic process, or does supervision build a theoretical and clinical construct that permits the ongoing development of personal analysis? The answer probably lies somewhere in between, shifting from one side to the other depending on the actions of the supervisee.

When supervision includes analyzing a supervisee by focusing on his or her work, the boundaries are not always clear and objective. Without invading the privacy of the supervisee, a supervisor can inadvertently touch on sensitive points or shadow areas that may be causing blind spots in therapy. I think that introductory supervisions are always more about the analytical process of the supervisee, while in later sessions there is a greater opening for an exchange between colleagues. However, the main focus in supervision is always on the conscious and unconscious processes of the supervisee in relation to the client and the development of his or her analytical capacity. Clearly there are supervisions involving supervisees who are more reserved, whereas others are more susceptible to interventions of a personal nature.

Composition of supervision sessions

In supervisions involving the supervisee's analytical process, the transference between supervisor and supervisee is one of the key factors that can – or not – reflect the transference between supervisee and client. Knight (2003) speaks of a reflection process or parallel process when the relationship between analyst and supervisor duplicates that between client and analyst.

We can observe that in many supervision sessions there are at least three people (the supervisor, supervisee, and the supervisee's prospective client) "present" plus the various linkages that arise from their interrelationships. These linkages include the following.

Negative transference of the supervisee

One supervisee complained about clients who unexpectedly broke the transference connection, leaving her totally disorganized and with a sense of abandonment and worthlessness. A few sessions later, she did the same with me – breaking off the supervision work by telephone, with no explanation. I insisted on a private meeting, where it was possible to analyze her feelings of inferiority and competition with me, which had stopped her from bringing her difficulties into the supervision. Her inferiority complex affected the supervision via projective identification: She attempted to make me have the same unpleasant feelings that her client conveyed to her. In this way, the supervisee also tried to make me feel the same abandonment and inferiority that she felt with her clients. Some supervisors contend that this question should only be dealt with in analysis, but I believe it is also a supervision question, in as much as the unconscious material of the supervisee emerges during this process.

Positive countertransference with client

The supervisor "empathizes" with the client when identifying psychological similarities with him or herself and feels antipathy toward the treatment that the supervisee is giving the "victim" of poor help. This negative countertransference from supervisor to supervisee can make the supervisee seem incompetent and incapable of helping the client. The supervisor analyzes the circumstances by criticizing or even ignoring the supervisee's comments in an attempt to protect the client from the supervisee's lack of preparation.

Negative countertransference with the client

The supervisor feels antipathy toward the supervisee's client. In this case he or she treats the supervisee more repressively and demands that he or she act in a similar fashion. One supervisee's client complained most about not being able to contain his aggressive impulses, which led him to physically abuse his wife and children. The supervisor, who had also been a victim of this same type of abuse, unconsciously tried to induce the supervisee to take a tougher stand, advising him to phone his client's wife and get her to call the police or find a lawyer in case the client lost control again. The analysis of the client's unconscious and an understanding of the case by the supervisee took a backseat to a primary plan that involved the police and vindictiveness.

Negative countertransference with the supervisee

The supervisor starts noticing only the supervisee's faults and finds him or her incapable of following reason or acting professionally. The supervisor then begins to interfere directly, advising the supervisee on how to act with the client. The dream of one supervisee illustrates this situation well. This young supervisee dreamed that he tried to enter an enormous library but was unable to find the key to the door. The supervisor analyzed the dream as indicating pretentious behavior of the supervisee, who, even though inexperienced, had tried to read everything in a library. Unaware of his destructive envy of the young man's talent, out of the blue he made a snap interpretation whose unconscious purpose was to reinforce the supervision hierarchy.

Positive countertransference with the supervisee

The supervisor sees the supervisee as an apprentice and someone who can continue his or her work, and the supervisee has a *positive transference with the supervisor*, filling him or her with confidence and knowledge. In this case, a healthy environment of mutual trust will allow them both to reach deeper levels of the supervisee's psyche, leading to greater personal and professional growth. Being immersed in the situation will be of benefit here to the extent that the defenses can be lowered, allowing not only an intellectual understanding of the process, but also an equally enriching experience for the supervisee and supervisor.

Supervision while part of the analytic process

Once conscious of the transference relationships involved in supervision, an evaluation of the supervisee's work can be made only when the supervisor's focus of attention is on the supervisee and not on the client. Although the dynamic of the scenes, the symbolic representations, and the type of miniatures used can provide vital information for the supervision process, and in fact become indicative of the situations and their structure, supervision is more effective when it is centered on the emotions and resonances of the supervisee with the client.

The anxiety of the supervisee and the areas that are repeatedly difficult or blind for him or her are indicative of a possible complex that can cloud the work. One supervisee had great difficulty working with a client who was a very powerful businessman and whose chief complaint was extreme anxiety and trembling hands when he had to close a deal. The supervisee's countertransference feelings hampered the therapeutic field from opening up so that new material could emerge. Even when working with sandplay, without noticing it the supervisee ended up reducing any unconscious expression to a moral judgment and could not see the client's seductive and powerful side, which in turn hid substantial aggressiveness and fear.

When analyzing the scene in Figure 9.1, for example, the supervisee "saw" the same thing as his client did: a father and son playing tennis on a beautiful beach. Although the man was holding a whip, this was seen as a tennis racket. In this case, the supervisee and client seemed to have great difficulty perceiving the aggressive and abusive shadow of the client due to his charming and seductive persona. During supervision, the supervisee had difficulty detecting what was bothering the client so much, because the seductive powers of this strong and aggressive man had already affected the countertransference. In time, the client told of beatings meted out by his father and the fear and shame that arose from these events. To protect himself he had built up a rigid and defensive persona that camouflaged the marks on his body and fooled everyone (including the supervisee) with his thundering voice and arrogant behavior.

After supervising the same supervisee for some time, a supervisor can note scene-analysis patterns that are repetitive or even monotonous due to the interference of unconscious factors of the supervisee – who always ends up seeing the same dynamic regardless of the situation. Therefore, supervision is most effective and elicits analytical effects when the supervisor understands, in analytical terms, what is bothering the supervisee. Naturally, though, the supervisee's capacity for self-restraint, theoretical and

Figure 9.1 Sand tray of adult male client

educational background, and depth and time in analysis must also be taken into consideration.

Theory and patterns underlying the supervisory experience

A good relationship in supervision also depends on the theoretical orientation followed, not just on the personalities involved and the transferential "game." Although this area is not generally discussed – because sandplay is part of a Jungian analytic process that features the verbalization and interpretations of dreams, and other sources of analytical material – the theoretical backgrounds of the supervisor and supervisee will also have a determining influence. For example, sandplay practitioners who center almost all their work just on the box differentiate themselves from those who only occasionally bring the box into the analytical process. Here, although the styles of the supervisor and supervisee may or not mesh, the tolerance for differences is vital for the work to continue in a "free and protected space" without one participant forcing the other to conform.

The supervisor's background contains the theoretical matrix that both participants can use to capture the expressions of the client and monitor his or her growth. Here, the idea of the transduction of an organic symptom, for example, inside a limited and protected space (the box), needs to be understood within the Jungian theory of psychosomatics (Ramos, 2004). This framework can sharpen the view of the supervisee to details of the process that could, without this reference base, pass by unnoticed. It is often necessary to almost "deconstruct" supervisees' outlooks, because they are accustomed to seeing scenes in an almost standardized way: "right side – more progressive, left side – regressive," and so on. They can even forget, for example, to note where the client was when he or she placed miniature figures or the client's movements toward where the therapist was seated.

Seeking patterns is always tempting, because it allows a certain standardization of processes by symptom category and age group. Admittedly, there is nothing better than finding similar patterns in scenes by clients with similar pathology. On the other hand, the risk is to virtually force the emergence of these patterns by practically paving the way to the placement of the miniature figures, or even use of additional figures from a specific category. For example, I wondered why one of my supervisees, who worked with children, never showed any sandplay pictures that contained animals until I found out that the shelf with animals was the highest one in her office and impossible to be seen by small children.

To ensure that there are sufficient figures to cover the principal categories, the sandplay supervisor must make a personal visit to a supervisee's office, or look at a photo of the collection, or know the number and categories of figures being used. Of course exceptions can occur when the material is insufficient, but only for reasons of circumstance. In common practice, however, the shelf and the material made available to clients must be assessed by the supervisor to see if these are in accordance with general guidelines.

As noted, the search for patterns can lead to interpretative monotony, wherein the supervisee always "sees" the scenes within a single dynamic. The simple sharing of images is enough to hinder the process of sandplay as a solipsistic event, that is, it hinders the supervisee from unconsciously internalizing the process of the client. Externalizing what happens in this very close relationship increases objectivity and allows the angles of different viewpoints to be expanded. This sharing occurs within a relationship of equality, but also of hierarchy, once the supervisor is recognized by everyone as having more experience and awareness of the process.

This sensible interlocution diminishes the anxiety of the supervisee and helps support the possibility of reflecting on the complex questions that lead to the supervision. The supervisor has to see through the eyes of the supervisee, as well as the eyes of the client – his or her style, way of moving the sand, and accompanying verbal expressions – and not jump too quickly at analyzing an otherwise easily accessible scene. Perhaps the biggest challenge is giving enough latitude to the supervisee, letting him or her rely on his or her own experience during the development of the scene – his or her sensations, the resonance felt (Amman, 2004), and the images and fantasies formed – so that later on they can be separated from the process of the client.

The establishment of an alliance between supervisor and supervisee allows for greater freedom of expression for the latter, creating a common "virtual" experience. They look at the photos of the scene together – a scene that occurred at another time and place – as if it were happening right then, and they imagine other angles and points of view without fear of rebuke. They simulate various possibilities and formulate hypotheses. By taking this route, the supervisee compares his or her views with those of the supervisor, which helps him or her to identify blind spots, resistance points, and anxieties, thus opening new possibilities for his or her clinical practice and personal analysis. At these times, it is relatively common for the supervisee to gain insight into his or her own process.

This point in the dialogue also allows a "cleaning" of possible psychological contaminations and even recognition of the stress of the supervisee and supervisee's work. In time, the supervisor can then introduce the supervisee to a community, providing him or her with a professional and singular identity.

Supervision in the sandbox

Often, the supervisee's anxiety over supervision and providing treatment results in countertransference qualities that are not always perceptible. In this case, the sandplay itself can be the instrument that clarifies the mechanisms underlying the process.

One supervisee complained about having great difficulty in taking care of a client and was relieved when the client missed a session. During the sessions she felt constrained and a little nervous about the client, who was well respected in academic circles. She later remarked that whenever she was treating this client, she remembered she had to wash the curtains and improve her office décor, although she had nothing in her conscious plan to explain these feelings.

In this case, the box was the best place where the supervisee could express her conflicts with the client (see Figure 9.2).

In this scene the supervisee identifies herself with a child hidden behind a mirror, while the all-powerful client sits in a large, comfortable chair. When viewing her own scene the supervisee felt like a scared girl in front of a powerful grandmother-teacher, a memory from her childhood. When detecting the inferiority she felt in the presence of the client, the supervisee could also identify the authoritarian and inhibiting pattern of her client, who complained of loneliness and depression. Also in this case, because the client and the supervisor were of a similar age, supervision became torture for the supervisee, who even began contemplating a career change. Working with these parental complexes was vital in allowing her professional work to continue.

Figure 9.2 Sand tray of female supervisee

When we observe what happens in supervision sessions, we generally see that they are heterogeneous. Some periods are directed toward the process of the supervisee, whereas others are more focused on the process of the client. The use of sandplay as a focal point where the supervisee can place his or her conflicts, difficulties, and perceptions of the clients is, without doubt, a creative way to bring about major transformations.

References

Amann, R. (2004). On resonance. In E.P. Zoya (Ed.), *Sandplay therapy: Treatment of psychopathologies.* Zurich, Switzerland: Daimon Verlag.

Knight, J. (2003). Reflections on the therapist-supervisor relationship. In J. Wiener, R. Mizen, & J. Duckham (Eds.), *Supervising and being supervised.* New York: Palgrave Macmillan.

Ramos, D. (2004). *The psyche of the body.* London: Routledge & Kegan Paul.

Chapter 10

The field of relationships in supervision

Maria Ellen Chiaia

Many factors, conscious and unconscious, verbal and non-verbal, influence the complex dynamics that occur between the therapist and client over the course of therapy. These complicated relational dynamics are also known as the *field of relationships*. This field is influenced by the relationship between the therapist and client, but also by earlier and current relational fields to which both belong outside of therapy, such as familial and cultural relationships. In supervision, all these dynamic fields must be kept in mind, as well as the field established in the supervision itself. To add to this complexity, underneath all these relationships is a large, multifaceted base of interconnected relationships within a sea that holds aspects of the personal, cultural and collective psyches of the therapist, client and supervisor, and all of the interacting fields of meaning.

Fields, triads, and parallel processes

The field of relationship between the therapist and the client has been called an *interactive field* by Nathan Schwartz (Jacoby, 1995), an *intersubjective field* by Stolorow and Atwood (1992), and a *transindividual field* by Chiaia (1997) and Grand (1999). In analytic literature, the idea of a field grew out of Jung's description of the dynamic interactions that occur in psychotherapy; it is used in Jungian analytic and sandplay literature to describe the analytic couple and all the conscious and unconscious processes in which they are involved. Jung wrote eloquently about the therapeutic or analytic couple in *The Psychology of the Transference* (1966), wherein he described and illustrated the personal and interpersonal conscious and unconscious of the therapist and client as interacting in a container in which many different alchemical processes affect the analytic couple. This definition expands the notions of transference and countertransference as discreet separate entities of interactions to a larger and more complex set of interactions encompassed in the relationship field.

One aspect of this crucial set of interactions is the cotransference, in which there is "a feeling with" or "inter-feelings that occur more simultaneously" (Bradway, 1991) from the therapist or the client and then are enacted interpersonally between them. In supervision yet another field is created when a supervisor and a therapist meet to discuss and attempt to create meaning about the therapist–client field. In doing supervision, we have the intersection of these two fields of meaning, but there are many more fields of meanings that enter into any supervision session, and these I describe in this chapter.

Two other concepts from psychoanalytic literature describe some of the dynamics within the field and are important to this discussion of supervision: the notion of a triad and the phenomenon of parallel process. Supervision has been referred to a "triadic system" (Wolkenfeld, 1990), because the third (the supervisee's client) is always present and forms the basis of all supervision. In this triadic system, parallel process inevitably occurs. According to Wolkenfeld, "Parallel process phenomenon is a multi-directional representational system in which major psychic events, including complex behavioral patterns, affects, and conflicts, occurring in one dyadic situation – analysis or supervision – are repeated in the other" (p. 96). Thus, what is happening in the client–therapist relationship field may be duplicated in the supervisory relationship, and vice versa. Whether doing either individual or group supervision, we might think of a triadic system as another aspect of a larger field wherein parallel process is occurring. Parallel process can start and/or reverberate simultaneously in any or all of the following relationships: therapist–client, supervisor–therapist, agency–supervisor, institution–supervisor, or supervisor–supervisor.

Example of intersecting fields

Here is an example of how the training institute and the supervisors impacted my client and me during my analytic training. It elucidates the multidirectional nature of parallel process as well as the mysterious movement of the unconscious. As Wolkenfeld (1990) states, "The feeling of the uncanny when we, as supervisors, are confronted by a parallel reenactment is due to the reminder that the unconscious has no regard for time, place or seniority" (p. 108).

In the final stage of becoming a Jungian analyst, the candidate studies a case in depth, and this case is supervised by two analysts. Eventually a certifying committee, which represents the Jungian institute, and later a certifying board, which includes representatives from the larger Jungian community, evaluate the case. During the last six months of this process, when I was writing and discussing my final paper on a client and our eight years of analysis, the following occurred:

> The client arrived for our session and asked to do a sandplay. She created a scene in the sand that expressed one of the main and current

areas of our analytic work. The center contained two figures in conflict, representing the core of one of her complexes. A circle of helpful figures surrounded the two figures, personifying parts of her psyche that had witnessed, assisted, and supported her analysis. This tray expressed her experience of the process of our work together. The sandplay also had a quality of calm and resolve, which had recently emerged between us – a progressive aspect of the work toward which she was moving. She stopped and reflected aloud what I have just described and then returned to the shelves of figures. She gazed around and then picked out a figure of Freud, smoking a pipe, which I had received from a fellow candidate (I did not have a miniature of Jung). Going back to the sandplay, she made a hill to the left of the original scene and placed this figure on the hill. She said, with great affection and warmth, "This is Freud – no, it is Jung, and he is overseeing our work together." I was surprised by this statement, because she "did not know" that I was presenting her as my final case for certification. She had been referred for psychotherapy before I was in the training program.

I had chosen this client for my final case, rather than other clients, because of how she and I responded to this ongoing intrusion of such focused and evaluative "supervision." I monitored psychic events by paying attention to her dreams, my dreams, as well as patterns, affects, and conflicts as they occurred in the cotransference. I determined that the supervision work was not experienced by her or by me as a negative intrusion but as a helpful one. However, I had struggled with the intense scrutiny and focus of the training committees and the two supervisors and knew that it had an impact on our therapeutic relationship. By placing Freud/Jung on the hill in the sand tray and saying that Jung is overseeing our work, my client is letting me know that her psyche "knows" what has been "going on" with her and me and that it is helpful. The relationships from my training had entered the room and, fortunately, had "helped" her and our relationship. I saw this helpfulness in the circle of allies surrounding the figures in conflict. These allies included spiritual figures and gods and suggested the solidifying of helpful emergent aspects of her self. This sandplay mirrored and solidified the way I was now feeling about the work with the training committees. Helpful forces surrounded the struggling, evaluated analytic pair: the multiple fields of relationship, which I could now experience as allies.

As would be expected, I was greatly relieved by this sandplay and was full of gratitude that it was created before my final meeting with the certifying board. It was a wonderful affirmation of our work that contributed to my having a positive experience with the certifying board. This is a good example of the reverberations among multiple levels of meaning throughout the many relational fields intersecting with the client, myself, my control analysts, my analyst, the training institution, and the larger Jungian community.

Multiple fields of meaning

In sandplay, we must consider the multiple levels of meaning and relational fields created by the therapist's sandplay collection and also by the many clients who use the collection. Unlike other expressive arts therapists, the sandplay therapist collects figures, both animate and inanimate, including found objects: shells, driftwood, feathers, bones, teeth, rocks, stones, leaves, petals, branches, pieces of glass, metal, or plastic. Each of these objects is chosen by the therapist and comes with its own meanings, derived from cultural stories and myths, natural history, and fairytales from all over the world.

Many collections also include objects made by the therapist and sometimes objects that clients have made and donated to the therapist's collection when leaving therapy. All of these objects belonging to the therapist have multiple but specific meanings and feelings and stories connected to them. Some of these meanings come from the therapist and some, of which the therapist may be unaware, come from the object. And then, as the objects are used over and over again by clients, these meanings and feelings and stories grow, expand, and deepen, and begin to have a life of their own. Over time the collection becomes full of feelings and meanings, connected with the therapist, the collection itself, and all of the clients who have used the collection.

Another aspect to consider in the fields of meaning is what is involved in becoming a certified sandplay therapist. It includes the study of Kalffian and Jungian theory and practice, and also the study of symbolism in history and culture, through religion, mythology, fairytales, art, and nature. These areas of study help the student understand the language of the unconscious and create a deeper and more complex picture of the psyche and psychological processes. However, we must consider that every therapist and supervisor brings to this study his or her own unique racial, ethnic, cultural, religious, historical, and personal experiences, as do clients. These multiple factors add another level of interacting fields of meaning. An understanding of any sand tray image or series needs to encompass what the therapist and supervisor have studied and learned and how they "hold" this knowledge, given their individual cultural biases. Kimbles and Capitolo have addressed their respective writings about the cultural complex (Kimbles, 2000) and the racial unconscious and sandplay therapy (Capitolo, 2004).

In studying a sand tray, we need to consider the following interacting elements: the archetypal meaning of the images, the cultural lenses of the client and the supervisor, relationships between the figures, the therapist's and supervisor's knowledge, uniqueness of the therapist's collection, and the therapist's conscious and unconscious understandings of these symbolic meanings.

Importance of listening and empathic attunement

I want to emphasize that any sandplay image is an intrapsychic *and* an interpersonal experience and expression of the many intersecting fields of relationship and meaning. When we study a sandplay image or process (i.e., a series of images created over time), we begin to see the complexity of what may be experienced when a sandplay is created and then described. How does one teach or model a way of listening that honors and respects this complexity and enables the supervisee to become an "instrument" that "resonates" with the client's material? Empathic attunement is an essential tool for engaging these interactive fields of meaning. When studying any sandplay image I start by asking the supervisee to join me in paying attention to what is evoked by the tray. I encourage the supervisee to express any feelings, images, somatic sensations, and thoughts that arise so that we may engage the triadic system, trusting that parallel reenactments will occur. It is by modeling this way of listening, of experiencing empathic attunement with the client, that I conduct supervision.

Here is an example of how I teach supervisees to listen. In a group supervision session, a supervisee was showing a sand tray of an African-American boy. The sandplay scene showed many Roman and Greek gods and goddesses arranged in groups. A little brown boy was sitting with his head down, observing the groups from a distance. After observing the tray silently, the following associations emerged from the group. The boy seemed sad and lonely. The group of gods and goddesses felt celebratory, and there was a beauty and joy found in these groupings. Then one of the members began telling stories about the wisdom and gifts that these Olympians might hold for the little boy. We all joined in associating from Greek and Roman mythology. One woman and I began to feel uneasy for the little boy. As we followed these sad and uncomfortable feelings, the therapist began to tell us about the boy's schooling. He attended an elite college preparatory school and was struggling to fit in and keep up with his studies. Now we had something personal and cultural that needed to be understood about what may have been experienced by this boy in making this sandplay.

By this kind of listening we were able to learn something about the cultural unconscious and how it was impacting the boy. As a group of mostly white therapists, when we skipped over the feelings and began amplifying from the collective unconscious with myths and stories, we almost missed what was being expressed about the cultural unconscious. By listening with empathy to the sandplay, we began to feel the aloneness and suffering of this African-American boy who attended a predominantly white school and was seeing a white therapist. The western myths and stories certainly had something to offer this boy, but the cultural issues and how they had impacted the personal were heard as well. This focus on empathic attunement and "feeling into the tray" helped the supervisee to bring consciousness to the work with this boy and what was happening in the cotransference. As the supervisee brought this awareness into relationship with the boy, the sandplays began to change. Later in the year we saw African figures struggling with the Roman and Greek figures and then sandplays appeared which showed African and Greco-Roman gods and goddesses celebrating *together*. In this process of struggle and integration, the supervision group viewed and experienced the intrapsychic healing within the client between his African and American roots and an interpersonal healing in the relationship with the white therapist. At this time, he began to function better at school.

Notice the use of musical terms in this description of supervision: listening, conducting, resonating as we attune ourselves to the sounds, waves, rhythms, and reverberations created by all these interactive fields of meaning. We must model for supervisees this way of listening, which includes reflecting and musing with an acceptance of ambiguity, uncertainty, and not knowing. Holding the space for reverie is an essential part of sandplay supervision so that an attitude of respect for the psyche and the unconscious can be learned, and emergent meaning may occur. This way of approaching supervisees encourages them to resolve their idealizing transference and awe of the supervisor, so that they may become finely tuned instruments of unconscious processes attuning to the multiple meanings that have arisen between client and therapist.

Communicating unconscious dynamics

Let us assume that the therapist has acquired an ability to listen to his or her client and to perceive the unconscious dynamics occurring between them. As we know as supervisors, and as therapists who have been in supervision, communicating unconscious dynamics to the supervisor is tricky. Wolkenfeld (1990, p. 108) wrote that, "our supervisees . . . have observed more than they can readily verbalize." In sandplay we also have an image that gives us a non-verbal way of communicating in therapy, in supervision, and in teaching. This image can be a benefit, but it could also be a distraction. The benefit is that images have a language of their own, and, if we allow an image to "speak" before we verbalize what we are seeing, we can gain a great deal of information.

The distraction is that people who have not learned to "read" the language of the images become uncomfortable with not knowing and tend to apply verbal concepts and ideas to the image. They do not give the image a chance to "speak" for itself, and therefore they do not experience what the client is trying to say. If supervisees begin with an internal reverie about the image, then they can begin to learn the language of images.

Next comes the task of putting into words the non-verbal understandings and meanings that the images evoke in us. I ask the supervisee to start by describing feelings, sensations, and images, leaving amplification with myths, fairytales, concepts, and theories until later. It is only after the supervisee's associations have been given that I encourage amplification and theories to enter slowly and carefully so that a collage full of multiple fields of meaning can be created. As the supervisee(s) and I engage with all of these interactive fields of meaning, emergent meanings may appear; that is, new meanings emerge and a pattern of psychological understanding may occur. Careful attention to this process eases communication of what the therapist and client are experiencing and what is being experienced and expressed in the sandplay. Jacoby (1995) wrote: "It is not easy for candidates to transplant, so to speak, their patient/analyst field to the interactive field with the supervisor" (p. 82). This is true in sandplay supervision as well. However, having images that speak non-verbally to us when we use reverie, reflection, and empathic attunement facilitates this process of engaging all the interactive fields of meaning and what the client is trying to express non-verbally.

Here is a simple and sweet story of a supervision session as an example of parallel process, interacting fields of meaning, and emergent meaning:

> A supervisee and I were observing a series of sandplays created by a 5-year-old girl. The first sandplays felt chaotic and confused and we sat together with this sense. We reflected on the lack of containment and holding in the trays. Some of the trays had both wild and domestic animals, usually alone and wounded. These trays felt disorienting and sad.
>
> During a few supervision sessions, the supervisee had trouble finding her notes and sandplay images, and she had trouble keeping the sandplays in order. I became frustrated with her and she was annoyed with me for my lack of patience. As we wondered together about what might have been happening, the supervisee remembered how much animosity and hostility there was in the sessions with the mother and father. The supervisee also reported feeling frustrated and sad toward the little girl, because she acted angrily and aggressively when she played in the sand and "hurt" or "killed the animals." The supervisee was also frustrated with the parents and was wondering about continuing the treatment. The parents repeatedly questioned the value of therapy, and sometimes they did not show up for their scheduled appointments.
>
> Together we began to understand how disoriented and angry the little girl was feeling, and I became more patient with the therapist. The therapist became kinder and more caring toward the little girl. She worked with the parents to help them see how their angry words and behavior impacted the little girl and to contain their feelings in front of

her. The therapist was also very protective of the little girl's time and worked with the parents to become more consistent with the therapy schedule and time. After a few months the sandplays began to change. The little girl was now creating scenes with families of animals, especially dogs and cats, who were protected and safe in caves and other natural shelters. The supervisee and I became aware of how she and the client were connecting at this point in the therapy.

The girl's use of miniature animals in the tray, particularly one dog that was a gift to the therapist when her dog of many years had died (the figure looked like her dog), was very moving to the therapist. Also, many years ago the therapist had written a thesis on the meaning and importance of animals, especially dogs. Animals and dogs were also important in my own personal healing. All of this enabled the supervisee and me to connect in a deep way and to trust in the process of the work with the little girl and of our work together.

In this example we see the multiple interacting fields of meanings and how they impacted the supervision. First the disorientation and anger, which created chaos and a lack of connection in each of the fields of relationships: parents and child, therapist and client, and supervisor and supervisee. Later, a deeper understanding and connection were established through animals, particularly dogs, in the therapist–client relationship and in the supervisor–therapist relationship. The many meanings of dog reverberated and resonated throughout the multiple fields of meaning in which we were engaged together and apart. The use of the special dog that meant so much to the therapist deepened the feeling and connection of the cotransference. Staying open to and allowing all of these feelings and meanings to enter into supervision is essential because they continue to reverberate throughout all fields of relationships and have an important impact on the therapist–client relationship.

In summary, essential and important qualities that need to be developed in supervision are empathy, reverie, and imagination. These qualities enable us to listen to the unconscious and encourage fields of relationships and all their interacting meanings to emerge. I teach my students the importance of honoring and holding the space open for what we do not know. A lifelong openness to learning is important, but most important is an attitude of openness to what it is in us that continues to try to express itself throughout our lives and in all of our relationships.

References

Bradway, K. (1991). Transference and countertransference in sandplay therapy, *Journal of Sandplay Therapy*, 1, 25–43.

Capitolo, M. (2004). The inter/interpersonal racial unconscious, *Journal of Sandplay Therapy*, *13*, 117–129.

Chiaia, M.E. (1997). *Imagination in dialogue*. Ann Arbor, MI: UMI Dissertation Services.

Grand, I. (1999). *Collaboration and creativity*. Ann Arbor, MI: UMI Dissertation Services.

Jacoby, M. (1995). Supervision and the interactive field. In P. Kluger (Ed.), *Jungian perspectives on clinical supervision*. Einsiedeln, Switzerland: Daimon.

Jung, C.G. (1966). *The psychology of the transference, vol. 16. collected works of C.G. Jung*. Princeton, NJ: Princeton University Press.

Kimbles, S. (2000). The cultural complex and the myth of invisibility. In T. Singer (Ed.), *The vision thing: Myth, politics, and psyche in the world* (pp. 157–169). London & New York: Routledge.

Stolorow, R.D., & Atwood, G.E. (1992). *Contexts of being: The intersubjective foundations of psychological life*. Hillsdale, NJ: Analytic Press.

Wolkenfeld, F. (1990). The parallel process phenomenon revisited: Some additional thoughts about the supervisory process. In R.C. Lane (Ed.), *Psychoanalytic approaches to supervision* (pp. 95–112). New York: Brunner Mazel.

Part IV

Moving into the cross-cultural world

Chapter 11

Supervision in an international, multilingual, and multicultural therapy world

Ruth Ammann

As a Jungian analyst and sandplay therapist, I have been doing analysis, teaching, and supervision for many years and in many countries throughout the world. At our C.G. Jung Institute in Zürich, Switzerland, and also when traveling abroad, I am confronted with very unique multilingual and multicultural issues. Routinely, for example, I work with candidates who do not speak my mother tongue and are familiar with only their own culture. These differences create very specific challenges and are the topic of this chapter. For example, I might supervise an Italian trainee who is working with an Italian client, or an Australian trainee working with an Australian client. Then, in individual supervision, I speak Italian or English, languages that I know well enough. However, I still have to keep in mind that my supervisee and his or her client's culture are different from my own Swiss cultural background. And these are the easier cases!

More difficult are situations I encounter frequently at the C.G. Jung Institute in Zürich. The Institute has many multicultural students. Officially, courses are taught in German and English, but our students come from many different countries and cultures – sometimes more than 30! Consequently, there are many mother tongues. It is possible that a Swiss analyst, such as myself, who has grown up speaking three languages – German, French, and Italian – as official languages of my country (but mainly speaking and thinking in German), may supervise the work of an Italian candidate who works with a Turkish client. The supervisee and I may talk together in Italian, which is at least fluent for both of us. The candidate and his or her client, however, may be communicating in English, which is for both a foreign language and creates, of course, a variety of problems.

Another example comes to mind. I supervised a Japanese clinician who worked with a South African client. In this case all three of us spoke English, but the cultural and social backgrounds were even more complicated than in the previous case.

What difficult and delicate situations we find!

In these cases, it is extremely important that the clinician learns to understand both the spoken and the unspoken language of the client; that is, the language itself, the client's body language, and the personal, social, and cultural backgrounds of his or her client. The supervisor, in turn, needs to have a good enough understanding and empathy for the language and the culture, not only of the supervisee, but also of the supervisee's client. This understanding is especially important because the supervisor must not only follow and survey the progress of the client's therapeutic process, but also help the supervisee to disentangle his or her personal and professional issues with the therapy.

Multilingual and multicultural situations call for very subtle and empathic ways of working and, in my experience, are indeed very demanding and exhausting. Let us remember that in a supervision hour there are actually three complex personalities involved: (1) the client, who is suffering and seeks professional help; (2) the supervisee, an individual with strengths, personal problems, and complexes, as well as professional questions; and (3) the supervisor, who holds the threads of the supervisee's therapeutic work in hand and must master his or her own personal issues and projections! It is self-evident that supervision under these conditions is very demanding for all three participants.

Supervision can also be very rewarding because it enlarges the psychic and spiritual horizon of all participants and develops a beautiful intercultural understanding and awareness between them about their own and others' sociocultural origins. The human psyche, or the *mysterium*, as we Jungians dare to call the soul, is so much wider, deeper, and older than we could ever imagine. It is for us, as supervisors, an enormous opportunity to work in an international and intercultural context and help create a profound connection between peoples.

Supervision also provides an opportunity to learn that, not only does human consciousness consist of many different layers, from the very personal to the most collective one, but also that, between the personal and the collective unconscious, exists a most interesting layer of the cultural unconscious.

Even the little miniatures we use in sandplay contain various layers of conscious and unconscious meanings: perhaps a personal meaning, an archetypal meaning, or a culturally conditioned meaning. A psychotherapist, especially a sandplay therapist, learns something new in every session, day after day.

When talking about the method of sandplay, we often like to say that the symbolism suggested by miniatures speaks a universal, archetypal language. We like to think that the symbols of the miniatures are universally understandable and form a bridge over different languages and cultures. There is a certain truth in this view, but it can also be misleading. To see the miniatures only from an archetypal point of view can be quite deceptive, because we can miss the client's individual feelings and emotions connected to that specific figurine. And, when missing or misunderstanding the client's emotions, which are rooted in his or her social and cultural background, we miss an important part of the client's soul life.

There are far fewer archetypal symbols that have the same meaning all over the world than is usually believed. And even an experienced therapist cannot assume to know what stimulates a client to use a specific miniature – even less so, a supervisee. Especially when working with clients from other cultures, the therapist absolutely needs to find out what a specific miniature really means for the client. To explore the meaning of a figurine by gently asking for the context or letting the client tell a little story about it is indeed an art, but an art that is absolutely necessary to learn for all those who use symbol-oriented therapies. The supervisor must teach this art. It seems to me a very difficult but important part of a supervisee's learning process to learn how to ask about the client's sensations, emotions, feelings, and motivations without being intrusive or blocking the conscious or unconscious flow of energy. Even in the context of our familiar culture we can easily fall into the trap of pure projection when we believe that a cow in a client's sand picture is just a cow in the way we understand it. How much deeper is the trap when working on other continents! Especially religious figures have very different meanings from people to people. It would be presumptuous to believe that we know their meaning. This attitude would prevent us from being able to empathize with our clients. What is the meaning of the crucified Christ for a Chinese person? A figure of Buddha for a Swiss? Lots of questions to be answered!

There are so many other aspects to observe for the supervisor. The method of sandplay does not consist only of placing miniatures in the sand. We don't speak of "*miniature*play," but of "*sand*play." In that moment, sensations, emotions, and thoughts arising from this basic bodily contact with the sand (the matter, the earth) are already culturally defined. In cultures where people have little contact with the earth – where the earth is seen as dirty – the contact with the sand will be difficult and awaken aversions. Or, in cultures where children have few possibilities to play or playing is seen as a loss of time because performance is the goal of education, the young people start crying or happily laughing when they touch the sand and finally are allowed to play.

Therefore, the supervisor must ask the supervisee to carefully describe the beginning of a sandplay session: "How did the client touch the sand? What kind of movements did he or she make in the sand? Did he or she show emotions, feelings?" Too often supervisees show only the final picture of a session and forget that sandplay therapy is a complicated process of movements, sensations, emotions, feelings, and reflections over a specific time span and that the final picture is only the last static result of this dynamic process. Wherever we supervise, we need to teach our supervisees that sandplay is a dynamic process, and it is not just the beautiful, impressive final sand picture that is important.

I like to compare the sandplay process with a pilgrimage. The pilgrim, called "client," wanders from chapel to chapel. By wandering slowly from one place to the other, clients experience many things in daily life and maybe even more internally. When coming to a chapel, they meet a person, the therapist, who is with them in an attentive way. They then create a sand picture, a half conscious and half unconscious image. We could call it a *status quo* picture of what they have experienced and processed during their wandering. When they finish the picture and say what they want to say, they leave the picture behind and go on walking and digesting what they have just experienced. They also ponder the therapist's spoken or unspoken messages. After a while, they come to another chapel, for they have now had additional external and internal experiences and are therefore different. They meet the therapist again and create a picture. And so the process goes on.

However, the therapist also reflects on what the pilgrims created and what they had talked about together or silently exchanged. The therapist tries to understand and disentangle the pilgrims' tangible and intangible messages. This is hard work because he or she needs to differentiate his or her own perplexity and confusion from the mysterious psyche of the client, the sand creation, and the open or hidden messages.

From time to time the therapist needs help and goes to see another person, the supervisor, who does not live along the pilgrims' way. The supervisor does not know the pilgrims and does not want to influence directly their pilgrimage. The job is to help the therapist become more knowledgeable and skilled. The supervisor first wants to hear the therapist's experience and interpretation of a client's session. Secondly, the supervisor is interested in an interpretation of the client's sand pictures and wants to know "Who is the client? What is his or her origin, life story? What was the approach to the sand? What did he or she do? What, if anything, was said? What was not said but implied? Was the transference phenomenon present? What was the trainee's countertransference reaction?"

And so on. The supervisor also asks questions that elicit the projections and unconscious personal or cultural complexes of the therapist.

In addition, the supervisor needs to know the context in which the client creates his or her tangible and visible sand pictures. Many of these questions can only be answered if the therapist knows the client's personal, social, and cultural background, as well as the particular personal and cultural complexes he or she has experienced.

Many cultures have hidden social and emotional inferiority complexes that can negatively influence the therapeutic process. Social inferiority complexes can originate in racial experience, skin color, or religious or economic difficulties of a country. However, in my experience, profound war traumas that have been experienced culture-wide can be the most difficult complexes to treat.

I often notice another complication, not a cultural but a professional one (perhaps we may call it the psychotherapist's culture). Some young, idealistic supervisees may secretly nourish fantasies of grandiosity, of being able to heal their clients. Or, both supervisees and clients project the possibility of an almost magical salvation onto sandplay therapy. I have found this phenomenon in many places, but most of all in countries where the development of Jungian psychology or sandplay therapy is just beginning. Behind these projections and fantasies operates either an attitude of naivety or a compulsion for performance and resulting materialism. In the latter cases, the unconscious is not seen as a serious, helpful partner, but rather as a servant or even a slave of the performance-oriented consciousness.

A sand picture may be seen as a fortune-telling experience and the therapist as a fortune-teller. Once a young Asian person showed me the sand picture she had done in a corner of the room out of my sight. "What does it mean?" she asked. "Tell me what it means. I want to get an answer from my unconscious. My unconscious must give me direction about how to get to my desired goal!" I was speechless.

How far away from our understanding of sandplay therapy is such a young person – so far away from the internal sense of direction that develops from participating in a deep sandplay process. One of the most difficult and least rewarding tasks of the supervisor is to teach supervisees that therapy doesn't progress with seven-league boots but unfolds slowly, like a turtle, and that sand pictures cannot be forced to reveal their meaning. The best foundation for sandplay training in all countries and cultures is thorough, well-founded knowledge in Jungian psychology (or in another depth psychology) and a personal experience in making one's own sandplay creations. Knowledge of Jungian theory and personal experience in sandplay provide a carpet on which supervisors and therapists from various cultures and languages can work together.

Another observation I have with regard to working with supervisees: I have noticed that, in some cultures, the relationship between the conscious and the unconscious is very different from my own Swiss experience. Even in Europe there are many differences; for example, I have found that the consciousness of people of Celtic origin is less split from the unconscious than the consciousness of people with a Greco-Roman background. In my travels and supervision in Asia, I have learned that, in the Japanese culture, the conscious ego seems to be more connected with the unconscious than in western cultures. Of course, this topic needs much more observation and elaboration, but I find it worthwhile to mention this theme to stimulate others' observations of this phenomenon, because it influences essentially the ongoing dialogue between the conscious and the unconscious in a sandplay process.

For many years I worked at the Zürich Jung Institute with an Italian-speaking supervision group. My Italian is quite good, but sometimes when all the trainees started to speak simultaneously (which is definitely a characteristic quality of this culture!), I had great difficulty in following the hot discussions. Eventually I stopped trying to understand intellectually what they were saying. Instead, I switched to another level of understanding, namely to an emotional and bodily level of perception. The group's dynamics spoke directly to my heart and belly, so I was able to understand the group's underlying emotions, such as repressed aggressions, undifferentiated mothering tendencies, etc. I often grasped the emotions and feelings among the supervisees, as well as the group's reactions to the presented case, much more clearly on this "subconscious" level than I did when trying to understand rationally all the details and dates of the case presentation. I developed a kind of subconscious, non-rational, emotional, and physical/instinctual way of understanding.

I also use the same kind of *abaissement du niveau mental* when supervising groups in other countries and using other languages, but only if I can build up a bodily and emotional resonance to the group members – that is, if their emotional life and its expression (body language) are somehow familiar to me and not too deeply repressed. If I do not understand the language and need a translator, and if I cannot read the emotions of the participants, and even their body language does not tell me something about them, then supervision becomes very difficult. In these cases, perhaps intuition can still be reliable – but unverified intuition is very tricky! I believe that working in a very alien culture sets its own clear limits on good psychotherapeutic supervision.

To close my reflections on supervision with multilingual and multicultural supervisees and their clients, I would very much like to encourage all clinicians to learn as much as they can about the people of the world – their myths, religions, art, rituals, languages, and history, as well as their happiness and suffering! Everything we learn about other people teaches us something about ourselves.

One of my students, who came from very far away to study at the Jung Institute in Zürich, stated, "I have to live and suffer in this very different and difficult country and culture in order to understand my own origin!"

Chapter 12

Sandplay supervision in a community mental health center

Sachiko Taki Reece

Introduction

This chapter focuses on the supervision of therapists who are working with low-income and ethnically diverse clients. First, I will provide an example of this subject by discussing my therapeutic experience with Asian and Asian-American clients.

I began providing services for Asian-Americans and Pacific Islanders at the Los Angeles County Mental Health Outpatient Clinic in 1977, after receiving my license as a marriage and family therapist. I quickly realized, painfully, that my counseling skills and the approaches I had acquired in graduate school were not very applicable to these clients, most of whom were not verbally articulate. In addition, they preferred a tangible cure, such as acupuncture, to the intangible process of "talking therapy." Gradually, the seven ethnic groups of bilingual and bicultural therapists working at the clinic learned from experience and research (Yamamoto, Lo, & Reece, 1982) that even within Asian ethnic groups there are distinct, sometimes subtle, differences as well as different expectations of therapy.

Because the clinic staff were all trained in the United States and expected therapy to be a long-term process, we assumed that we were doing something wrong when clients stopped coming after a few visits. We felt that we had failed. In addition, we were taught that clients should verbalize their thoughts and feelings and that the inability to do so should be interpreted as resistance or a lack of psychological sophistication. In fact, we found that these preconceived ideas were way off the mark. We realized that we needed to rethink and revise what we had learned about how to practice psychotherapy with Asian, Asian-American, and Pacific Islander clients.

When I introduced sandplay therapy to my Japanese and Japanese-American clients, they responded well, perhaps because sandplay is a tangible process where thoughts and feelings can become visible. Although these clients were not verbally expressive in the way European-American clients are, through their sandplay expressions they easily talked – without prompting from the therapist – about memories and present and future concerns. Images and metaphors in their sandplay expressions bridged language barriers and facilitated self-disclosure, and they opened up and eagerly talked about their life histories in depth. This openness in the context of sandplay suggests that they "forgot" the cultural stigma and shame attached to disclosing troubling thoughts, at least for the moment.

Sue and Morishima (1990) report that about 50 percent of Asian-American clients who utilize mental health services drop out after one session for various reasons, compared to a dropout rate of 38 percent for European-American clients. Major factors related to dropout status included "cultural reasons, i.e., shame and stigma attached to mental health, seeking help outside of family meant weakness of the family and self etc., and unavailability of bilingual and bicultural therapists" (pp. 33–34). More recently, Sue observed: "The numbers of ethnic minorities and ethnic researchers have increased in the United States . . . Research and training on cultural diversity issues have become more of an integral part of psychology" (as cited in Rockwell, 2001, p. 5).

Setting for supervision: diversity among staff and clients

For the past 15 years, I have worked in a community mental health center in south Los Angeles as a training consultant, teaching sandplay therapy and Jungian child psychotherapy to a multidisciplinary staff and supervising prelicensed therapists, Licensed Clinical Social Work (LCSW) associates and Marriage and Family Therapy (MFT) interns in California.

Recent demographic data of this clinic's service area, south Los Angeles, indicate the following population composition: Hispanics 59.7 percent, African-Americans 34.7 percent, European-Americans 2.7 percent, and Asian-Americans 1.4 percent. Those living below the poverty level constitute 31.5 percent of this population. This area, which had traditionally been predominantly African-American, is now dominated by Latinos due to a rapid shift in demographics during the past ten years. According to the Index of Relative Need (1992), 39 percent of children and youths under the age of 18 in this area live below the poverty level. The area is characterized by poor and overcrowded housing, a high rate of unemployment, parental and teenage substance abuse, and involvement in the criminal justice system, along with a low level of educational achievement.

The majority of our clients have inner-city socioeconomic backgrounds. Sometimes parents or caregivers are illiterate, with only a few years of schooling. Often they are new, legal and illegal immigrants. Therapists and interns, who are mostly from a middle-class background with a higher education, are forced to make adjustments in building a therapeutic alliance by overcoming various psychosocial and cultural gaps with these clients. One major hurdle is language. We don't have enough bilingual, Spanish-speaking therapists, and therefore we must rely on translators in our therapy sessions. This is especially frustrating for novice therapists. Many therapists also come from diverse ethnic and cultural backgrounds (Europe, Asia, South Africa, etc.). Of course, some of the American-born therapists belong to minority cultures, too. Only a few are European-American therapists.

When faced with difficult therapeutic situations, therapists need to re-examine basic questions regarding sociocultural background to assess if they have overlooked an important factor. Where did this client come from and when? How did the person and family live in their native country – what was their life like – and how did their situation change by moving to Los Angeles (or elsewhere)? What is the religious background? Then the therapist needs to explore his or her own feelings and understanding about the client's issues and background to know how to best serve him or her. Individual and family therapy for ethnic minority clients requires so-called multidimensional approaches. Falicov's (1995) definition of "multidimensional" incorporates culture into the thinking, teaching, and learning of family therapy. We cannot provide services to our clients otherwise.

Sandplay therapy in a medical-model setting

Training therapists in a medical-model setting involves various constraints in the practice of individual and family therapy. Supervisees face time limits on treatment plans and therapeutic approaches, affecting, for example, the frequency of visits. Another complication is the need to identify a diagnosis; the client has to demonstrate "medical necessity." Therefore, the thera-peutic goal focuses on symptom reduction, aiming for visible cognitive and behavioral changes. Various day-to-day irregularities are also a struggle (e.g., missed appointments, coming late to appointments, bringing young children without notice). Clients are often not motivated to change, and they tend to take a long time to build a therapeutic alliance with the therapist – often a discouraging situation for eager and goal-oriented young therapists.

And finally, a high percentage of clients are court referrals, for whom therapy is mandatory. In these cases, therapists often need to spend at least a few sessions focusing on clients' resistance and mistrust toward the system before getting into the real issues. The supervisor needs to be quite inno-vative in inspiring supervisees to learn about, and make new discoveries, in the seemingly murky areas of inner-city work.

Role of a clinical supervisor

I believe that the clinical supervisor's responsibilities are multifaceted: (1) to teach basic clinical knowledge, including legal and ethical issues and the particulars that apply to public service systems; (2) to coach supervisees in the clinical and therapeutic approaches that would appropriately match their unique personalities and personal styles; and (3) to support supervisees' learning and development of professional identity. Of course, in addition, the supervisor is responsible for protecting clients from unethical or unprofessional conduct by their supervisees, as well as preventing any unnecessary delay in treatment.

Use of sandplay for supervision

I've found that sandplay is a powerful tool for teaching, coaching, and supporting the learning and discovery process of supervisees. Sandplay pictures often provide clues about the quality of the client–therapist relationship, the therapist's capacity for empathy and containment, and the supervisee's utilization of supervision. Although self-disclosure in supervision may intimidate the supervisee, it becomes less egocentered when the third element – sandplay pictures and concomitant narratives – is involved. To the supervisor, sandplay pictures can clearly reveal the client's pathology and coping mechanisms, thus providing a guide for further inquiries into the broader scope of the client's past, present, and future life situation. Having a concrete sandplay template on which to base feedback to supervisees is comparable to how a surgeon instructs medical students; that is, in an actual surgical situation. Usually, psychological supervisors and students have no such visible demonstration methods. The hands-on approach for teaching and coaching that is afforded by sandplay creates an experiential, case-by-case learning environment for both the supervisor and supervisee. Sandplay richly enhances the supervisory relationship and the quality of supervision.

Example 1: individual therapy

Our outpatient clinic provides services for children and youths (ages 5–18) and their families. Peter was a European-American marriage and family therapy intern with intellectual and philosophical inclinations. He came to supervision with many clinical questions and was quite eager to share his experiences. I had the impression that he had difficulty staying focused on clients' emotional states and that he had a tendency to introduce his own ideas as a way to divert attention from their emotions, or possibly his own. I noticed that he was extremely reverential toward me and idealized me. He probably acquired this style from his Asian martial arts training. I am from Japan, and he may have projected this tradition onto me. His manner suggested to me that he was uncomfortable in emotionally charged situations. I felt I should wait until some situation arose before gently confronting him.

Figure 12.1 Sand tray of 16-year-old boy

One day a client was referred to Peter by the Department of Probation. He was an extremely depressed 16-year-old Hispanic boy, who was reluctant to discuss anything in his sessions. I suggested to Peter that sandplay might be applicable for this client, because he was so inhibited and uncomfortable. Peter agreed. It was decided that they would have a regular verbal session for a half hour or so, and then they would go to the sandplay room for the remainder of the session. After one such session, I happened to be around, and Peter proudly showed me the picture his client had made (Figure 12.1). The picture was rather empty except in the middle of the tray.

At the center was Jaws and, in front of the deadly maw was a small boat. There were three other ships encircling or moving toward the center. Peter said, "I thanked him for making this picture. He was quiet about it. So we ended the session." I asked, "Did you say anything?" Peter responded, "I said, 'See you next week.'" I was disturbed by his nonchalant words to his client. I said, "Look what's happening here! Tell me what your response was while witnessing his play." I was hoping to get a sense of his 'gut' feeling response. He said he was excited that the client had engaged in play and that it was good that he had made a sand tray. I replied, "What do we see here? This is his inner world." Because the action in the sand tray was taking place at the center, my guess was that it had something to do with the client's ego–Self relationship. The spatial symbolism offered a beginning point for inquiry and exploration. "You said, 'see you next week.' Are you sure he will come back?" Peter had a puzzled look on his face. I continued, "Psychologically or metaphorically speaking, this little ship or vessel was traveling about at the center of the world and suddenly, in front of the ship, a huge creature, the Jaws, surfaces." Peter exclaimed, "Oh, no, it's a nightmare!" He explained that his client has nightmares. Peter looked quite shaken. Finally this picture made sense to him. "So," I added, "he has shared his innermost fear with you, which is the confrontation with the darkest part of himself, the devouring Dark Self. He fears that despair and rage may engulf his little ego, his ship."

Sandplay therapy works if the therapist and client can share in the transference experience in the "here and now." Bradway calls this mutuality *cotransference* (Bradway & McCoard, 1997). It is based on the mother–child experience of oneness, a *participation mystique*. In this case, Peter was not in tune with his client. His own difficulty with intense feelings colluded with the client's. Supervision needed to take this dynamic into account. Because sandplay images often hold strong emotions and ideas, the therapist needs to develop a special relationship to the client, one that is in tune with non-verbal exchanges and builds on what the Japanese understand as a *hara-to-hara* (gut-to-gut), embodied communication (Reece, 1995).

Peter was relieved when the client came back the following week. In our supervisory session, we held in our minds the client's psychic conflict and fear – the ego's fear of facing the danger of its extinction. I also associated this sand tray's imagery with the story of Jonah and the whale in the Hebrew Bible, a story *par excellence* about the ego–Self relationship. However, because Jonah was a mature man and this young client had not yet developed his identity or ego strength, I did not mention the story in our supervision sessions.

Example 2: family therapy

A family preservation program, whose goal is family reunification, is a tough place to work for a novice therapist. Bob was my new supervisee, with whom I'd had a few sessions. He is an African-American marriage and family intern, and a musician as well. He was feeling overwhelmed by the routine of a new workplace, his caseload, and other responsibilities, such as paperwork. His supervision hours, in addition to focusing on how to work with severely disturbed clients and families, became his survival container for all the frustrations and anxieties he was undergoing. I sought to support his learning as he developed his own grounding base from which to work.

His new assignment was a family of seven: parents in their mid-40s, two teenage sons living at home, and three younger children, a girl and boys in foster care due to the mother's inability to care for them (i.e., child neglect). The goal of therapy was family reunification with the three younger children.

As Bob explained how his session with this family went, his arms thrashed about and he rolled his eyes, as if exasperated. With a big sigh, Bob mentioned that the father had recently been arrested and sent to a psychiatric hospital when a neighbor called the police because he was acting peculiarly. According to the father, he was searching for intruders (para-noid?) under his own house with a torch! This man had had a car accident a few months ago and, since that time, he had been exhibiting other odd behaviors as well. Bob told me that the man's wife seemed to be reacting to this situation by "responding to her inner stimuli." I was confused and felt disturbance in my body, as though I had to steady my own bearing. I knew almost immediately that my feeling was a result of "parallel process," which occurs in supervision when the psychological dynamics of the client–therapist dyad emerge in the supervisee–supervisor dyad. I discussed this manifestation to reassure Bob by saying, "Probably your disturbed feelings were influenced by this family's psychic state, psychological field, or coun-tertransference." Then I said to him, "I need to understand how they are as individuals and as a family." I asked if he would be interested in asking the whole family to create a sand tray picture. I then instructed him on the basics of sandplay therapy. My purpose was to give him a way to contain the chaos and create a therapeutic environment, as well as to protect himself, a novice therapist, from overwhelmingly disturbing family dynamics and pathology. The sandplay structure would give Bob time to observe each member's non-verbal behavior and witness their sandplay expressions of both pathology and coping. In turn, this information would help him find appropriate ways to interact with the family as a whole and give him a chance to learn sandplay therapy firsthand, with my weekly coaching and supervision. As a supervisor, I would learn more about this puzzling family from photos of their sandplay pictures and their narratives. I then would be better able to assess how Bob's work with this family was progressing than from just his report of the sessions.

The first photos were truly eye-opening and "shocking," even for me, an experienced sandplay therapist and a seasoned clinician. "No, wonder!" I exclaimed. My surprise and reactions to these photos were reassuring for Bob. Both of us discovered a core factor in their symbolic expressions that contributed to the family's difficulty. Although the teenage sons' pictures were age appropriate and showed a psychological situation of normal range, the parents' pictures contained odd and puzzling features. The mother placed a regular-sized baby doll in the center of the tray and two large horses. The proportion of these figures was huge in the space. She also hung an empty bag over the front of the tray. Why didn't she use miniature figures? Perhaps, this was a way to convey her dominating preoccupation with, and longing for, her infant and toddlers in foster care.

The father's picture was divided at the center. Only the left side contained objects (a house, people, etc.); the right side was totally empty (Figure

Figure 12.2 Sand tray of adult male client

12.2). He explained that his family is the most important thing to him, and he wants to have a house so that they all can live together – but he has no job to support them. He has an 18-month-old baby, 2- and 4-year-old toddlers, two teenage sons, and a wife, who may be pregnant with a sixth child.

We made a referral for the wife to have a psychiatric consultation, and I consulted with a neurologist, a Jungian analyst who understands sandplay, to see if the husband's picture suggested hemineglect. Manifestations of *hemineglect* occur often in the acute phases of brain injury, such as tumor and head injury. Its core element is an inattention to one side of space, and with a right hemisphere lesion, it is caused by brain injury. I took several sandplay pictures of hemineglect cases for comparison. We made a treatment plan based on the finding that our client's empty half was not due to a neurological deficit, but to a psychological one.

With the help of housing services, this family received a three-bedroom apartment, and the younger children were returned to their parents. When the children came home, one of the teen sons moved out to live with his friend. We thought, afterwards, that he experienced the mother's behavior change to be "crazy-making," and he removed himself for his own survival. As Bob continued family therapy, the mother's sandplay pictures revealed a deteriorating, psychotic range of confusion and chaos. Bob told the service agency that the mother needed immediate help for day-to-day care and supervision of the young children at home. Bob also revised his treatment plan to empower the father by using a direct, educational approach.

Example 3: children's day treatment program

Janet is a marriage and family therapy intern of African-American background working in a child day treatment program. She is an extravert, probably an ESTJ (i.e., extraverted, sensation-thinking with decisive type). She is bright, articulate, and has a great organizational mind. She prefers goal-oriented, cognitive-behavioral interventions. Early on, she faced difficulties with her clients – that is, children and their families – who had a hard time following her directions and her well-focused treatment plans. She could not, nor did she know how to, shift gears, so to speak. Then Kevin, a 6-year-old boy, was referred to her. He was known as an "impossible" kid who kicks, hits, and bites while screaming foul language. Many times a day, Kevin gets into fights and has tantrums.

I introduced sandplay therapy to Janet, who later explained in supervision, "He was a different child when he started to play." That day, Janet saved Kevin's two sandplay pictures for us to consider during supervision. (Normally we take a photo and then dismantle the scene and clean up the space immediately after the child has left the playroom.) The first tray had a castle in the center. Ferocious large dinosaurs and dragons were invading this kingdom, and all the soldiers and knights had been eaten up by those monstrous creatures. It was a fantastic battle scene; each monster had a human in its mouth and the town was destroyed; the monster seemed victorious. Kevin moaned and groaned during the play fights. Then he wanted to make another tray. He said that this one was different from the first one because "humans thought how to defeat these monsters." Kevin again placed a castle in the center with monsters roaming around. He said, "See, people are going around and attacking them [monsters] from the back." I was so surprised to see his drama. He had showed us the nature of his sufferings and how to tackle the enemy, indirectly.

Communication through images and metaphor

I requested that all CDT staff – mental health workers (paraprofessionals), case workers, and therapists – see his work. Kevin's drama told us, "If you don't want to be chewed up by monsters, go, sneak around and attack them from behind." His extreme behavior problems had not altered for the better in quite some time. The therapist felt stuck and his condition seemed to escalate to endless repetition. But his play gave us a direction. Staff at every level understood his "play language" and the images and metaphor in his drama. We discussed how to approach his complex, that is, his aggressive behavior and despairing affect.

All staff members received a clear message from his sandplay drama: "Don't get sucked into a confrontation with his monsters." Rather, this drama suggested that an indirect, disarming, ignoring, or gentle, empathic approach would be the most effective.

Janet continued to report on his sandplay sessions, and we were utterly surprised by his new development. At one point, Kevin asked if he could remove the sand from the tray. His therapist answered, "You can play any way you want, as long as you keep three rules. The rules are, don't throw sand intentionally, don't break toys intentionally, and don't borrow toys (or steal)." He then scooped sand with a cup and poured it into the next tray. He repeated this process in silence until the tray was completely emptied. With a brush, he then swept the tray's blue surface clean and put several marbles here and there. "This is a sky," he said, and he was ready to go. While witnessing his play, Janet experienced a deep relaxation or reverie that she had never experienced "in my life!" She said, "I didn't do anything while he was making this [sky]. I was simply being there for him." In the next session, he played in a similar way, emptying out the sand, cup by cup, from one tray to the other. Then he placed marbles in the empty blue tray and a single circular object in the right upper corner of the tray he had filled with sand.

How did this sandplay work affect Kevin's daily life? This was a surprise to us. His problematic behavior changed dramatically – no more catastrophic incidents. This experience helped Janet to feel that this boy was no longer a completely hopeless (basket) case, as she was previously convinced.

Jungian perspective of the case

The boy's psychic energy had been stuck in the primitive affective state, day in and day out, with extreme affect dysregulation and behaviors as well. Consciously we tried to "unstick" his condition but were not successful. Jung (1953) described the sort of stagnation that occurs when a tension of opposites is missing: "There is no energy unless there is a tension of opposites; hence it is necessary to discover the opposite to the attitude of the conscious mind . . . Repressed content must be made conscious so as to produce a tension of opposites, without which no forward movement is possible" (pp. 53–54).

When the boy was invited to play in a safe space, he was able to play freely, to "his heart's content." Then his internal turmoil took shape in the tray. His inner world was a horrific place, as though the kingdom and humans were cursed to destruction. But we found that he also had a well-functioning mind that conceived a strategic move and showed us all how to deal with the enemy monsters, that is, the primitive affect. After we gained this understanding of his psychological state, we modified our approaches to his behavior. In the following sessions, his psychic energy swung to the opposite end, quiet reverie, and thus he unstuck himself from the terrible affect. In the quiet reverie, he created the beginning of the mythic time; a starry sky and the morning sun, night and day. Jung (1959) states this condition as:

> The symbolic process is an experience in *images and of images*. Its development usually shows an enantiodromian structure like the text of the *I Ching* and so presents a rhythm negative and positive, loss and gain, dark and light. Its beginning is almost invariably characterized by one's getting stuck in a blind ally or in some impossible situation; and its goal is, broadly speaking, illumination or higher consciousness, by means of which the initial situation is overcome on a higher level.
>
> (pp. 38–39)

The boy was in touch with a rhythm of universal order, a manifestation of the Self. This archetypal order can regulate or extinguish raw affect and stabilize one's world. Kevin's progress was sustained until he heard that the school had decided to transfer him to non-public school at the end of school year, which was a few weeks away. His behavior became rocky again, but not as disturbed as it used to be.

Janet felt that she herself has changed with him; she has embodied the experience of psychic healing and affect regulation from within.

How did these experiences change the therapist?

Janet said that she now felt confident that she can wait without talking and be able to reflect without busily trying to figure things out in the session all the time. Non-verbal and wait-and-see approaches were an unfamiliar territory for her, but now she has gained a non-verbal dimension to her therapeutic repertoire. In our supervision sessions, I have observed her changes in perspective. She became a better listener of children and especially their families, which used to be "impossible" for her. And she became more reflective of her own inner feelings and voices. She used this embodied experience with Kevin as her reference point to modify her therapeutic stance. She said, "I gained a useful metaphorical language and also an example of how the psyche can work itself out from the impasse when we provide a safe enough place." She has also expanded her existing strategic and articulate capacities with a depth therapy approach. From this grounding, she has developed a felt sense of mastery in her identity as a psychotherapist.

Feedback from supervisees

The following feedback from supervisees arrived while I was preparing this chapter. I include some of their points:

1   At the initial stage of training, a supervisor's experience may cause the supervisee to feel inadequate, not capable to take sandplay on, or the supervisor may introduce new fears to a supervisee. Example: "I presented a client whom I considered stable and ready for discharge, but the sandplay picture indicated that the client might still be in crisis. I panicked and found myself walking on pins and needles. Even the client noticed the difference." This therapist had a tendency toward perfectionism, so this was a blow to her self-image. In time, she has grown out of that unhelpful attitude through formidable effort and discomfort on her part.

2   Sandplay allows a therapist to present additional findings of a client's case that can be helpful for the supervisor.

3   Sandplay helps a supervisee understand aspects of a client's problem that may not be manifesting in the physical world during therapy sessions. Example: "I introduced an 8-year-old girl's picture that had a lot of darkness and snakes in it. During supervision, the supervisor asked if the child had a history of abuse. I asked the client's mother, who later admitted to secrets of sexual abuse of the client in the past. (Note: of course this was when I first started sandplay!)"

4   Sandplay allows supervisee and supervisor to develop a more intimate relationship that is empathetic with client's sandplay pictures. Example: "Using clients' pictures and stories that are tragic, hopeful, or simply touching will provoke a reaction in supervisee and supervisor, which may be the client's inner cry that needs to be heard."

5   Sandplay makes multiple contributions to many areas: assessment, treatment plan, rebuilding and restructuring therapy, growth of the client and therapist, building therapeutic relationship between both the client and therapist and the supervisee and supervisor.

Final thoughts

In 1992, I was fortunate to meet John Griffith, Ph.D., through my dear friend Lorna Bernaldo, whose vision it was to introduce Jungian sandplay to the Kedren Mental Health Center. Dr Griffith and his staff, Frank Williams, MD, Lorna Bernaldo, MD, and Madalaine Valencerina, MD have supported my efforts to provide Jungian sandplay therapy as an essential therapy, among other modalities, for the inpatient children's unit. By supervising therapists in such a diverse and multidimensional environ-ment, I have had a unique opportunity to introduce sandplay wherever it was needed and applicable for clients at Kedren, as well as for therapists. Thus, sandplay has also been implemented in outpatient services, the family preservation program, the children's day treatment program, and the school satellite program. Sandplay enhances supervision and the supervisory relationship. I have enjoyed exploration and discovery in each supervision session utilizing sandplay.

References

Bradway, K., & McCoard, B. (1997). *Sandplay: Silent workshop of the psyche.* New York: Routledge.

Falicov, C.J. (1995). Training to think culturally: multidimensional comparative framework, *Family Process, 34,* 373–386.

Jung, G.C. (1953). *Two essays on analytical psychology* (trans. R.F.C. Hull). Princeton, NJ: Princeton University Press.

Jung, C.G. (1959). *The archetypes and the collective unconscious* (trans. R.F.C. Hull). Princeton, NJ: Princeton University Press.

Reece, S.T. (1995). Mound as a healing image, *Journal of Sandplay Therapy, 4,* 14–31.

Rockwell, S. (2001). *Stanley Sue earns kudos for improving minority psyches,* available at www.dateline.ucdavis.edu/042001/DL.

Sue, S., & Morishima, J.K. (1990). *The mental health of Asian Americans* (4th edn). San Francisco, CA: Jossey-Bass.

Yamamoto, J., Lo, S., & Reece, S. (1982). Diagnostic interview schedule for Asian Americans, *American Journal of Psychiatry, 139,* 1181–1184.

Chapter 13

Supervision of sandplay therapy in preschool education in China

Gao Lan

My first personal encounter with sandplay therapy was in 1995 when I attended the thirteenth International Conference of Analytical Psychology in Zurich, Switzerland, and participated in a workshop on sandplay therapy led by Harriet Friedman. When I returned to China, I set up a sandplay room in my home and soon after that I initiated sandplay therapy rooms at three kindergartens in Guangzhou, China. Over several years, 38 sandplay rooms were developed in various kindergartens and schools in different areas in China.

Background of preschool education in China and related sandplay work

In China, preschool children, from 2.5 to 6 years old, live at the schools for five days a week. In these residential schools, much is dealt with beyond academia. An important aspect of the work – perhaps the most important one – is the child's psychological development and emotional well-being. Many children miss their parents and their homes very much and feel unhappy. Other children have difficulty coping not only with the separation, but also with the adjustment to disciplined living, such as asking permission and following rules. Some of these children come from homes where parents had worked all day and left them alone without limits. The shift to a contained environment can be difficult. In addition to issues of separation anxiety, some children have special difficulties, such as attention-deficit hyperactivity disorder (ADHD), and other physical and mental disorders.

As a team of five graduate students of child psychology and preschool education and six preschool teachers, we started our work in these schools as a research project entitled "Psychological Education for Children," and adopted sandplay therapy as a technique to study psychological development. I supervised the research and sandplay practice.

Our understanding of sandplay in the preschool setting

Our first step was to learn the theory of sandplay therapy and to combine the theory with preschool education. For example, we wanted to incorporate the concept of the "free and protected space," as taught by Dora Kalff (1991) and related ones of safety and empathy, as discussed by Bradway and McCoard (1997).

The environment of preschools in China today is more restrictive than open. Therefore, when we introduced sandplay into the kindergartens, we were also introducing more freedom and trying to create a healthier psychological environment for the children. With the introduction of a free and protected space, sandplay became not only a means of psychological education, but also a therapeutic environment for the children.

Ammann's book (2005) was the first we read on sandplay therapy. She stressed that sandplay therapists needed to be centered, creative, and psychologically healthy. This clear delineation was very helpful in our work, for these characteristics are also important for a good preschool educator.

I learned the importance of providing the free and protected space and the healing function that it facilitates from Harriet Friedman and Rie Rogers Mitchell, my sandplay teachers.

With this basic understanding of sandplay therapy, we started our research on the use of sandplay in preschool education.

Case discussion and reflection

We began our work as "sandplay without therapy," using sandplay as a way to provide psychological education; however, the therapeutic effects of sandplay were still apparent during the work. We held case conferences every week with the research group. The following is a typical case.

The client, "Sam," is a 4.5-year-old boy, who was labeled "the most difficult" child at the kindergarten (where about 800 children live four to five days and nights every week). He was overly aggressive, often biting other children; whenever he was corrected by the teachers, he withdrew to himself, and refused to participate in most of the activities that day. It appeared that he wanted to find a way to escape from the kindergarten.

Sam is the first child in the family. When he was 3 years old, his mother gave birth to his brother. Since "one family, one child" is still the national policy of China today, his mother sent him away to the countryside. He cried all the time because of the separation and became sick after three months. After that, his mother sent him to the kindergarten. When we started the sandplay work with him, he was in his second year in preschool. His teacher suggested to his mother that he needed "psychological work

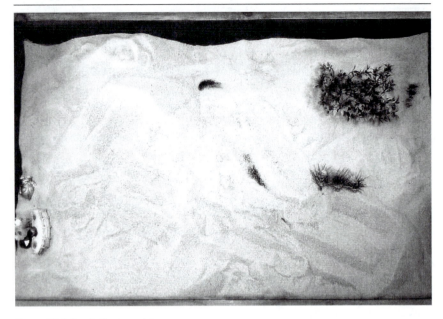

Figure 13.1 Sam's first sand tray

with sandplay." We received her permission for him to participate in this activity.

Sam started sandplay spontaneously as soon as he entered the room. One of the graduate students was the therapist and sat at the right side of the tray. Sam first played with the sand for a few minutes and then made the following initial tray (Figure 13.1). The picture was taken from the front of the tray, where Sam worked.

At the right side he placed two pieces of shrubbery, one that contained two small flowers. Near the left front corner is an overturned bridge, a car turned on its side, and a cartoon boy lying on his side. The process took about 15 minutes, and just before he left, Sam placed both of his hands in the sand, leaving his imprints.

When we looked at Sam's initial sand tray during group supervision, we all felt the difficulty that he was experiencing. The vast emptiness seemed to reflect Sam's situation at the school; that is, his inability to take part in the activities and his mistrust and withdrawal. The three miniatures at the left side (the bridge, car, and cartoon boy) were overturned, reflecting the wounded theme (Mitchell & Friedman, 2003). However, at the same time, we can see and feel some positive expression from the greenery with two small flowers. Then, close to the therapist, the two green bushes suggest a positive transference. Also, the wounded left side (the past) is clearly separated from the positive right side (the present and future). We wondered if he would be able to make the necessary bridging.

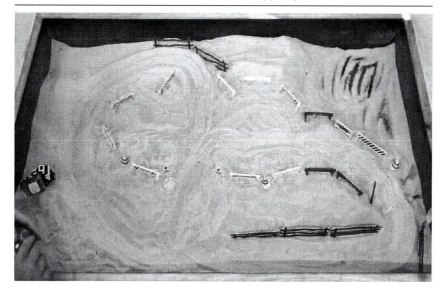

Figure 13.2 Sam's second sand tray

The therapist worked once a week with Sam, each session for 40 minutes. In his second tray, Sam used the same car and left it overturned, almost at the same place as in his first tray. He selected many traffic and road signs, many fences and two guardrails. He placed the fences at the upper and lower sides of the tray (Figure 13.2).

When we observed this tray in group supervision our first feeling was that it was difficult and dangerous for Sam to run his car. But what was the meaning of this? What was Sam trying to say to us with the sand picture? We thought his sand tray was a vivid picture of the difficult and dangerous situation he faces at school. For Sam, the road to school is rough and bumpy, full of difficulties and danger and needing additional construction.

We compared it with the first tray, where Sam had left a vast empty space on the left side of the tray. Now in this tray, he is cautiously starting to move; the tray told us how difficult and dangerous it was for him to start.

Sam used the same miniatures for his third tray: the traffic and road signs and some pieces of guardrails. He added some water into the left side of the sand tray (and even left the cup he used there), and placed the pieces of green that he had used for his initial tray in the wet sand at the left, as well as adding much more greenery and flowers at the right side (Figure 13.3).

We were able to see the improvement, comparing this tray with the first and second trays. Sam is trying to find and make his way.

The fourth tray is quite simple but meaningful. First, the ground of the tray is very flat and smooth. Second, the tray looks much more constructed

Figure 13.3 Sam's third sand tray

and balanced. Sam's life at school was changed too; it was not as difficult and dangerous for him, and he began to take part in everyday activities with the other children (Figure 13.4).

In his fifth tray, Sam is still using almost the same miniatures as before. It is clear that he still needs protection, as well as free expression. More greenery and flowers are placed at the right side. A small change – the green flowers at the bottom left corner – seems to have an important meaning. After this place was watered in his third tray, it now contains green grass with flowers growing (Figure 13.5).

Sam's sixth tray has good structure, form and balance. He used exactly the same number of traffic and road signs at the left and right sides, and made a good structure in the center of the tray. An important change for Sam is that, when he used the overturned bridge from the initial tray, he placed it upright and balanced (Figure 13.6).

Sam's final tray is the most touching one. Three weeks before the end of the school term, Sam knew that we would stop working in the sand. So, after three months of sandplay work, he created this closing tray (Figure 13.7).

Sam made a protected space in the tray. On the flat and smooth ground, the car freely moves. Sam seemed very proud of himself, for he placed a flag in the top left corner and put four flowers at the four corners.

This is a big change compared with the first and second trays. We were all touched by Sam's trays. How to understand the big change? What happened that caused the healing? These were the main issues that we discussed during the supervision process.

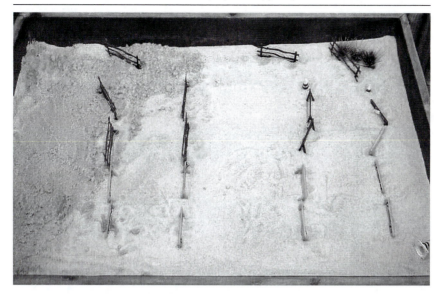

Figure 13.4 Sam's fourth sand tray

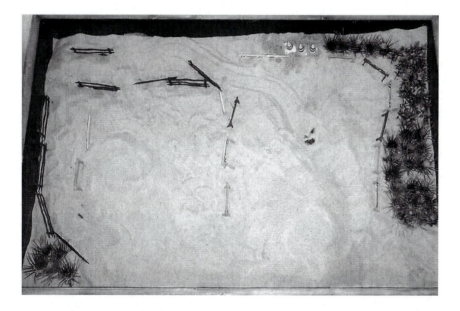

Figure 13.5 Sam's fifth sand tray

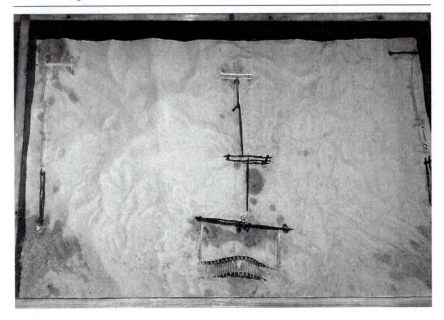

Figure 13.6 Sam's sixth sand tray

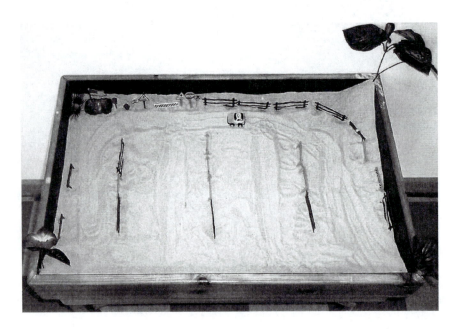

Figure 13.7 Sam's final sand tray

First and foremost, the free and protected space created by the therapist was an important factor. From using sandplay, we learned and understood much more about this basic principle of sandplay therapy.

The main cause of Sam's disorder was separation anxiety. Being sent away by his mother at 3 years of age caused a "crack" in his trust. The five days and nights in kindergarten, separated from his mother and his home, made him again feel abandoned by his mother and distrustful of her. Because he could not trust his mother, it was difficult for him to trust teachers and other children. The sandplay work, with the free and protected space provided by the therapist, rebuilt his trust in others and in his own world (the flag).

The therapist is the most important "technique." Clearly, Ammann's three characteristics (i.e., psychological health, centeredness, and creativity) were present in Sam's therapist. If the therapist can provide a free and protected space, then the client can also feel more stable, centered, and creative, as Sam's final tray illustrates.

Sandplay "without therapy"

All the children who took part in the sandplay research were quite concentrated in their "play." That gave us the confidence to carry on with sandplay therapy in the kindergartens, where we used it as "sandplay without therapy." These children expressed their creativity during the sandplay process. We can see that creativity in Sam's sand trays.

The next pictures are of two sandplay trays created by other children in the research project.

Figure 13.8 shows a tray created by a 5-year-girl diagnosed with ADHD at the hospital. After five months of sandplay work, her behavior improved in the kindergarten class. As we can see from the black and white design and the orderly way in which she places the cars, she was focusing on her sandplay work.

Figure 13.9 shows a tray created by a 5-year-old boy after three months of sandplay work. After much quarreling and fighting, his parents finally divorced. He often played with houses and furniture. This tray was made at the end of our work. My feeling is that, even though we can do very little about the outside family situation of our client, he was able to find a warm home within himself. This warm internal home can help our client, especially at this period in his life.

From the children's pictures in the sand, we learned much about them, specifically their emotional development and learning styles. Our supervision session also contributed to our learning about sandplay and helped us become more confident in its use. Mostly, though, we learned from children themselves when we observed and shared the joy they felt in freely expressing their creativity, feelings, and spontaneous images in the sand.

Figure 13.8 Sand tray of 5-year-old girl

Figure 13.9 Sand tray of 5-year-old boy

References and further reading

Ammann, R.A. (2005). Foreword to the Chinese version of *Healing and transformation in sandplay*. Guangzhou: Guangdong Higher Education Press.

Bradway, K., & McCoard, B. (1997). *Sandplay: Silent workshop of the psyche*. New York: Routledge.

Chen Guying (1992). *Laozhi: Modern translation*. Changsha: Hunan Publishing House.

Jung, C.G. (1965). *Memories, dreams, refelections*. New York: Vintage Books.

Kalff, D. (1991). Introduction to sandplay therapy, *Journal of Sandplay Therapy, 1*, 7–15.

Kalff, D. (2003). *Sandplay: A psychotherapeutic approach to the psyche*. Cloverdale, CA: Temenos Press.

Mitchell, R.R., & Friedman, H.S. (1994). *Sandplay: Past, present & future*. London: Routledge.

Mitchell, R.R., & Friedman, H.S. (December, 2003). Development of transformational themes in sandplay. Symposium conducted at meeting of mental health professionals, South China University, Guangzhou, China.

Part V

Supervising special groups

Chapter 14

Mentoring supervisors: a process model

Rie Rogers Mitchell

One day last spring, I received a phone call from Anne, a colleague supervising at a local mental health clinic. As I listened to her strained and subdued voice, unlike her usual energetic speech, I knew something was up. She said, "I think I need to talk with you. I am feeling frustrated and worried about a couple of people in one of my supervision groups."

When we met a few days later, I noticed her troubled expression and, as she spoke, the furrows in her brow deepened and her eyes looked so sad. Initially she had some difficulty in expressing her concerns, and she began the conversation by stating that she doubted whether two or maybe three of the eight interns in her supervision group would even "make it" as therapists.

She continued, "I've never had so many people in one group that concern me. They just don't seem to get it. And I don't know how to help them."

Introducing Anne's interns

As she spoke about each intern, the issues became somewhat clearer. Maya, an Asian-American woman in her early 30s, joined the clinic staff about a year ago. She had not previously worked with children, nor had she elected to take a course in child counseling during her academic training. In fact, in the first group supervision session, Maya announced that she was only interested in seeing adults and older adolescent clients. Maya said, "I feel so uncomfortable with children. I'm just not cut out for that. I know I can work well with adults; I love to listen to them and I like trying to figure out what is going on in their lives. But children seem like a whole different breed to me."

In reflecting on her own thoughts about Maya's unease with children, Anne said that she didn't believe that all therapists needed to be able to work with every client. "However," she added, "Maya just can't seem to see any other approach except 'talk therapy'." She thought Maya was far too narrow in her approach to therapy and wondered what might be underneath Maya's reluctance "to spread her wings." She was worried that this attitude might hinder Maya's effectiveness and growth as a therapist.

The second intern, Natalie, a young Caucasian woman in her mid-20s, had joined the staff quite recently and was very interested in counseling children. However, she saw children as simple, "sweet angels," who were mostly victims of their parents and other adults in their environment. The ideas that children's behavior could also affect their environment, that their behaviors in therapy may be metaphors for their experience in life, and that the symbols they use in play or sandplay might suggest a deeper instinctive awareness seemed to escape her. Anne said, "When I talk about the symbolic life or the power of imagination, Natalie just looks at me blankly. I don't know what to say to her that will help her see beyond her preconceived ideas and begin to move towards a more psychological outlook."

By this time, I was thinking, "Oh my, how can I help Anne and indirectly help her supervisees? I'm not sure what I have to offer." I was aware that my feelings of inadequacy were beginning to surface. And then, my attention became riveted on Anne's next comment. She said, "In some ways I'm most concerned about Ned – not about his ability as a therapist – but because I see him becoming disheartened."

Anne described Ned as a talented therapist, working equally well with children and adults. His African-American background and wide cultural experiences contributed to his understanding of the clinic's clients. However, Anne reported that recently he had said to her, "I like to use sandplay, art, and play therapy, along with traditional talk therapy with the children and adults I see, but I find myself asking, what am I really doing? What is this all about? I think my clients are getting better, but maybe it's just my imagination – maybe the children are just getting older and the adults are telling me that things are better in their lives because they want to please me. Sometimes, when I look at all the sand tray pictures, especially the chaotic child pictures, I just feel lost and wonder what I can do."

As Anne spoke about these three interns, I understood how distressing it was to be entrusted with their professional development and yet feel that perhaps she would be unable to nurture their growth. She was reaching out to me to help her discover ways to support and guide these interns along their paths of becoming professional and competent therapists.

Understanding the supervision group

I knew that Anne had been selected as a supervisor by her clinic's administrators because of her proficiency as a therapist. To prepare for this new role and to meet state licensure requirements, she had attended a day-long workshop on supervision techniques, but she had received no specialized training in the supervision of sandplay therapy, play therapy, or other expressive arts therapies, nor had she pursued advanced certification or specialization in these areas. However, she was knowledgeable, skilled, and clearly sensitive in the use of these approaches with her own clients. Even a seasoned therapist may not, however, have developed the necessary skills to be an effective supervisor/teacher. For example, new supervisors sometimes find that they don't have the necessary language to successfully communicate to students/supervisees what a competent and experienced therapist does naturally to help a client. Sometimes there simply are no words to describe what supervisees need to know. Thus, the supervisor is left with the critical job of exploring new, creative, and meaningful ways for supervisees to relax enough in order to learn and absorb therapy skills so that these become a natural way of being with clients.

The eight interns in Anne's supervision group were typical of many supervisees earning hours towards licensure. They all held at least a master's degree and were fairly new to the profession. They attended group supervision sessions once a week for two hours and saw eight to ten clients per week. They had been assigned by the clinic to attend Anne's supervision group without knowing her theoretical orientation or anything else about her. In addition to participating in her group, some of the interns were also in another weekly supervision group or individual supervision either at the same clinic or another one, as well as possibly being involved in their own therapy and attending professional training workshops. Some clinics sponsor workshops that are designed to enhance interns' knowledge and skills, whereas in other clinical settings the supervisor is responsible for additional training, as was the case in Anne's mental health clinic.

This general type of supervision group is quite different from the majority of sandplay supervision groups in which licensed therapists who are interested in studying sandplay choose to come under the tutelage of a chosen certified sandplay teacher. Nevertheless, these pre-licensed therapists, usually with only a modicum of training, use the clinic's sand tray and miniature collection with their clients, and their supervisor is called upon to supervise their cases, no matter whether or not the supervisor feels comfortable and knowledgeable about sandplay and play therapy.

Reminiscing about internship

After Anne talked about the concerns she had regarding the three interns, I asked her if she would be willing to try a relaxation exercise followed by a visualization to explore her feelings further about the situation. She readily agreed. After getting comfortable, I asked Anne to close her eyes and led her in a short relaxation process. Then I asked her to go back in her memory and visualize herself when she was a new intern sitting in the supervision group at her first placement. Giving her enough time to consider and feel each of the following situations, I suggested that she try to remember how it felt to be there. Then I asked her to focus particularly on her thoughts and feelings about herself and her relationship with her supervisor and other members in the supervision group at that earlier time in her career.

I have found that empathy and reflection deepen through simple relaxation and visualization exercises. Supervisors are often able to recall difficult times during their first internship and connect with how they felt. They realize that their interns are experiencing some of the same anxieties and fears.

When we had completed the exercise, Anne was surprised and pleased with herself that she had no difficulty recalling her feelings and thoughts.

She said, "I had been chosen to be an intern at a clinic with an excellent reputation. However, I didn't feel that I really deserved to be there. I felt scared most of the time and kept hoping no one would notice how 'green' I was. I remember being really 'off my center' – I usually spilled coffee on myself or someone else during supervision. My group teased me about being a danger to myself and others," she laughed. "Most of the time, I tried to be invisible, hoping I wouldn't have to say much. When I did talk, my vocabulary seemed to leave me and I found myself stuttering and groping for words."

Reflecting on possibilities

I said, "I'm wondering how you got through that period and were able to work through your feelings. What happened that helped you do that?"

"Well, as I think about it now, in hindsight," Anne said, "I believe several things helped. Of course, just being at the clinic for an extended period of time helped – I just couldn't maintain my high level of anxiety indefinitely, and I finally settled in. Also my clients helped me indirectly. Although some of my early clients dropped out of therapy after a few sessions, I did have success with a few clients. I especially enjoyed the children I saw. When I was with them, I could relax and play with them, and that seemed therapeutic for me as well as for them. Also, I was seeing a therapist for myself at the time, so I received support from her. And then, after a while, I realized I wasn't the only intern who was scared and we began to talk about our anxieties in supervision. My supervisor was wonderful; she understood how difficult this all was for us newbies. She seemed to have confidence in us and dealt with our mistakes with kindness and forgiveness."

"Do you see any parallels between what you experienced early on and what your current supervisees might be experiencing?" I asked.

"Well, Natalie does have that 'caught in the headlights' look at times. I know she has very little experience. Maybe she's just scared. Or perhaps she has not experienced how therapy can work on a deeper level – how the psyche is able to heal itself – in either her own therapy or with clients. This could explain why I get a blank look from her when I talk about non-verbal therapy, the instinctual push toward health, and the importance of symbols in expressing the inexpressible."

"Let's think more about that together," I said. "If we assume that she needs to gain more experience in working on a deeper level, how might that happen?"

Anne replied, "Well, I don't want to make suggestions about Natalie's own therapy, but maybe if I presented a sand tray case or two during supervision, the pictures themselves might help her understand."

I chimed in, "That sounds like a good idea, and it might help Maya too."

Anne responded, "Yes, I think it would, and . . . taking that idea a little further . . . maybe sometime after I show a case and talk about how I go about understanding the sandplay process, Ned would be willing to share one of his sandplay cases. Of course, I'd help him beforehand. There's nothing quite like seeing a sandplay case, in its totality, to deepen understanding of the sand pictures and the client's unconscious processes. And studying one case in depth, especially if it is one of your own client's sandplay process, is even better."

Anne went on, "But I think Ned also needs to talk more about the feelings he expressed of not being effective in therapy. When he said this during supervision, he sounded anguished, on the one hand, while on the other hand it seemed that he was thinking of his clients' progress in an almost magical way, something that just happens and is out of his hands. I think I need to help Ned talk about and understand on a cognitive level what he is actually doing to facilitate his clients' psychological growth and help them learn to support themselves in the process."

After a couple of moments of reflective silence, Anne said, "Another activity I've previously tried during supervision might work. Here's what I do. I ask a supervisee to hold an image of a client in mind and then select miniatures from a more intuitive, non-cognitive state of mind. The type of miniatures that are selected usually surprises us initially, but with reflection we often come to a deeper understanding of the client. I don't think I've done that exercise since Natalie joined the group. Of course, I'd want other supervision group members to do this activity first before I ask Natalie, so she won't be so scared. I hope this might help her better understand the power of the unconscious."

I nodded in agreement and then asked, "What other ideas do you have?"

"Well, of course," Anne responded, "the best way to learn about the deeper aspects of the psyche is to create your own sand tray pictures." She continued, "I don't feel comfortable in asking Natalie to do that, especially since she is currently in therapy, but perhaps she'll think about going in that direction after she sees a case. Whenever I show a sandplay case, I emphasize the importance of making one's own sand trays with a sandplay therapist in order to have a better understanding of the process. Natalie may pick up on this suggestion. She really does want to be a fine therapist."

Anne's belief that Natalie would benefit from participating in her own sandplay process is congruent with the current thinking in the field of sandplay therapy. Sandplay therapists believe that not only creating trays, but also having the opportunity to experience a transformative personal sandplay process, is the most significant, foundational requirement of training. It is what Lee Shulman (2005), president of the Carnegie Foundation, refers to as *signature pedagogy*. Just as physicians view grand rounds as the centerpiece of their training or their signature pedagogy, sandplay therapists view the completion of a personal sandplay process as fundamental in the education of future sandplay therapists.

Accessing the wisdom of the unconscious

I felt pleased about how the consultation session was progressing. However, I noticed that Anne was spending much more time talking about Natalie and Ned than she was about Maya.

I said, "I notice that we haven't talked much about Maya."

Anne responded, "Humm, that's interesting, I wonder what that's about." After thinking for a short time, Anne said, "Actually, I think I feel less connected to Maya than anyone else . . . in the group." At that moment Anne seemed to drift off. She seemed to be thinking hard about something.

I waited.

Then she said, "My mind just went to a strange memory. Let me tell you about it. About 15 years ago, I saw Jon, a 9-year-old boy in my therapy practice who had told his parents that he wanted to kill himself. They were of course concerned and talked with his pediatrician. The pediatrician referred him to me. Although the boy had been born in the US, his parents were fairly recent immigrants from Cambodia. His father spoke some English, but his mother spoke only her native language. During my first session with Jon, he talked openly about his sad feelings and other things that were on his mind. At one point, when our talking had slowed down, I noticed that he was glancing around the room, looking at the toys. I suggested that he might like to play with them. (I hadn't, as yet, started using the sand tray in therapy.) He shook his head and then told me that his parents didn't allow him to play anymore. According to Jon, when he turned 8 years old, they took away his toys. They told him that he was too old to play. Instead they wanted him to spend his time on schoolwork."

Essentially this is a story about a boy whose parents were misguided. They thought they were acting in his best interests. However, when he could no longer play, a meaningful and necessary part of his childhood was lost to him. This loss left him bereft, depressed, and unable to express his feelings in a natural way. For children, play is instinctual behavior and their most natural mode of expression. It is through play that children explore, create, release stress, rehearse roles, master skills, and integrate their experiences of mind and body. Play also opens up the path toward healing, balance, and internal harmony. Jon's parents wanted him to be successful and have a good life. But the means they selected (i.e., to stop his play) to reach those goals did not consider his necessary needs as a child (i.e., to play). Their mistaken approach had caused not only a psychological wound, but also the possibility of a symbolic or actual death, that is, his initial threat to kill himself would be realized.

After telling me Jon's story, Anne stopped, looked at me, and said, "I wonder why this story came into my mind now? Is this memory in some way tied to Maya?"

I waited, but I was also thinking about suggesting that Anne create a sand tray. I knew that Anne had excellent thinking and analytical skills and would easily be able to identify connections between Jon's story and Maya. I was worried, however, that the conscious connections she made might not touch into that unconscious part of her that had sent the gift of Jon's story when she was struggling with issues surrounding her relationship with Maya. I felt there was a need to access an even deeper, intuitive understanding of the connection, even though such a use of the sand tray is unconventional.

I finally decided that both approaches could be used – the verbal and the non-verbal – but that it would be best to start with a right-brain, hands-on physical approach (a sand picture) before moving to a left-brain, cognitive approach (verbal analysis). Anne readily agreed to my suggestion and after touching the sand in the damp tray, she moved to the shelves of miniatures and quickly began to select items, seemingly without much cognitive thought.

The first miniature she placed in the tray was a Native American woman sitting astride a white horse that pulled a bundle secured to two poles. Most of the remaining miniatures were placed quickly, although she did spend some concentrated time positioning flowers and vegetables in rows.

After the sand tray picture was completed, we looked at it together. Anne said, "I wanted this tray to come from the least cognitive place as possible, closest to the most unconscious space as it can be, so I only selected miniatures that caught my eye. However, when I saw the flowers and vegetables, those seemed to really fit. I knew at once that I wanted to create a garden somewhere in the tray. As I made the picture, I was amazed how each miniature seemed to find its place in the tray."

Anne went on, "Now that I look at the tray, I see some miniatures that I really like: the old woman in the right corner sitting at the spinning wheel, the goddess near the center back with her arms outstretched holding snakes in her clasped hands, the Middle Eastern man standing at the left side holding a hookah and watching the action, and the stone with the word *hope* written on its top. I do hold hope about Maya. And, of course, I love the garden – it is so vibrant and plentiful and it's being protected by the umbrellas. I also feel good about the Native American woman on horseback. She seems to be on a journey, moving from the cave in the left corner towards the garden. I think she could be Maya . . . or perhaps me."

After studying the tray for a few moments in silence, Anne added, "I don't know what the vacuum cleaner, army medal, and surfboard are doing here. Also, I have no idea about the mouse sitting by the cave entrance. Anne then pointed to a large chalice and said, "This chalice is really too big for the picture and it seems empty . . . well, actually it seems like it's waiting to be filled – maybe with rain water."

Then Anne exclaimed, "Oh, I didn't see this before! Look! In the center of the tray is a bunch of yellowish flowers that seem to be growing wild. They aren't part of the organized garden."

We spent a few more minutes just standing and looking at the tray, and then we seated ourselves once again.

Anne said, "I'm so glad I made a sand tray with Maya in mind. If I had just used my *thinking self* in considering the connections between Maya and Jon's story, I would have said that both Maya and Jon are from Asian cultures. However, I noticed that the sand tray contains miniatures from several cultures – all different from my own, plus I don't understand why some of the miniatures are even in the tray. It may be that my feelings of distance from Maya may not just be because we are from different cultures. Perhaps there are many more things about Maya that I do not understand. Maybe I need to listen and observe more."

"What else did you notice about the picture?" I asked.

"I noticed that the flowers are in full bloom and the vegetables seem ready to eat," Anne responded. "When I saw this, I thought about my relationship with Maya and the development of her skills. Maybe Maya has already enhanced her skills. However, I also noticed that the garden is full – there didn't seem to be much room for anything new to be planted or grown. Maybe Maya has enough on her plate right now – she doesn't need anything more. Yet, a group of wild flowers grows outside of the garden in the center of the tray. Perhaps something natural and beautiful, but unexpected may emerge during her journey. I think that's the hope I hold."

I then asked, "Can you come up with any connections between Maya and Jon's story – either from thinking about it or from the sand picture?"

"Let me see . . ." Anne responded. "Well, Jon's parents thought they knew what was best for him, but when they told him that he must stop playing, he became depressed and had suicidal thoughts. It seems to me that he essentially lost his way." After a brief hesitation, Anne said, "Oh, my, as I think about it now, I realize that I've had an agenda for Maya all along – from the very first day! When she announced that she didn't want to see children, I think I heard her statement as a refusal to consider any approaches outside of verbal therapy. Therefore, I believe I've been on a campaign to broaden Maya's outlook on therapy. In fact, I've been thinking about assigning a child to her for therapy, even though she doesn't want to counsel children. What's been stopping me from making such an assignment is that I believe a child would immediately pick up on Maya's reluctance and, therefore, the connection would not strong enough to support a therapeutic alliance. Now I realize that if I had made such an assignment, I would be a lot like Jon's parents – believing that I know what is best for her, rather than trusting her own natural path."

Anne then made a surprising observation. She said, "Rie, did you notice that the surfboard had a name written on it?"

"No, I didn't see that," I said.

Anne said with wonder, "On the surf board it says *Natural Breath* . . . That certainly says it all, doesn't it?"

Processing the session

In their small book, *Mentoring: The Tao of Giving and Receiving Wisdom*, Huang and Lynch (1995) define mentoring as the giving and receiving of wisdom. They state that through interactions with others, mentors share the "gift of wisdom and [have] it graciously appreciated and received by others who then carry the gift to all those within their sphere of influence" (p. xii). Huang and Lynch emphasize the point that mentoring occurs within a community, and mentoring activities help to promote a culture of wisdom throughout this community.

I am sometimes asked, "How does a mentor differ from a supervisor?" In the introduction to this book, Harriet and I define a supervisor as both "a teacher and a mentor (not a personal analyst or therapist), who is able to establish a collaborative relationship in a free and protected environment." As a mentor, the supervisor becomes a trusted ally, guide, facilitator, sounding board, and advocate, and above all invites and nurtures the "total autonomy, freedom, and development of those he or she mentors" (Freire, 1997, p. 324).

In mentoring Anne, I was mindful that the nature of our interaction was as important, if not more important, than the information she took away with her, and further I knew that both our process and content would have a subsequent impact on her interns, and they, in turn, would have an impact on their clients.

Throughout the session, Anne and I worked collaboratively. At times, I suggested a verbal or a non-verbal activity that I thought would facilitate the process and help her come up with ideas or ways of solving her concerns or defining the issues in a different manner. I tried to resist the impulse to give her direct suggestions or options. Instead I asked questions to open up the possibility of her thinking in a different way. For example, I asked if she saw any similarities between Jon's story and her relationship with Maya.

Anne was particularly open to the wisdom and reality of the uncon-scious. She was willing to tell me Jon's story and she recognized that the story was important, not a random memory of the mind. She also created a sand tray enthusiastically, using an unorthodox approach and being able to hold Jon's and Maya's stories with her during the entire process. And, after the picture was completed, she thoughtfully reflected on the tray and its possible messages. All of this helped me see that she felt protected and safe enough with me to express herself within the container of the consultation room.

The interns she discussed with me were typical of many pre-licensed people we supervise. Natalie was a young, inexperienced intern who wanted to learn but seemed anxious and overwhelmed by her new responsibilities. It was hard for her to take in information and relate it to her practice, because the intensity of her anxiety and tension was so high that it blocked access to her authentic feeling state and inhibited her connection to the unconscious. I wondered if her anxiety also limited her being able to experience a deeper level of therapy. As Anne deduced, Natalie needs time to settle in, see clients, work in her own therapy, and develop a mutually trusting relationship with Anne. Anne's idea to present sandplay cases to her group is a good one; believing the deepening of the psyche as it evolves through sandplay will speak to Natalie on an entirely different level than just a cognitive one. When Natalie is ready, it is essential that she experi-ence first-hand the movement of the psyche through creating her own sandplay process, especially if she wants to work with young children using non-verbal play and creative arts therapies. In the meantime, Anne's exercise of having the interns select miniatures with a client in mind and then reflect on the miniatures' symbolic meanings could help Natalie recognize and begin to understand the symbolic language of the psyche.

Ned's questioning of his effectiveness as a therapist and his current need to understand cognitively what he initially understood intuitively, and now doubts, is quite common among advanced interns and even some experi-enced therapists. As a supervisor, it is extremely important to recognize and address these concerns with a supportive, understanding attitude as well as offer as much cognitive, resource information as possible. Without this approach, therapists may become frustrated and move from using both talk therapy and expressive arts therapies with children and adults to working only with adult clients using traditional verbal therapies. Anne's idea of giving Ned the opportunity to discuss his concerns and present a sandplay case will provide an opportunity for him to think about and discover answers for himself. Students of sandplay therapy and other expressive therapies often attend workshops and consult with a number of different teachers in order to broaden and deepen their knowledge. A training workshop given by a certified sandplay teacher may help Ned better understand how and why sandplay therapy is effective, and an individual case consultation would help him prepare for his case presentation.

Pre-licensed therapists often state initially that they don't want to see children in therapy; however, over time, that belief usually fades as the supervisee hears in supervision about other therapists' child cases, realizes that child therapy is fun and gratifying as well, receives more training in non-verbal therapy, and becomes more confident. Nevertheless, most supervisors usually allow the supervisee to have some choice in the types of clients they see. Anne's attitude was much the same; i.e., therapists don't have to work with every type of client. Yet, Maya's vehemence worried her and, in the year Maya had been at the clinic, her attitude had not seemed to soften. Anne didn't think that the primary issue was working with child clients versus adult clients. It seemed that Maya would not allow herself to try anything new or different. Anne wondered, "Was Maya shut down in some way? Why was she so rejecting of approaches other than traditional talk therapy? Was there something in Maya's background that didn't allow her to participate in imaginative play or expressive arts? Would Maya's hesitation to 'spread her wings' hinder her growth as a therapist?"

During the mentoring session, it became apparent that a deeper dimension needed to be accessed to understand the forces at play between Anne and Maya. When Anne became aware that she was focusing her attention on Natalie and Ned, she realized that she felt distant from Maya. Then memories about a previous client, Jon, came into her mind and she wondered about the connection between that client and Maya. To understand more, Anne created a sand tray while thinking about these memories and their possible connections with her work with Maya. From that experience, she intuited that perhaps there were many things about Maya she didn't understand; she needed to observe and listen more. Contrary to her fear that Maya was not developing as a therapist, Anne's sand picture suggested movement and growth, with the possibility that something unexpected and natural might emerge – perhaps for Maya, or for Anne, or in their relationship. Connecting Maya and Jon's story, Anne realized that from the beginning she had held expectations for Maya, and she almost acted on what she thought was best for Maya, rather than allowing Maya to follow her own natural path.

My mentoring session with Anne was satisfying and meaningful. Within a free and protected space we worked together collaboratively using our thinking, feeling, intuitive, and sensate functions to illuminate issues arising in supervision. Normally, I like to make a summary statement at the end of a session, but this time I chose not to do that. I felt that Anne's reflections concerning her three interns were still in process and that, over time, additional creative thoughts and ideas would emerge.

References

Freire, P. (1997). A response. In P. Freire, J.W. Fraser, D. Macedo, T. McKinnon, & W.T. Stokes (Eds.), *Mentoring the mentor*. New York: Peter Lang.

Huang, C.A., & Lynch, J. (1995). *Mentoring: The tao of giving and receiving wisdom*. New York: HarperSanFrancisco.

Shulman, L. (2005, February). *The signature pedagogies of the professions of law, medicine, engineering, and the clergy: potential lessons for the education of teachers*. Paper presented at the Math Science Partnerships (MSP) Workshop, Irvine, CA.

Chapter 15

Group training in a crisis: an urgent response to 9/11

Rosalind Winter

Large rectangular tables covered with perhaps a thousand miniatures stood at the front of the training room in New York City (NYC). As 50 "Ground Zero" school counselors and social workers entered the room for the monthly scheduled guidance meeting, there was a sense of curiosity, wonder, and skepticism. The counselors had grown accustomed to presenters sharing their various methods of response to the trauma of 9/11. And, certainly, they had been exposed to play therapy, but so many toys and sandboxes – just what was this "sandplay therapy?" And how could it, with all this "stuff," possibly work in a school setting? Intrigued, the counselors were receptive and willing to explore another possible response that might be useful for "their children, their students"; those who were struggling with the after-affects of 9/11.

Not all of the children in the Ground Zero school area were responding well to the traditional forms of trauma interventions. Cultural values were impacting the use of verbal therapies, particularly in Chinatown, where expression of feelings was considered inappropriate. Supervising guidance counselor Sheila Brown and director of the 9/11 response Marjorie Robbins were deeply concerned about this population. Ms Brown was searching for resources that might work with this underserved ethnic group. That morning, after my first presentation to the school counselors, Sheila canvassed the group and identified the counselors whom she believed would be able to commit to the required ongoing training if the program were to be truly effective. We met later in the day with the interested group, described the high level of commitment that we would expect of them, and then selected 20 of the interested counselors who would begin our program the next day.

Little did I know or understand the implications and significance of what was to develop over the next four and a half years for both the participants of the training and myself. In this chapter, I focus on three significant issues that emerged in our work together: (1) diversity of the group; (2) multiple role relationships for both myself and group members; and (3) group dynamics. The extraordinary diversity of experience, spiritual orientations, ethnicities, and talent of the group would require care and attentiveness. As a consequence of running a long-term training program, I would have multiple roles that included trainer, mentor, supervisor, cheerleader, advocate, and evaluator – roles that could and would conflict with each other. And thirdly, as a result of the ongoing nature of the training and its focus on a personal depth experience as the means of developing clinical skill, we would all face group dynamics that could and would either thwart or enrich the training program.

For me personally, the work was challenging, immensely rewarding and demanding. I maintained a full private practice in Montclair, New Jersey; taught at the Jung Institute of New York; ran an ongoing sandplay training group; and had a teenage son at home. I was also president of the New York Society of Jungian Analysts, which would split into two societies during the third year of my work in the schools. In its own way, the symbol formation project became a grounding focus in my life. It allowed me to re-enter the larger collective, apply my knowledge of Jungian views of the psyche and society, and expand the level of therapeutic knowledge in the educational system, where I had first started my professional career as a teacher. This was profoundly gratifying. My participation in this work was not a choice; it was a moral imperative, or in Jungian terms, it was directed by the Self, something greater than my personal ego. Each obstacle became an opportunity to move beyond some limited view of what was possible. Whenever I had the thought that this was too much, that I could not go on, I would be inspired by the counselors or by the symbol formation/sandplay work itself. I would get caught up in what Sheila Brown called the "warm energy system" of the group, which constantly generated support and an irresistible and gratifying self-exploration. It was a sacred *temenos*, a free and protected space in which we all felt held.

Symbol formation, an adaptation of sandplay therapy, began as an urgent response on 9/11 in the Montclair, New Jersey, schools. On 9/11, as I worked with a group of 60–80 students at Montclair High School, who did not know whether their parents, relatives, and close friends were alive or not, I experienced the intense affect that overwhelmed us all. We were flooded with emotions and images, and we traumatized ourselves by watching the attack on the World Trade Center (WTC) over and over again. We wanted our students to show up at school, we wanted our teachers to be able to lead and to contain the chaos we were all experiencing. It was nearly impossible to function, yet we had to. In the midst of the chaos of the day, I recalled (reminded myself about) the power of symbols to hold unbearable affect. I knew the depths of our psyches would find the exact images and symbols that would help us, if we provided an opportunity to access them by tapping into the resources of the collective unconscious. Archetypal symbols, the shared universal images deeply embedded in all of us, tap into patterns and energies of healing. Perhaps we could foster the process.

With the leadership of a receptive principal and assistant principal, Elaine Davis and Bruce Dabney, the Sandplay Therapists of America (STA) community, and family and friends, I was able to install a set of miniatures, a sand tray, and sand in a walk-in closet in the freshman building of Montclair High School. As a result of a grass-roots movement among school counselors, social workers and nurses, within two months symbol formation sets were in each of the 11 schools in the Montclair School District.

In time, we came to describe symbol formation as a non-verbal, tactile medium for the creative expression and containment of disturbing feelings and experiences through the use of a sand tray, sand, and miniatures. In this process, a person has an opportunity to create an image/symbol of his or her inner experience in a free and protected space. This type of non-verbal expression and mirroring leads to the binding and containment of emotions, which results in increased tolerance of frustration and greater impulse control – a basis of ego stability and growth. Symbol formation, with the appropriate selection of miniatures and attitude of play, is a culturally and gender-free medium that provides an opportunity to express, concretely and symbolically, what is most urgent in a person's life. In its use of play, it manages to bypass the typical defenses, resistances, and impingements of the client and counselor, giving the person the opportunity to work at the level that is most authentic for him or her.

A few months after 9/11, I was asked by Linda Lantieri, the representative of CASEL (The Collaborative for Academic, Social, and Emotional Learning) at their Ground Zero Satellite Office to present my work with the Montclair School District to the NYC Ground Zero, District #2 leadership as well as representatives from major funding groups and trauma centers. Sheila Brown, representing the Ground Zero schools, had the awareness that symbol formation could potentially draw on the non-verbal and aesthetic strengths of the Chinese culture and as such might be an effective immediate response to the both 9/11 and other daily trauma experiences in the Chinese-dominated Ground Zero schools. As a result of that meeting, Sheila Brown suggested that we try symbol formation in the Chinatown schools.

We decided to present an introduction to symbol formation to all the counselors in District #2 in a morning experiential training session, and then select 20 counselors for the full two-day training program. By the time we had finished our two-day training, many of the counselors saw the potential of moving symbol formation training into sandplay training. We openly explored which counselors would want to commit to more extensive training. They all had cases that were difficult, that required a more therapeutic stance and would seem to respond to the depth that sandplay work could offer. This training would include twice-a-month personal process (adhering to the basic tenet that a therapist can work with only a client to the level that he or she has reached him- or herself), twice-a-month super-vision groups, a weekday monthly basic training, and monthly Saturday meetings with certified sandplay teachers from around the country. There would be no remuneration or cost for this extensive commitment. But it was clear that all would benefit from the training, both personally and pro-fessionally. The group enthusiastically moved into a deeper level of training, with 18 of the original 20 choosing to go forward. Sheila Brown took up the cause of finding the resources to make the in-depth training possible.

Diversity

The group of 18 was diverse in a multitude of ways. It was composed of Asian, African-American, Hispanic (from various Latin countries), and Caucasian social workers, crisis counselors, and guidance counselors. There were 17 women and one man. We had mixed levels of therapeutic talent, skills, and knowledge of psychological development. Diversity was clearly our asset. It provided us with a tension, moments of struggle, and opportunities for growth. Fortunately, we had so much diversity that any two participants might find themselves in disagreement or on different sides of an issue at one moment, but aligned in another moment. This kept the group energy in motion, never allowing for totally fixed positions.

Not everyone agreed that a therapeutic response was appropriate in a school environment. Some counselors believed that therapy did not belong in schools. Others felt that a therapeutic response was the only way to effectively deal with the level of trauma that the children were experiencing. This diversity of psychological interest was reflected in the different levels of professional training among the group members. Some had advanced training at psychoanalytic institutes; some were faculty at New York University (NYU) in the Social Work and Art Therapy Schools; and a few were new interns, not completely finished with their graduate education. Some had limited knowledge of therapy and had never experienced their own therapy. Some had ongoing private practices, others worked part-time for social agencies, and others would never dream of doing any work outside the school system. Some, with psychoanalytic training and depth orientation, wanted to work as deeply as possible. They typically had experienced depth therapy themselves. Others were more familiar with concrete services and were hesitant to open up the issues that would come up in any trauma work. This reluctance would be challenged by the reality of the situation. We were dealing with trauma constantly. Extensive 9/11 resources brought a multitude of trauma trainings to this group. Being trained in trauma eventually forces us to face our own traumas. In some cases, this opening up of personal traumas was contrary to the cultural norms of the counselor. The Asian culture frowns on the expression of feelings, whether verbal or nonverbal. The Chinese counselors in general, but not all, were challenged by their own personal and cultural experiences and did extensive work to be able to move from their cultural-based values to those held by the larger therapeutic community.

The diversity and range of religious/spiritual attitudes and experiences impacted the group. These beliefs would come to the fore as we worked with the symbolic realm, bringing deeply-held beliefs into potential question. Some participants struggled to imagine that there was something greater than one's own ego. Others, as part of their religious beliefs, felt that there was only one true image of the divine. An openness to a multitude of images and symbols of the divine is a significant aspect of sandplay theory, which is based on a Jungian understanding of the psyche. For some in this group, coming to terms with a theory that was in contrast to deeply-held atheistic or religious beliefs was a life-altering process. These counselors worked deeply and valiantly in their own spiritual and sandplay processes to be able to hold alternate realities. For some, a transcendent experience emerged, leading to profound changes in personal, professional, and spiritual lives. Eventually, it became clear that those who remained in the program would have to be committed to a deep individuating process that would shake their sense of reality, open them to the unknown, and often bring them into conflict with their familiar ways of being.

An unexpected factor was that the Chinese counselors, in general, had little connection to their ancient Chinese traditions. Reconnection to these traditions, through an experience and understanding of universal, sometimes ancient Chinese symbols was both awakening and occasionally resisted. A split-off piece of the psyche's heritage was moving into consciousness and value.

There was a diversity and range in the level of personal chaos in the trainees' lives. Family businesses of some had been shattered by 9/11. Others had lost people dear to them. Some struggled with profound loss during the training program, including the loss of siblings and spouses. Others had to work with the life-stage issues of aging and ailing parents. A significant number of our participants struggled with cultivating new marriages, difficult pregnancies, and the realities of having young children while being in training. Some members experienced limited change or chaos in their lives and were eager to move ahead in the training. They wanted extra readings, more time spent on supervision, and a quicker pace. The tension between these varying needs was worked with by both the leaders and group members. Even though efforts were made to accommodate personal realities, including the bringing of babies to workshops on Saturdays, for some the timing was just not right. They could not spare the psychic and physical energies required for an in-depth training. We all had to be flexible and adjust to the realities and limitations of our lives. Life continued as we continued the training process.

Two training tracts seemed to emerge in the group: one focused on the use of symbol formation as a short-term immediate response to a crisis situation, and the other interested in pursuing the depth training of sandplay therapy. We worked hard to provide an environment that would accept and foster both levels of training. Additionally, it was important to provide the opportunity to change one's mind at any point in the training and move from the symbol formation focus to sandplay therapy focus, or the reverse. Over time, it became clear that this training was possible only if there were enough personal and professional resources in place. All of our participants had personal resources and support available to them. For some it came from a spouse, a child, a sibling, or their school principal. In addition, Sheila Brown, the counselor in charge of this program, became a personal support for all of the counselors involved. She was aware of group members' personal and professional conflicts and often tried to facilitate their continued participation in the training. Ms Brown gained release time for trainings, made sure that other trainings for the same group of counselors would not conflict time-wise with our meetings, and negotiated with district-wide as well as individual school staff who did not understand and thus did not welcome the sandplay modality in the school environment. Upon occasion, she even facilitated the transfer of a counselor to another school. She used her power and influence to find funding and to free up grant money when it was being bureaucratically blocked. She was able to communicate its success to those who needed to hear it. She stood up to the criticism inherent in the use of sand and toys, i.e., it was just play, sand would be on the floor, it would make a mess, kids would steal the toys, and so on and so on. She kept the training running. I could never have done both her and my role. I can't imagine that any clinician could. It was our joint effort that brought the program to life and then sustained it over time.

There was also diversity in the actual training. We made our mistakes, especially in designing the program. Ideally, I would have thought it out more clearly, had I realized that the training would go on for four-plus years and that we would bring in new people yearly. Instead we tended to design curriculum in response to what the counselors seemed to be dealing with in their work with the students. As we entered our second year, it would have been best to change our design to a modular one that would help us fill in what the new counselors needed. For example, we found that some group members had attended two sets of colloquiums on alchemy, whereas others had attended one session on only one of the alchemical operations. We did begin with a basic structure. Each time we added new members, we offered the first two days of symbol formation training again. We gave the new group extra hours of supervision, but at minimum they were missing a year's worth of training. Some of the new members were able to do extra readings, attend other workshops that I led, or go to conferences to gain additional training. However, one core group did not have the same exposure to the material. Additionally, and more troublesome to me, I became confused. Because I had to teach the same material several times and did not track exactly what I had taught in each session, I was unsure who had had what parts of the training. A certain amount of chaos resulted from the ever-changing nature of the group, the removal of the requirement that all participants attend all training, my lack of record keeping, and my spontaneous style of teaching.

Regardless of the diversity of group members, all were highly valued in their work environments and had a strong therapeutic background. They were all connected by time, location, and shared tragedy. They experienced themselves as a group deeply concerned about each other. Additionally, from their own experience at the first morning of training, they had a sense that there was something powerful in the symbol formation work and they all thought it would help them fulfill their own personal commitments to working with the school children at Ground Zero. We might hypothesize that they all had access to, and were driven by, varying degrees of rescuer archetypal energies. They were all affected by the circumstances in NYC Ground Zero schools on 9/11. They felt called to a purpose greater than their own personal or previously defined professional lives. These universal aspects deeply served the group and its process during difficult times.

Dual roles

My collaboration with Sheila Brown was my first dual-role relationship. We organized the training program, struggled with those who seemed to be questionable in their commitment, determined how to approach funders, selected the miniatures and sand trays to purchase, and deliberated on whether to ask a person to leave the training program or not. Although I held the clinical authority on what was necessary in the training, she held the authority on what was possible. We worked together intimately and, without her, the work could not have been done. We became friends. The reality of my role as her trainer and possible evaluator was uncomfortable. Fortunately, Sheila decided not to become focused on her sandplay training but rather to manage the training for the group.

The most obvious of my many dual-role relationships was a result of the limited number of Sandplay Therapists of America (STA) certified sandplay therapists and teaching members in NYC. Only three STA teaching members worked in the larger New York area. Therefore, all of us had to be involved in the personal process aspect of the training in NYC. I was one of the three. Initially, symbol formation was emerging and evolving through the counselors and my working together on almost a daily basis. I created and did the trainings and supervision as a direct response of what was going on with the counselors and their students. As the program became more stable, well funded, and moved into sandplay therapy, other STA teaching members came to NYC to assist in the training. I assigned the counselors their personal process therapist. I elected to do the personal process part of the training with those counselors whom I felt could best handle dual relationships. They tended to be those who were more mature, with more life experience and more dual roles in their own lives. It worked, more or less, with a good deal of processing and consciousness on both sides. This set of dual roles led me to be careful, in both individual process and the larger group, about sharing my personal life. However, teaching is significantly different from clinical work. Because I used case material in my trainings, the counselors who worked with me in their individual process knew more than was ideal about my style and the theoretical underpinnings of my work. This sometimes caused confusion and tension. What would I say about them if I were presenting their material? Are they like such-and-such example that I discussed in the large group? Some felt an extra privilege to be working with me individually; others felt pressure to be more "right/perfect" in their work as a sandplay therapist, since they were getting the "best" training. Others were negatively impacted by believing that those working with me knew me better. Issues of sibling rivalry and envy surfaced in the larger group.

Additionally, my son was involved in setting up the miniature sets for the symbol formation and sandplay training. Many of the counselors met him and saw him work. This proximity actually created less difficulty than I had imagined. He kept fairly quiet, and the counselors did not ask him many questions. In this case, I think everyone was protecting him and themselves from too much involvement.

I served as an advocate for the counselors, requesting a modification on their requirements to become STA members. Eventually, I petitioned the STA Board of Trustees to consider other levels of membership for the entire STA organization that might serve those with limited financial resources and the areas of the country where it was difficult to obtain a sandplay process. I was not neutral in promoting STA membership and advanced training among my students, the counselors. As a result of my advocacy role of wanting a larger number of certified sandplay therapists in the NYC region, I found myself not waiting to see if becoming an STA member or sandplay therapist grew organically out of an individual counselor's personal process or psyche. In most cases, I just encouraged the commitment to the symbol formation/sandplay training program. And although part of me wanted to be indiscriminate or universal in my positive attitude that all of the counselors could become symbol formation or sandplay therapists, I knew in my other role as evaluator that they would and could not. How could I hold the possibility for growth and development as a clinician for each counselor when I had serious doubts about their capacity for consciousness and symbolic depth work? There was tension in these two roles as advocate and evaluator. I periodically would feel a need to have a conversation with a counselor about where he or she was in the process. Naming it honestly seemed to be the way I could hold the tension and the role conflict. The counselors I was most concerned about did leave the program. Was it because I was evaluating them (perhaps not spoken directly to them, but I am sure it was felt), or was it because in truth they were not appropriate for the level of sandplay training we were doing as we moved through the years? Of course, we do not know the answer.

Conflicts in my roles of cheerleader, evaluator, and psychotherapist were exacerbated by our decision to offer certification in symbol formation. This decision grew organically from our funding efforts. The funders wanted to know what the counselors could expect to gain from doing this training. Certification in the basic skills of symbol formation seemed quite appropriate. Symbol formation certification standards were based on the STA certification criteria. For example, STA requires two ten-page symbol papers. For symbol formation certification, we required two one- to two-page symbol papers. My goal as cheerleader and advocate was to launch the counselors into the process of meeting STA certification requirements. However, the certification process put me in the role of evaluating whether or not the counselor's work was "good enough." My general educational role stance had always been that it could be good enough if the student would just give it more attention. In the end, I continued with my educator's stance. I mostly evaluated their effort and quality of work on the papers and more minimally evaluated their clinical skills. Of course, my role as evaluator impacted a counselor's individual process. For some it was a struggle not to participate in the certification program. For those with whom I worked individually, this issue of certification, and whether to do it or not, was dealt with more consciously – which is not to say it did not have both conscious and unconscious ramifications for all of us.

In my role as a trainer, one of the ramifications was simply that I felt frustrated with the limited effort that some of the counselors were willing to put into some of the training requirements. I had to remind myself consciously about the nature of the individuation process, my academic bias, and my interpretation of "work ethic." I would tell myself, not everyone wants to put effort into the written requirements for a variety of valid reasons. I found this reality difficult to tolerate in those I thought were gifted in their clinical skills. I particularly wanted them to move forward in their training to become "certified." Eventually, I was able or forced to become congruent with the principles of depth psychology as they applied to my students. The individuation process of each member became more important than the training goals of our program.

Sheila and I agreed to support those who were most committed to the training. It was exciting to have some people who were both talented and committed in the program. We made sure that this select group had access to outside speakers for individual supervision first, and, when we had some extra money to spend on individual supervision, they would be the first to be involved. However, I think those who were less interested in "certification" received fewer benefits of the possible training. Our resources were being used to support collective "legitimization."

In the STA organization, sandplay candidates receive an advisor or mentor. The counselors frequently approached me with their questions and concerns about their individual paths to becoming sandplay therapists. I often responded to four or five emails or phone calls a day. This level of interaction became time consuming, sometimes interfering with training or process sessions. I tried to take the first 15 minutes of large group trainings to respond to the more general questions. However, a good deal of support was needed to understand the requirements and to clarify them for those for whom English was a second language. I asked STA members outside of New York to take on the role of advisor. There was some positive response. I would find the details of both managing the training program itself and organizing the data on the counselors overwhelming. I had always let those training with me be responsible for themselves. In this group there was pressure for me to organize the data for them. I did not want to do that, and eventually some of the counselors who were more naturally sensate oriented made up forms and kept track of all the topics of training sessions. As we brought in other people to work in the grant, I also had to mange their invoices, their schedules, and their particular issues and needs. This work level was also overwhelming sometimes, as I was trying to keep the rest of my professional life going. Additionally, although our monthly guest presenters were a treat for all of us, the presentation usually required an additional Friday night and a full Saturday of my time and energy. Often the guests would stay with my family. Sheila Brown was aware of the time I put in and suggested I charge for some of it. A minimal amount was billable, but most was not. There was significant tension in wanting to do everything well and thoroughly and keep all the pieces working.

Dual roles were inevitable in this crisis-based group training process. We clearly did not have enough STA teaching members available for the different aspects of the training. Some of the role conflicts certainly made it impossible to do a "clean clinical" process for all of the counselors. Fortunately, the sandplay work itself took over in the sessions, providing each counselor with a valuable depth experience. It was in our imperfection that we worked and struggled together to sort out what would be best and what they should not do with their students, in part based on our own "difficult" experiences.

The nature of responding to such a total crisis in a school or perhaps in any environment requires (1) flexibility; (2) a willingness to work with administrative personnel in an intimate manner; and (3) quick response time in order to develop the trust of the organization. The person responsible for the training must understand the essence of the organization and be willing to meet its needs. I believe that it was because we were willing to be messy, to do what seemed necessary in the moment, and in fact, to openly make mistakes that this training process actually happened. We all had to be able and ready to say, "Let's try that again in a different way." Anyone who had thought it all out methodically would have said it couldn't have been done. And I am sure they would have been correct. We learned what was possible as we experienced the process ourselves.

Group dynamics

The group ethos was one of support, reliability, and deep concern for each other and the students who did symbol formation/sandplay. Its shadow was competitiveness, envy, and cliquishness. Although like many groups in their strengths and vulnerabilities, the symbol formation/sandplay group was unusual in its commitment to stay focused on the purpose of the training and take responsibility for mediating their own shadow qualities. More specifically, the strengths of the group were (1) a shared commitment; (2) an emerging sense that the training was serving professional and personal development; (3) a task leader with authority; and (4) personal ego resources. The counselors reported that they were deeply engaged in the training at first because of sandplay therapy's role in healing the children. Many said that the training gave them another tool in their toolbox. Some saw it as an opportunity to further their professional options, including possible membership in STA and the possibility of a private practice in the future. However, most significantly, almost all stated that eventually they realized that they themselves were developing psychologically and spiritually as a result of the training. As one counselor put it, "This is for us." Sheila Brown, as the leader within the group who had legitimate authority within the school system, was a powerful force who had to be reckoned with, and the issues she brought up could not be avoided. In some ways, her voice kept the integrity of the group's training function prominent. Additionally, each member brought a sense of fairness, a willingness to explore personal issues, and a capacity for self-reflection that supported and sustained the group's process and the task of training and personal development on a daily basis.

It is important to look at how the group was formed, the nature of its members, and key interactions that determined the ethos of the group. District #2 counselors were deeply bonded as a result of both sharing the tragic experience of 9/11 and their collective roles of caretaker in the midst of the chaos and uncertainty of that time. We began with a group that was both selected and then self-selected. The sense of being chosen to do this special training added a feeling of coherence to the group. The group shared a sense of "being in on something big." In some ways Sheila and I worked to foster this feeling. We were aware that the counselors were going to need to make a significant commitment to the training, and we wanted them to feel it was worth it. There was a powerful felt value of the training and support for being in it. This valuation and support remained an underlying foundation for the training program throughout the years. Although there were the expected acting-outs one would find in any group, the foundation of mutual support and shared vision was available to enough people, at any given time, to redirect the group back into a cohesive whole that could withstand its own group process.

Eventually, issues of scarcity, deprivation, and sibling rivalry surfaced, as they would in any group, and most often manifested around the concrete materials of the training, miniatures, and trays. Initially, perhaps for the first six to eight months, group members were willing to share all resources with a high level of sensitivity to each other's needs. Each member of the original group received a full set of miniatures and a tray with sand. As we obtained additional miniatures, more conflict arose. Some of the counselors were in the same school and we felt a need to spread the resources among the schools. This meant that some individuals who were at a school by themselves got more "stuff." Additionally, some counselors used their own money to augment their collections: when new "stuff" was being handed out, others felt that they had less and were therefore entitled to more. Those who purchased their own materials were annoyed that they "lost out" because they had gone out and invested in their own collection of minia-tures. Additionally, several counselors were in the same school; many became proprietary about their miniatures, because they had used their own resources to develop their collections.

Another area of unsettledness emerged later in the first year. As the diversity of levels of skills and commitment became clearer, we made a decision to allow the more experienced clinicians to move from symbol formation work into sandplay therapy. This group received an additional sand tray and the permission to use water with their students. This change caused some bad feeling among some of the clinicians, who demanded that each person have two trays, and then struggled with my assessment that some of the counselors were more skilled than others. Some felt that it was flatly unfair that they had only one tray and others had two. Although this was difficult, I openly stated and made decisions based on my evaluations of clinical skills. Inevitably, this caused tension within the group. Did this cause alliances between the "haves" and the "have not's"? The acting out seemed to center around who got the "new miniatures" that Sheila and I brought to group meetings, and whether a counselor could use another counselor's miniature collection if hers was unavailable at a particular moment. Officially, Sheila and I managed the issue by supporting those who added to their own collections and insisting, whenever possible, that the trays were for the children's work and needed to be shared, and holding to the decision that each counselor was only allowed to use a wet tray when officially deemed ready by me. (In all cases, we supplied the trays.) No one seemed willing to let the tension risk the group training. I noticed that some of the counselors who were more intimate with the upset members might intervene and smooth the way. They found nuanced methods of keeping themselves intact as a group.

Our goal was not to work out emotional issues in the group, though we occasionally did in order to remain a working group. Sheila held the role as the distributor of "stuff" and the arbitrator of conflict. She was exceedingly fair, and her decisions were accepted as law. She rarely reprimanded the group, and when necessary, returned to the overarching vision of serving the children. She was quite cognizant of individual investment into the materials and wanted to support and not punish it. This created an ethos for the group. If a conflict was brought to me, I would send the person to Sheila to work it out. Between ourselves, Sheila and I would vent about a group member's behavior; I believe that this venting kept us both able to process the group and reduce our acting-out. In this way we were co-leaders of the group. With Sheila as the authority on administrative issues, I was free to stay out of most of the daily issues and hold a more neutral position within the group.

In general, especially the first year, miniatures and trays was fairly equally distributed. Notes and forms that one person created were often shared with the entire group. Parent consent forms were created in Chinese and Spanish, and all counselors used them. There was a high level of attentiveness to each other's needs, experience and strengths. One counselor might remember that another was lacking a particular miniature and would be on the lookout for it. If a counselor had worked with a child at an earlier time, files might be pulled out and shared, or emotional support on the difficulty of the case might be offered.

The situation became more complicated as we brought in new members as part of a turnkey operation, planning to institutionalize symbol formation/sandplay in the schools. The inadvertent "out-ness" that we created when conveying the "specialness" of those in the training reverberated as we integrated new members into the program. "When" a person joined the group was the key method of identifying oneself within the training program. It became the most consistent issue for most of the members not in the original group. One of the ways this issue manifested was in the view that you were more special, luckier, and perhaps more significant, if you had had more years of the training. If you had been around a long time, you had more miniatures, more hours of personal process and supervision, and were further on your way to possible symbol formation certification or sandplay therapy certification.

One of the most "special" experiences we offered the initial group was an opportunity for members to do their own process with an STA member, every other week for a year. This arrangement took place during the second year of the program. The third year of our program, we did not have enough money to replicate this opportunity for the new members. Instead we required new members do three or four sessions with a mentor, an advanced student from the original group. We tried to match up people who were not friends and not in the same school. For some, doing several trays with a "peer" was workable; for others, it set up issues of power, vulnerability, and alliances. In neither case was a safe *temenos* created. The training was deeply impacted by this mistake in planning and judgment. Often the required sessions did not happen, and thus the new member did not have the experience of doing his or her own trays. This absence of personal experience had a significant impact on members' understanding of the power of the work and thus the training itself. The following year we decided to use our monies to have all the new members do three sessions with an STA therapist. In hindsight, this was one of my more significant mistakes. I let the circumstances divert me from the fundamental training truth: that a clinician can take a person only to the level that they have experienced. With more focused consciousness, I may have been able to resolve this problem differently.

Using very broad strokes and generalizing, I would say that cultural and ethnic ethos were part of the group dynamics. Over time, the group became increasingly Chinese in ethnicity. Occasionally, Chinese members would speak to each other in Chinese, and the non-Chinese-speaking members were cut out of the conversation. Meanwhile, the Jewish members occasionally resorted to Yiddish. Most of the time there was a questioning of what was being said, and the conversation came back to the larger group. The Chinese and the Jewish members almost always brought food to our meetings. The Chinese were often the ones we asked to shop for us in Chinatown, where they might get a better deal on miniatures. Jewish and Italian group members tended to be more verbal than the Chinese. Most of our Chinese counselors were also Christians and struggled with multiple symbols of divinity, which were more comfortably accepted by our Hispanic, African-American, and Caucasian Christians. One of the nicest characteristics of the group was members' sharing of their ethnic and cultural diversity. For example, we collected many versions of Cinderella when we were studying fairytales, as each cultural group contributed tales from their heritage. Symbols and stories were naturally explored from many cultural points of view, leading us all to feel enriched.

As group members developed at varying rates and the group grew in size over time, the level of training needed to become more differentiated. Two counselors with the most clinical training and experience joined my ongoing NYC sandplay training group. I felt confident that these counselors were receiving the appropriate level of training when they joined a group of equally skilled and committed professionals. Many of the NYC counselors knew about the "special status" of these members. Since one of them had recently retired and the other ran another therapy training program in the schools, I do not think there was much resentment on the part of the larger group. Interestingly, as the NYC counselors talked about their training in the ongoing group, some of the ongoing members became resentful of the "free" training opportunities afforded the school counselors. Becoming a certified sandplay therapist is quite an expensive training process. Fortunately, Sheila Brown readily invited all sandplay students to our Saturday presentations by out-of-town STA teaching members. The opportunity for the counselors and my ongoing training group to interact enriched each of their experiences. The Chinese counselors brought their heritage and understanding of symbols and the Chinese psyche to the non-Chinese group; the school counselors gained a greater appreciation of the potential depth of sandplay work; and the ongoing group gained an awareness of the application of sandplay work to an institution and the difficult realities of many children's lives.

More complications arose in the fourth and final year of our training. Several in the last group of new counselors were recent graduates of an art therapy training program and had previously been supervised in their school placement by one of the most experienced and well-trained clinicians from the original training group. (She was one of the two mentioned above who moved into my ongoing sandplay training group.) She had trained them well and was a natural resource for them. They identified with her, often deferring to her opinion. Some of the other counselors experienced this subgroup as a clique, one that valued more depth work (not viewed as appropriate by all the counselors) and perhaps a group that understood more of the theory I was teaching. One of the overt manifestations of this subgroup was that they usually sat together at trainings. Additionally, members of this subgroup were of the same race. I am not sure if racial issues were stirred up, as I didn't see or hear of them directly. But I was aware that they might be present. There was an underlying sense of tension that was mostly felt and (to my knowledge) not expressed. My sense was that some of the counselors not in this subgroup naturally, and maybe even unconsciously, used their mediating skills to sooth the tensions. All of this said, the clearest identification of subgroup membership occurred the year that a counselor entered the training program.

An aspect of the group ethos was support for professional development. The counselors helped each other do the necessary work to become certified in symbol formation and to move toward certification in sandplay therapy by STA. Their deep commitment to the process (which had grown throughout the years of working together) was evident in the multitude of ways in which they supported one another. Some wrote their papers together, others made deals with each other about deadlines they would meet, and others just placed expectations on each other to rise to the occasion. They held informal peer supervision groups to support their clinical work. They purchased miniatures for each other, often showing up at a training session with a meaningful miniature for a particular counselor. There was always a good deal of warmth and celebration when a counselor received his or her certification in symbol formation.

As I review the dynamics of our group experience, I am aware that there was a surprising stability and cohesiveness in this training group born of chaos, loss and uncertainty. I am unsure of what really facilitated our group dynamics. However, I would suggest that key elements in our success as a group included (1) a shared experience of a profound nature; (2) strong values of trust, fairness, and respect for individual needs; (3) a deep spiritual orientation (a sense of shared service to a higher value); (4) a significant level of psychological skills in group members; (5) a task leader with compassion and legitimate authority; and (6) the use of an experiential mode of learning.

The original group members shared a profound tragedy and a resulting call to action. Just as they were unwilling to leave any child unattended on 9/11, they were unwilling to leave each other unattended. Perhaps the strong spiritual orientation and values of some of the members was reflected in their level of compassion for all of the group members. They in particular seemed to use their psychological skills to support their basic values, which had the side benefit of keeping the group intact. Some members were in a group work training program during the first three years of our training program. The skills they learned in that venue benefited us as well. Additionally, all the counselors said that they quickly became aware of the power of symbol formation and sandplay therapy and they wanted to know it and use it responsibly. These elements speak to the character and experience of the group members.

A task leader with compassion, commitment, and legitimate authority kept the group focused. She was able to bring up difficult issues, name acting-out, role model support, and remind the group of its ultimate value of learning symbol formation and sandplay therapy to benefit the children. She and I were able to comfortably co-lead when necessary, and at times I would turn the leadership over to her. My confidence in her commitment to the training allowed me to focus on teaching and clinical issues and not be overwhelmed by group dynamics.

An experiential mode of learning consistently brought the group members to their own individual experience. The process of discovering one's own psyche is powerful and equalizing. It was clear in each and every one of our trainings that we were all human, all had struggles, and all had a shadow (aspects of ourselves we would rather reject or at least not know about). I began the training with an exercise in which I asked the participants to pick the sandplay miniature they least liked. With much laughter, we identified what we hated and were able to move to the concept of the shadow and how we projected it onto others. We were able to work on ourselves with seriousness and humor.

When I began the training program in symbol formation/sandplay therapy I was unaware that this group of counselors would become one of the best trained groups in trauma response in the United States. The level of resources that were funneled into the Ground Zero schools to train and support the counselors and staffs to deal with the immense trauma that permeated the lives of the people of lower Manhattan was atypical. The group itself – in its range of ethnic diversity, skill, and psychological talent, with its commitment to a higher vision, significant levels of compassion, and willingness to explore the unknown and the unpleasant – was able to stay intact. We worked "well enough" through what might have been overwhelming circumstances in the outside community and with our own particular multiple-role relationships to do what we set out to do.

Chapter 16

Questions and exploration: supervising graduate students of analytical psychology in China

Heyong Shen and Gao Lan

The graduate study program in Analytical Psychology and Chinese Culture at South China Normal University (Guangzhou, China) began in 1998 with a masters degree, and in 2002 a Ph.D. program was initiated. For both of these degrees, sandplay therapy is the research theme and also the most attractive clinical technique. This graduate program in analytical psychology is the only one in China and has received excellent support from professional associations such as the International Association of Analytical Psychology (IAAP), the International Society of Sandplay Therapy (ISST), and Sandplay Therapists of America (STA).

As faculty members in this graduate program, we have been working on two levels with students: (1) supervising their research on sandplay therapy for their masters degree thesis or doctoral dissertation; and (2) providing basic training in the clinical use of sandplay. Most of the students have completed about 100 training hours (lectures and seminars) in sandplay therapy taught by ISST or STA members.

In this chapter we focus on the questions we are most often asked during supervision and training.

- What is the healing function of sandplay therapy?
- What is the role of the therapist during sandplay therapy?
- How can one become a good sandplay therapist?
- How can a western approach to therapy be used effectively in China?

As supervisors, our role is not to provide the "answers" but to explore the meaning and understanding of the questions with supervisees.

What is the healing function of sandplay therapy?

When our students first started to learn and practice sandplay, most were attracted by its healing power and intrigued by several questions: Why does sandplay heal? Is its healing function similar to that in Buddhism? Where does its healing power come from? Is it magic or can it be understood empirically?

As professors and supervisors in analytical psychology for many years, we have asked ourselves a similar question: What is the most important healing factor in the process of analysis? This is an important question because it stimulates reflection about our therapeutic work and, overall, a deeper understanding of our profession.

Even though healing is usually a complex phenomenon of emerging from chaos to order, we can still explore identifiable variables related to it. The five variables we often discuss are the therapist, client, the therapist–client relationship, the setting for sandplay, and the sandplay technique itself. We believe these variables are the basic conditions for change and healing.

With the five basic variables in mind, we center our discussion on three key terms in understanding sandplay therapy:

1   *Unconscious*: we believe that sandplay works on the unconscious level.
2   *Image*: as manifested through the use of symbols.
3   *Ganying*:[1] the meaning of Hexagram 31 in the *I Ching*, touching by the heart and responding from the heart.

The key to healing can be found in the heart. Dora Kalff understood this point very well. She ended her book (2003) with a quote from the *I Ching*, Hexagram 29 (Kan, abysmal, water): "It flows on and on . . . if one is sincere when confronted with difficulties, the heart can penetrate the meaning of the situation. And once we have gained inner mastery of a problem, it will come about naturally that the action we take will succeed." Kalff added, "Remember this in Sandplay. And remember that when we do succeed with the work of bringing about the inner harmony that defines a personality, we speak of grace" (p. 140).

An old Chinese saying states, "Distress of heart needs heart medicine." The saying points to the view of the healing process in Chinese culture. As Hexagram 29 states, "If you are sincere, you have success in your heart, and whatever you do succeeds" (Wilhelm & Baynes, 1961, p. 115). So a sincere heart can make *Ganying* happen, and the power of *Ganying* can open and penetrate all of the difficulties. That is how we, using the wisdom of the Chinese culture, view healing.

There is another old Chinese saying, originally from Zhuang Zi, the butterfly Daoist: "Getting from heart, and responding through the hands" (Zhuang Zi, 1997, p. 261). Movement from the heart to the hands is an embodied process in sandplay. It is also a hands-on creative process, as Ammann notes, that encourages a transformation from vague bodily sensations or emotions into a visible, tangible, three-dimensional image created in the sand tray: "Those sand pictures are like windows of a person's soul house and allow the therapist or analyst a direct, deeply moving contact with the analysand's inner life" (Ammann, 2005, p. 2).

In analytical psychology, contact with the inner life is the way of healing. As Jung (1965) acknowledged, "confrontation with the unconscious" was the real beginning of his creative work as well as his own healing and growth process. "The years when I was pursuing my inner images were the most important in my life – in them everything essential was decided" (p. 199). Here Jung is underscoring the reality of the psyche, the psychological meaning of Philemon (representing superior insight), and the emergence of the Self through symbolic imagery, i.e., the mandala, and the use of active imagination. Images from the depths of the unconscious can help us to understand the workings of the psyche and the healing function and power of sandplay therapy.

What is the role of the therapist during sandplay therapy?

Sandplay is often described as a non-verbal and non-directive form of therapy. However, students then wonder what role the therapist has in the therapy. They want to know everything that the therapist needs to do during the sandplay process.

We emphasize the importance of the sandplay therapist. Usually we discuss with students what Dora Kalff taught us: to create a free and protected space for therapy. This is the first principle and a fundamental step in sandplay change or transformation is possible only if a therapist is able to provide such a space.

We use the Chinese term of *Jingjie* (heart-imagery, level of understanding, state of thought) to convey the role of the sandplay therapist in relation to the following basic meanings: the therapist is the container of the therapy, and the therapist's personality also influences the therapeutic process. The Chinese story of the rainmaker helps us understand the role of a sandplay therapist. Jung advised his students to never give a seminar on active imagination without telling this story. When the rainmaker, who made rain for a drought-plagued village, was asked, "What did you do?" he said, "Oh, that's very simple. I didn't do anything." Then he explained to the puzzled people, "I come from an area that is in Tao, in balance. We have rain; we have sunshine. Nothing is out of order. I come into your area and find that it is chaotic. The rhythm of life is disturbed . . . When I am able to get myself in order, everything around is set right" (Chodorow, 1997, pp. 19–20).

The meaning of this story is found in two Chinese words – *wuwei* (no-act or non-action) and *Ganyin* (responding from the heart, when stimulated by the heart) – at the core of Taoist philosophy. Lao-zi once said, "acting the no-act" or "acting without action" (Chen, 1992, p. 145). "Till one has reached inactivity . . . But by this very inactivity, everything can be activated" (Chen, 1992, p. 111). "No-act" is a highly mature, spiritual state of harmony and balance and influences the environment around us.

In the *I Ching* we also find the same teaching: "In the *I* (the philosophy of changes), there is no thought and no action. It is still and without movement; but, when acted on, it penetrates forthwith to all phenomena and events under the sky. If it were not the most spirit-like thing under the sky, how could it be found doing this?" (Qinying, 1993, p. 309).

Just as Dora Kalff's understanding and use of the *I Ching* (Hexagram 29) reflected these beliefs, we speak of the role of the therapist during the healing process of sandplay therapy in much the same way. It is the essence of *wuwei* and *Ganying*. When in a state of harmony and balance, "action" is unnecessary; the healing process will unfold.

How can one become a good sandplay therapist?

Our students are knowledgeable about the basic training requirements of ISST and STA, but most desire to move beyond these. They not only want to meet the requirements but also understand sandplay at its deepest level.

Dora Kalff (1991) said that, in order to be capable of carrying out the sandplay task, the therapist/counselor, in addition to psychological training, must be able to fulfill two all-important prerequisites: (1) have a profound knowledge of the language of symbols; and (2) be able to establish a free and protected space.

Along with these requirements, Kalff emphasizes the importance of the therapist's own personal development: "one must have experienced these symbols and their efficacy on the basis of one's own psychic maturation process. Only this practice makes it possible to accompany the client's experience effectively" (p. 14). And, "What we want to mediate for others should emerge from our own experience . . . an experience of one's own deep-seated positive potential – an experience which guarantees an inner security which thus enables one to create a protected space for others" (p. 15).

Using the inner healer archetype, Guggenbuhl-Craig (1998) also emphasizes the significance of the therapist's psyche: "Healing is a technique that can be learned. But the medical man or woman whose inner healer is very weak, despite a good learned technique and a wide knowledge, can do harm to the patient" (pp. 408–9). The ability to be an ethical healer, shaman, or alchemist must be developed at the deepest archetypal level.

A similar teaching by Hui-neng, the founder of Chinese Chan Buddhism, explains that, "the essence of heart is intrinsically self-sufficient." For Chinese Chan Buddhists, brightening the heart and seeing nature is the basic principle or purpose and, at the same time, a way of practice.

So, awakening and developing the inner healer is of primary importance in becoming a proficient Jungian analyst, as well as a fine sandplay therapist. We have found that supporting our students' inner healing, along with helping them learn and use the language of symbols and develop their ability to create the free and protected space, assists them in becoming capable therapists with a genuine understanding of sandplay therapy.

How can a western approach to therapy be used effectively in China?

This question conveys a hesitation or doubt about the effectiveness of sandplay with Chinese people. At the same time, people are curious to know if there are differences in sandplay therapy between West and East.

The movement of indigenous psychology is still going on in China. If students view sandplay as a totally western method of therapy, then the question about its effectiveness seems reasonable. But, in fact, if we go back in the history of sandplay therapy, another story emerges.

Dora Kalff used three main resources to found sandplay therapy: the World Technique of Margaret Lowenfeld, Jungian psychology, and Chinese philosophy. In the first chapter of her book, Kalff (2003) indicates that she uses Zhou Dunyi's philosophy as a fundamental principle in her therapeutic work with children and adolescents. Kalff effectively applied the *I Ching*, yin and yang, the five elements, and eight hexagrams to sandplay therapy, including the images and their changes, movements, and relationships (see Figure 16.1).

Martin Kalff (2003) said that his mother learned Chinese when she was very young: "As a young girl, my mother attended a girls' boarding school in the Engadine. Her Greek teacher inspired her to study Sanskrit and, later, basic Chinese. It was here she discovered her interest in Eastern philosophy, Taoism in particular" (p. vi).

According to Mitchell and Friedman (1994), Dora Kalff had two dreams that inspired her in the development of sandplay therapy, both related to China:

> Intimately connected with her interest in developing sandplay as an analytical tool was Kalff's long-standing attraction to Asian philosophies. During her time of redirection and change, her interest in Asia was brought into clearer focus through two dreams. According to her son Martin, her first dream was set in Tibet, where she was approached by two monks who gave her a golden rectangular instrument. Implicit in this gift was the understanding that she was to swing the instrument and, as she did so, an opening appeared in the ground that cut through to the other side of the world, the West, where she saw the light of the sun.
>
> (p. 50)

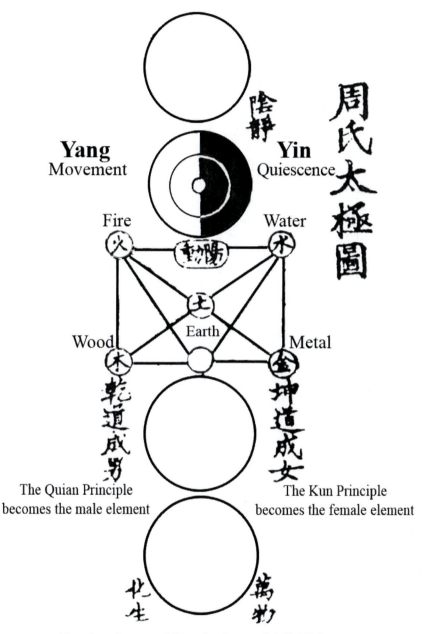

Production and Evolution of All Things

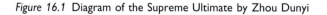

Figure 16.1 Diagram of the Supreme Ultimate by Zhou Dunyi

Kalff brought this dream to Emma Jung for analysis. We don't know too much about their work on the dream, but Mitchell and Friedman mention that, through her knowledge of the Orient, Emma Jung helped Kalff to understand the message of the East and encouraged her to work on the bridging of the two worlds: "The second significant dream of Dora Kalff came the night of Jung's death. In the dream Jung invited her to dinner. In the middle of the dinner table was a big mound of rice. Pointing to the rice, Jung indicated that Kalff should continue her exploration of the East" (Mitchell & Friedman, 1994, p. 51).

Jung died on June 6, 1961, the same day that Kalff had this dream. We can see very clearly the image of sand and tray in the dream – images of rice and a dinner table. Like Emma, Jung encouraged Kalff to learn more about the East. Dora Kalff's connection to the East is an important part of the history of sandplay therapy and can help us to understand its theory and principles.

In addition to the historical connection of sandplay and Chinese culture, we also discuss the universal language of sandplay therapy and its limitations in different cultural contexts. We agree that sandplay is a universal language, but at the same time, the sandplay process is still influenced by cultural factors. However, we do not see the cultural differences and influences as obstacles but rather as inspiring and beneficial. For instance, many symbols have culturally specific meanings, such as dragon, unicorn, fox, cricket, cicada, and trickster. We think that experiencing sandplay in different cultures, such as in China, offers a rare opportunity for students as well as practitioners to understand and accept cultural differences. Confucius said that men (and women) of honor can have unity in diversity. We hope that sandplay practice in China can also uphold the same spirit of developing unity and accepting differences.

Conclusion

That both C.G. Jung and Dora Kalff learned much from China and Chinese culture gives us a feeling of familiarity and confidence when we start our work on sandplay therapy. However, through the practice of teaching and supervision of sandplay, we realize that C.G. Jung and Dora Kalff are not Chinese. Hence we need to explore and reflect on our Chinese psyche through our own sandplay work. It is a hard journey, but rewarding.

Sandplay in China is a new development. With the support of IAAP, ISST, and STA, the first generation of Chinese sandplay therapists are on their way. They are learning this wonderful therapy step-by-step, and gathering experience through their practice. At the same time, their research and practice are reflecting and manifesting the Chinese meaning of sandplay and bringing the benefits of this culture to it.

Note

1 Author's Note – Heyong Shen. In the *I Ching* three important elements are: (1) *Qian* (Hexagram 1), heaven and yang principle; (2) *Kun* (Hexagram 2), earth and the yin principle; and (3) *Xian* (the first hexagram of the second part of the *I Ching*), human being and the principle of *Ganying*.

Hexagram *Xian* (*Ganying*) is created by combining two trigrams, *Dui* and *Gen*:

Dui   Gen

We refer to *Xian* by the Chinese word *gan* (influence, with feelings and emotions), which expresses the meaning of interaction, as well as the process of influence and response. The Chinese character *gan* 感 is the combination of *xian* (name of the hexagram) 咸 and *xin* (heart) 心 together, with *xian* written over *xin*, forming one character.

The hexagram *Xian* can give us a psychology of consciousness with unconsciousness. The image of the hexagram of *Xian* contains *Qian* and *Kun* (three yang lines in the middle, one yin line at the top, and two yin lines at the bottom), representing a situation of influence and response between heaven and earth as a whole. Such a situation is beyond ego-consciousness and forms the heart–mind state.

References

Ammann, R. (2005). Foreword to the Chinese version of *Healing and transformation in sandplay*. Guangzhou, China: Guangdong High Education Press.

Chen, G. (1992). *Laozhi: Modern translation*. Changsha, China: Hunan Publishing House.

Chodorow, J. (1997). *Introduction: Jung on active imagination*. Princeton, NJ: Princeton University Press.

Guggenbuhl-Craig, A. (1998). The necessity of talent. In M.A. Mattoon (Ed.), *Florence 1998 IAAP conference, destruction and creation: Personal and cultural transformations*. Switzerland: Daimon.

Jung, C.G. (1965). *Memories, dreams, reflections*. New York: Vintage Books.

Kalff, D. (1991). Introduction to sandplay therapy, *Journal of Sandplay Therapy, 1*, 9–15.

Kalff, D. (2003). *Sandplay: A psychotherapeutic approach to the psyche*. Cloverdale, CA: Temenos Press.

Kalff, M. (2003). Introduction to *Sandplay: A psychotherapeutic approach to the psyche*. Cloverdale, CA: Temenos Press.

Mitchell, R., & Friedman, H. (1994). *Sandplay: Past, present and future*. London: Routledge.

Qinying (1993). *Book of changes*. Changsha, China: Hunan Publishing House.

Wilhelm, R., & Baynes, C. (1961). *The I Ching, or Book of Changes*. Princeton, NJ: Princeton University Press.

Zhuang Zi (1997). *Zhuang Zi*. Wuang Rong-pei trans. Changsha, China: Hunan Publishing House.

Chapter 17

In the presence of the child: developing therapeutic language

Judy Zappacosta

For therapists desiring to use sandplay with children, supervision provides an opportunity to refine our clinical skills in both receptivity and observation. It also invites us to develop a deeper understanding of the ways in which sandplay promotes healing in the psyche of the child. In addition, the supervision experience increases opportunities to understand how symbol and metaphor act as healing agents in sandplay.

Children, through their play, sandplay imagery, and spontaneous stories, lead the therapeutic hour. The invitation to "just be" with children during this process calls for understanding on many different levels. Supervision offers the therapist an experience that expands awareness in what may be developing within the sandplay process. It invites the clinician to explore how experiences of deep attunement with the child impact the therapeutic environment. Supervision helps us explore and more fully understand how moments of reverie may arise during sandplay, promoting a healing atmosphere of containment and safety.

It is an accepted principle that sandplay, as a modality, provides a mediating process whereby conscious and unconscious material from the inner world of the psyche can be organized in new ways that offer healing and new outer stability to the developing personality (Kalff, 1980). In early supervision sessions, a culture that respects the free and protected space is established. This emergent culture contains the fundamentals of sandplay therapy, as developed by Dora Kalff, and builds a belief system regarding the importance of "presence" in the therapist. Next, beliefs in the importance of containment are fostered. This containment may be imagined as the early mother–child unity that develops in a healthy attachment and offers both safety and protection.

Unique to sandplay, containment is offered in three different configurations. It is offered within the parameters of the sand tray itself, within the therapeutic dyad, and within the therapy room, which provides a secure and insulated setting. The significance of a free and protected space for the child is implicit in sandplay, as is the idea that symbols used in the tray act as healing mediators.

Understanding metaphorical language

Supervision offers the opportunity to understand how children naturally use metaphor in play as a healing agent. The way in which metaphors operate as healing agents, and the ways they can be examined and amplified, is often a little understood factor during supervision. Metaphors can be observed in the language of children during play in the sand. Children may exclaim with excitement, "I can't believe I got these guys to stand up this way in the sand!" The therapist can translate the dialogue as, "I am able to look at something that has remained unconscious until this moment," hearing the metaphorical message tucked within the statement.

In early supervision sessions, clinicians often report feeling bereft, confused and inadequate when their main effort during a sandplay session is to work at being very present to the child's energy in the room and his or her activity in the sand tray. One supervisee stated, "I felt useless in the room when I wasn't asking questions, and I imagined that the child probably felt I wasn't 'there' for him."

Feelings of inadequacy in clinicians during a therapy session become very apparent when they are asked to observe and amplify an experience with a child using metaphorical language rather than engaging in questions or daily conversation. When the supervisee is unsure how to respond fully to what is being expressed, it may be important to realize that something still needs to be developed in the relationship with the child.

Contrary to some beliefs regarding sandplay, the therapist is not required to be a totally silent witness to the process. Often, therapeutic language must be forged with the child that offers amplification of scenery, symbol, or action during the session. The understanding of metaphor and its use as a form of communication and healing opens another layer of dialogue with a child's unconscious. This language and particular way of holding a dialogue can help anchor new understandings of inner experiences in the sand: "It is extremely important that the newly awakened energies are caught by the therapist and led into constructive paths" (Kalff, 1980, p. 69).

The timing of a specific intervention during the therapy hour may also be noted as an important junction that can build both understanding and trust. Many clinicians report thinking that they should say more; however, the child may be busy at work building a scene, with almost no attention focused on the therapist in the room. At the same time, if the therapist's attention wanders to a bird outside the window, the child may quickly respond to the loss of the therapist's focus with questions regarding where something in the room might be located. The child feels the resonance and reverie being held in the room by the therapist. When this presence disappears in lack of attention, it is likely the child may acknowledge the loss in some way. Supervision invites a review of how therapists are able to use themselves as an integral part of the sandplay experience, even within silence.

Teaching observation and acceptance

Developing a sense of presence as a therapist includes careful and very specific child observation, a very necessary task that supervision can support and expand. Supervision dedicated to the therapist's observation of treatment can heighten perceptions and provide a more refined understanding of how the sandplay experience impacts the child. The presentation of a child in therapy as either "acting-out" with explicit behaviors and activities in the sand or "acting in" with depressive features shown when the sand is barely engaged, provides immediate feedback to the therapist, which then can help set treatment goals with a family. The supervisor has the task of helping the clinician focus on how the child moves, talks, utilizes the room, makes use of the toys, and chooses to interact with the sand in the tray. Observation becomes important for noting what the child can engage in and what the child is not able to do within a therapeutic hour. Somatic features also may play a primary role in a child's presentation, as when headaches, stomachaches, or asthma present, focusing attention on both the physical and psychological aspects of his or her life.

Imagery that arises in sandplay can touch the unconscious with such power and immediacy that weekly supervision sessions are necessary to hold both the clinician and the child's work and allow a larger field of containment. Sandplay asks the clinician to be as accepting as possible and to provide an environment where it is safe for the child to act out behaviors and feelings that at first may appear maladaptive, inappropriate, or at times aggressive. Axline (1947) underscored the importance of acceptance of the child in her defining work on play therapy:

> Acceptance of the child goes further than establishing the initial contact or getting the child into the room and functioning. After the therapy is well underway, the therapist must maintain an accepting attitude for all the things the child does and says. The process of non-directive therapy is so interwoven that it is difficult to tell where one principle begins and another ends. They are overlapping and interdependent. For example, the therapist cannot be accepting without being permissive. She cannot be permissive without being accepting. She cannot leave the responsibility to make choices up to the child that she does not respect. The degree to which the therapist is able to put these principles into practice seems to affect the depth to which the therapy can go.
>
> (pp. 89–90)

The clinician is always asked to guarantee physical safety in the room for both the adult and child client. Supervision can help clinicians develop their skills in receiving and holding behaviors and feelings that may appear threatening or potentially dangerous in other settings. Discussions in supervision that highlight the developmental stages of childhood that may have been interrupted or unfinished help the supervisee understand how seemingly chaotic play can serve the child's learning to self-regulate.

Learning about nonlinear paths of healing within the psyche gives direct meaning to Michael Fordham's (1957) original theories of the changing states of integration and de-integration that manifest in early infancy. Progressive and regressive play are usually surprising to the supervisee, as new understandings and a deepening respect for the path of the psyche can be observed through children's sandplay. A child who has created imagery with context and meaning may return in a following session to play that appears very undifferentiated and chaotic. However, during supervision, the study of these "doing and undoing" moments provides direct observation and discussion of the natural healing that is provided in sandplay.

The natural elements of fire, water, and earth often become fodder for a child's inherent curiosity. Children may repeatedly need to fill a tray with muddy, murky water or light match after match to experiment with fire. Often, the supervisee arrives in supervision with urgent questions regarding what constitutes a healing environment. It becomes particularly challenging for the supervisee to allow aspects of play that challenge his or her tolerance for certain behaviors while still maintaining a permissive, healing environment. Most clinicians have their own personal limits tested in allowing and even inviting certain kinds of play. One supervisee was very worried that a child's use of matches would set off the smoke detector in the office in which she worked. It was clear that her discomfort and fear meant redefining the limits of play possible during sessions.

Children who require an exhaustive level of permission to safely act out their inner impulses will test the supervisee's tolerance on many different levels. These levels of permission are exactly what must be discussed and processed in supervision in order to continue to develop a sandplay culture that fosters the provision of a free and protected space that can contain the myriad childhood behaviors and feelings.

Behaviors that appear as a deep withdrawal and depression in the child can also challenge the ability of the supervisee to contain painful elements that present during sandplay. As stated earlier, painful scenes or play within a sand tray directly impacts the unconscious of the therapist. Without consultation and supervision regarding the deep sense of overwhelm, this pain can become a "cotransference contagion" within the room for both therapist and child. A therapist's own analytic work can strengthen his or her ability to hold and contain difficult imagery that arises within the sandplay process. It is often a challenge for the supervisee to hold the painful sadness that a child may reflect in sandplay.

Transference and cotransference issues

Supervision of child therapists requires cultivating the meanings of a free and protected space. It is a belief that must first be developed within the therapist as well as offered into the environment of the sandplay room. Siegelman (1990) notes, "Empathy, I have found in supervising and consulting, is limited by the range of the therapist's inner development. The more complex and differentiated the therapist, the more he or she can empathize with different kinds of patients" (p. 115). It is important for the supervisor to discern with the supervisee when issues arise within supervision that may need further exploration within individual psychotherapy rather than supervision. Transference issues that reopen core issues for the supervisee may best be addressed within personal psychotherapy in conjunction with supervision.

A clinician working with adolescent children found herself becoming more and more exhausted and angry during her tenure with this particular age group. During supervision, the clinician began recounting the distress she had felt as an adolescent when her father had died suddenly, leaving her both alone and vulnerable. Although she had sought therapy regarding this issue earlier in her life, the work with adolescents brought back many old feelings and reopened an old wound. It was interfering with her work and ability to observe objectively what she saw in the children she was working with presently. It was very appropriate to refer her to therapy to deal with this old core issue in her own personal life.

Countertransference issues of loss and grief can arise quickly during supervision when the therapist is challenged to hold the intense psychic pain reflected in the early life of his or her client. Because these issues arise from a pre-verbal stage, sandplay offers the unique possibility for primary primitive energies to emerge, possibly for the first time. Unresolved personal issues from a supervisee's own childhood may arise and overwhelm him or her, particularly when this kind of potent primitive imagery or play appears during the sandplay process. Jungian analyst Hayao Kawai (1997) of Japan explains this deep connection between the therapist and client as a "*hara* connection," a relationship that goes from "belly to belly." Kay Bradway noted the deep relationship that exists between the therapist and client during sandplay as the *cotransference*.

Observing children at play may also evoke a deep sense of wonder as well as reminders of unexplored feelings of loss that arise within the supervisee. During supervision hours, many clinicians report personal childhoods that lacked opportunity for curiosity, play, and natural exploration. These deep countertransference issues can take immediate precedence as the clinician working with the child is suddenly asked to be both observer and receiver for the young client's world of play in the sand. The grief of a therapist's lost childhood is processed within the safe and protected space of supervision, with the hope that it will transform and deepen the possibility for potential healing in the child's therapy.

The importance of the supervisee's own experience of a sandplay process, or other analytic modalities that offer the experience of a contained, safe experience in art, movement, or play, cannot be understated. Many times supervisees report that if it were not for their own personal knowledge of experiencing a free and protected space as an adult sandplayer, they really would not know how to sit and offer their presence in such a receptive way for a child. Hopefully, by the time supervision is in place for child therapists, they have already had the opportunity to do their own sandplay process with a certified sandplay therapist. Otherwise, supervisors must encourage supervisees to find a sandplay therapist as early as possible to deepen their own experience of play in this specific modality.

Interfacing with parents

Another important area of supervision is expanding the supervisee's ability to impart information to the parents of a child using sandplay as the primary modality in therapy. Many supervision hours are devoted to helping the clinician learn how to insulate and contain a child's sandplay work and inform parents regarding the support needed by them for their child. It is of utmost importance to protect and insulate the child's work, but it is equally important to develop and hold a relationship with parents while a child is in therapy. A relationship with the parent of a child in therapy is very essential to successful outcomes:

> Parents entrust their children to me for examination and treatment. However, it never takes long before it becomes apparent that – usually without realizing it – the child's mother or parents also need me to confide in. The child is sent ahead as a pioneer as it were to reconnoiter the new territory. I think this is perfectly legitimate, for I know how much of a struggle the parents may go through before they manage to entrust their child to a specialist, no doubt because they sense or know somehow that ultimately they are concerned at least as much as the child. It is probable that parents follow their child's therapy with such rapt attention or suspicion, as the case may be.
>
> (Kiepenheuer, 1990, p. 125)

Delivery of information to parents must always come with very deliberate attempts to protect a child's inner world. Supervisors must help the clinician learn to deliver "chapter headings" or themes of sandplay therapy, without giving away details of a child's work in the sand. For example, when a child has been reticent or careful in his or her play, the therapist can convey to the parents that the sandplay therapy is inviting the child to explore in new ways, and that the child is learning about investing and risking within the therapy. Often, if the therapist can translate how these skills can support success at school or home, the parents understand more fully how "just playing" can become very therapeutic.

It is also important to be able to explain to parents how play in the sand with miniatures actually can empower a child and offer him or her a renewed sense of agency. Maintaining the delicate balance of periodic meetings with parents to help them understand the work going on in sandplay, without disturbing the *temenos* of the therapy, is extremely important to the overall success of the therapy. Without parental support and understanding of sandplay therapy, a child may be withdrawn from therapy too soon, or the child's reports to the parent that "I just play" can undermine parental beliefs regarding the goals of treatment.

Imagery and symbol respresentation

For both adults and children, sandplay offers a very natural way to explore areas of internal conflict, trauma, tension, and distress. The symbolic language of miniatures allows a safe distancing and personal agency to emerge, particularly in areas of immense emotional charge or trauma. The invitation to create and build scenes with miniatures in the sand tray offers the possibility of developing new relationships to early experiences of hopelessness or helplessness, which then invites a stronger and emergent relationship to the Self. Sandplay also fosters a natural healing environment wherein symbols used creatively offer the possibility of a renewed inner stability to emerge.

Supervision of clinicians using sandplay provides an opportunity to deepen their understanding of how symbols offer healing to the psyche. In order to deepen a clinician's understanding of what is transpiring during sandplay, supervision hours are used to study the images presented in the sand. Observing how the scene is built, what presents as the theme in the play, and the general affect of the child, is necessary for the supervisees to gain an understanding of the metaphorical messages being expressed and transformed in sandplay.

Many times clinicians quickly go out and buy a symbol dictionary, hoping for help in analyzing a sandplay scene. Although a symbol dictionary may provide interesting information and an expansion of knowledge, it is usually little help in deciphering meaning in a sandplay scene because it lacks the ability to hold the context in which symbols have arisen. Symbols must also be viewed fluidly to remain alive and vital in sandplay. Supervision hours keep symbols alive and moving, rather than concretized, by building understanding of their particular use. The supervisee is taught to hold the sandplay as a moving, alive process wherein symbols may transform and offer unique meaning to the child. For children of divorce, for example, it can be a particularly pivotal moment in their treatment when they place a bridge in the center of a tray that has repeatedly been built to hold two separate worlds. The bridge signals the inner healing work of repairing both the outer and inner splits the child has experienced. It is myth-making, as well as healing, for the child, and it must be allowed to transform and keep growing. Otherwise, it becomes a concretized stereotype, like a dictionary term, and no longer lives as an object that can bridge affect and meaning for the child in spontaneous healing moments. These tenets further develop the culture and training of sandplay child therapists.

Symbols are imbued with an archetypal force, an energy that holds a magnetic-like charge, with both positive and negative poles. Symbols used in the sand can carry active archetypal messages that form bridges to healing. Symbols in the sand become transformative agents of healing in the therapeutic hour. The clinician is invited to hold and receive a child's experience as expressed in sandplay, even without full cognitive understanding in the moment by either therapist or child. The supervisor helps the supervisee develop a belief in symbols as agents of change and the ability to be steadfast in a receptive attunement that holds potential for growth and transformation. The supervisee is challenged to believe in a possibility of transcendent healing that may arise quite spontaneously.

The supervisor has the unique responsibility of mirroring a receptivity and potential for growth and change within the supervisory relationship. This modeling invites the supervisee to share the supervisor's strong belief in the healing capabilities within every psyche, and that this growth and change can happen quite spontaneously through sandplay. Total acceptance of an image or symbol as a metaphor for healing is important for progressive moments to evolve in sandplay therapy. This stance becomes a very challenging proposition when there is little or incomplete cognitive understanding of how the symbol is acting. There are moments in supervision when the meanings of a symbol remain elusive but seemingly very important to the child's work. Being able to model a belief in what we cannot see or know in the moment is an important principle for the supervisor to hold in sandplay. The supervisee takes this acceptance of symbolic healing that is mirrored in supervision back into the therapy room with a child. This belief system invites the child to continue playing and exploring using both the sand and symbols as healing agents in the sand.

This type of seemingly "blind receptivity" is a challenge to teach in supervision because it defies the principle of immediate cognitive understanding used in other kinds of therapies. The supervisor has the important task of convincing the supervisee that a forward movement in sandplay can occur in quiet acceptance of the child, a deep receptivity of the scene created, and belief in the potential for transformation that happens within the sand tray. Supervision provides a secondary *temenos* for the ongoing work between the supervisee and the child. The parallel holding of relationship in supervision imparts a mutual influence within the supervision experience and the relational field of the therapy. This relational field held within supervision can collaboratively affect the potential for growth in both therapist and the ongoing child work. Many times supervisees report that just after presenting their child case during supervision, there is a renewed energy in the therapy in the following week, or the child that has presented in supervision as "stuck" now seems to be progressing again. Whether the support for the therapist during supervision helps them and the therapist to hold the case more consciously or the relational field is supported in some new way remains a mystery, but clearly supervision seems to offer positive support to both clinician and client.

Understanding the use of metaphors as healing agents

Long ago metaphorical stories provided tools for transferring knowledge orally around campfires, hearths, and within the community. Stories told in metaphor provided collective messages that imparted values, morals, and spiritual teachings. Historically, metaphor became a bridge between logic, affect, and imagery – a process that we now know engages both sides of the brain. Symbols, images, and other nonrational processes engage the right brain, whereas logic and language are processed in left-brain activity: "Metaphor often carries not only affect but insight as well, so that the therapist needs to do very little. It is more a question of attentive receptivity" (Siegelmen, 1990, p. 78).

Explicit, intentional use of metaphorical understanding and language can amplify a healing symbol used in play. Metaphor becomes a nonthreatening way to contact particularly charged issues for the child and can help integrate non-verbal work and spoken language in a supportive, therapeutic way. Siegelmen (1990) describes a therapist's role in this way: "Through the therapist's heightened listening and his willingness to stay with the metaphor and unobtrusively enlarge its deeper meanings, he [was] actually doing a great deal to further the therapeutic exchange" (p. 63). Teaching the supervisee how to use metaphorical understanding and reflective language is crucial. The secondary issue then becomes the timely way in which metaphor may meet and amplify a child's sandplay.

Effective use of metaphor builds a rapport with the child that allows the clinician to communicate in a way that reaches both the child's conscious and unconscious. Rather than directly and cognitively discussing the painful aspects in a child's life, such as the separation and divorce of a child's parents, the clinician can offer metaphorical statements that reach a child on multiple levels of consciousness and support the child doing sandplay. When the clinician can join the child using metaphorical language, recurrent themes can be acknowledged and implicitly understood.

A 6-year-old child living in the midst of custodial battles around him may play out his own internal conflict with animals that are continually fighting in the jungle he creates in the sand tray. Hearing the metaphorical acknowledgment from the therapist that "It doesn't look like the war is over today between the lions and tigers" forms a bridge to the child's inner frustration and dissatisfaction. Intervention using metaphorical language allows a gentle distance that can move the therapy forward rather than any cognitive discussion of what it feels like to go back and forth between mom and dad's house. Most often a child shrugs his or her shoulders and changes the subject.

Asking the supervisee to develop metaphorical language can prepare both the clinician and child for the discussion that may occur weeks later when one day frogs, snakes, and turtles in a pond replace the jungle conflict. It becomes a marker for both child and clinician that the therapy is holding the potent possibility for metaphorical change and growth as well as scenes of intense struggle. Bridges may be used, joining new areas in the sand tray where previously scenes of animals eating each other stood. The child receives support in metaphor as he or she creates safe passage through a difficult and dangerous time in his or her own development.

One of the more difficult challenges reported during supervision is the clinician's report that a child's play has become increasingly repetitive. When play within the sand tray continues week after week, a distinction can usually be made within supervision as to whether the child needs a continued level of permission for that specific means of play or whether the supervisee needs to refine his or her understanding of how the play is serving the child in those moments. Often, when the supervisee has a clearer idea of how the play serves the child, there is potential for more progressive movement in sandplay.

Encouraging the supervisee to observe what the hands engage in while children are talking, even when not using the sand tray, becomes an important tool for discovering metaphorical messages. A 10-year-old girl braids the fringe on her poncho carefully while telling her therapist it really doesn't bother her that her parents no longer live in the same house together. She slowly begins to frame pieces of her hair before her eyes. As she reiterates her acceptance of their separation and how they will both be happier living apart, and that she will have little difficulty adjusting to these huge changes in her own life, she begins to intently braid three pieces of her own hair in front of her forehead and before her eyes. The hands are really giving the metaphorical message of trying to bring the three back together as one again. In that moment, the therapist is asked to hold a tension of opposite energies with silent acknowledgment. These feelings expressed through the hands of the child remain unconscious but apparent to the clinician. The consciousness and understanding that the therapist holds for the child in that moment can promote a strength and potential for the child to bring the feelings to consciousness when there is sufficient ego strength to confront the grief in the separation.

Summary

Supervision allows the full spectrum in children's behavior to be highlighted so that many features that might otherwise go unnoticed can be integrated as metaphors that offer a deeper truth of feelings.

It is essential to understand how play serves the child, the language he or she brings to it, and its particular expression when the major modality used is sandplay. In addition, teaching supervisees how to amplify and use metaphor in relationship and conversation is important to their development as sandplay clinicians. The successful use of metaphorical language in response to children's sandplay offers direct dialogue with the child's unconscious. The supervisee is encouraged to amplify the energy a child brings to his or her struggles in the sand tray with statements such as, "The fighting in this war is very fierce. Your noises even help me understand how those warriors are struggling." Many consultation hours are spent helping to translate and offer meaning to children's approach to three main areas: their developing relationship with the clinician; their choice and use of sandplay miniatures; and their interaction within a sandplay scene. Supportive metaphorical responses by the clinician to all these areas are the bridges to meaning for children.

Supervision in sandplay includes developing a culture of attunement and presence that can then be palpably felt in the therapy between the child and clinician. With this acceptance and security provided by the clinician and in the therapy, the opportunity for reverie, healing, and the ineffable may emerge within sandplay. The potential for this aspect to arise in both child and clinician offers deep satisfaction in the work of supervision.

References

Axline, V.M. (1947). *Play therapy*. New York: Ballentine Books.
Fordham, M. (1957). *New developments in analytical psychology*. London: Routledge & Kegan Paul.
Kalff, D.M. (1980). *Sandplay: A psychotherapeutic approach to the psyche*. Boston, MA: Sigo Press.
Kawai, H. (1997). '*The enlivened moment*'. Symposium conducted in Santa Cruz, California.
Kiepenheuer, K. (1990). *Crossing the bridge: A Jungian approach to adolescence*. LaSalle, IL: Open Court Publishing.
Siegelman, E.Y. (1990). *Metaphor and meaning in psychotherapy*. New York: Guilford Press.

Part VI

Making connections with other expressive arts therapies

Chapter 18

Midwives of consciousness: supervising sandplay and expressive art therapists

Gita Dorothy Morena

Birthing is not an easy process. An attentive, wise, patient, and responsive midwife is an important asset when a woman is struggling to give birth. Psychotherapists are the midwives of consciousness. Their presence facilitates the birth and development of the psyche and stimulates the healing of inner traumas and emotional pain. Just like midwives, therapists need training and education to unravel the confounding and intricate issues that arise during the therapeutic process.

Professional mentoring or supervision is the way therapists learn to apply academic knowledge to concrete situations. It is a complicated process that involves establishing a supportive relationship, sharing information, and modeling effective interventions and communication. In addition to transmitting therapeutic techniques, supervisors educate and guide students in the practical application of psychological theories. Although this is different from being a therapist, it requires the use of therapeutic skills as well as creative educational strategies. Supervisors are guides and mentors who encourage students to learn, develop, and integrate information in personal and deep ways. Furthermore, supervisors are charged with the activation of their own wisdom, skill, and sensitivity to creatively teach and interact with students. For an experienced clinician, working as a supervisor requires understanding his or her own psychotherapeutic orientation as well as guiding students in their development of effective psychotherapeutic tools.

Sandplay, art, play, music, and movement are the primary interventions of expressive art therapists. These artistic modalities are used singularly or in combination to bring a creative, right-brain dimension into a therapeutic process. Working with these approaches involves establishing a highly intuitive and penetrating relationship with the unconscious. As this connection with the unconscious deepens, hidden patterns, clinical issues, and unresolved feelings and attitudes are exposed. In therapeutic sessions, expressive art therapists generally respond to clients and their art as it manifests, trusting that a client's psyche is healing itself in the process of self-expression. They learn to speak and listen with the symbolic language of imagery as well as the language of words, and are trained to understand and receive the messages carried in creative art expressions.

One of the unique jobs of expressive art supervisors is to instruct students in understanding and working with the complexities of symbolic language. In addition to educating students about therapy and its execution, they are guides into the unknown territory of the unconscious, teaching and modeling how to navigate its terrain. Educating students about symbolic process involves many levels of training. The first phase of training occurs with the students' own sandplay or expressive art therapy. Here they encounter the complexity of the psyche, heal emotional wounds and traumas, find their own inner voice, and connect with the unconscious. Through their personal experience with expressive arts, they learn how to resolve inner conflicts and concerns.

The next phase of training involves exploring symbolic language by studying archetypes, mythology, fairytales, dreams, rituals, and art. Through classes, workshops, and engaging in personal therapy and supervision, students gain facility with the language of the unconscious. With group and individual supervision, personal experience is blended with academic knowledge to develop professional judgment. With the completion of training, a foundation is established for working with conscious and unconscious aspects of the psyche in a way that leads to emotional healing and transformation.

For clinicians who become supervisors, moving from a therapeutic to an educational relationship can be difficult. Remembering and recognizing the skills needed for effective psychotherapy is helpful, as supervisors assume the important tasks of instilling professional confidence, increasing understanding of case dynamics, teaching effective intervention strategies, and identifying and removing obstacles that interfere with students' effectiveness.

I was taught early in my career that the first and most important task of a therapist is to establish rapport. This magical and illusive ingredient creates a sense of connection, understanding, and safety within which vulnerabilities and insecurities can be explored. Without it, healing does not occur. When rapport breaks down, tension, defensiveness, and feelings of separation arise. This rupture must be repaired for therapy to continue.

Building rapport requires listening without judgment, speaking with authenticity and congruency, and maintaining awareness of the inner world as it opens and reveals itself. An expressive art therapist must also appreciate, understand, and respond to a client's symbolic and unconscious communications. The establishment of rapport in a safe and protected space is critical for a client to explore emotional pain, resolve inner conflicts, open unknown places in the unconscious, and create sandplay or art.

Just like competent therapists, supervisors must establish rapport and create a safe and protected space for their students. Without a supportive environment, the delicate issues of professional competence and confidence remain hidden and unexamined. After establishing a relationship, supervisors must educate and guide students about the therapeutic process, while modeling and teaching the positive communication techniques of listening without judgment, speaking with authenticity and congruency, and maintaining awareness of interpersonal dynamics. Supervisors suggest therapeutic interventions and provide constructive feedback as students bring in case material and questions from their work. This cannot happen without the establishment of a positive, healthy relationship. It is important for supervisors to track the degree to which students are able to incorporate their suggestions and feedback, for it determines the content and direction of future supervisory sessions.

Developing clinicians must learn to separate personal issues from client dynamics. Unresolved complexes and personal insecurities manifest quickly in therapeutic work. They influence difficult-to-recognize cotransference issues, cloud therapeutic judgment, and confound clinical observations. Without direct observation of their students' counseling sessions, supervisors have difficulty separating their students' well-meaning, albeit inexperienced descriptions from their own case considerations. By viewing sessions through one-way mirrors or computer linkages, supervisors can observe directly and give precise feedback for professional development. Working with one-way mirrors or computers is not always possible though, and sandplay and art provide other ways to observe case dynamics without student interpretation. Examination of sandplay photos and art also allows supervisors to assist their students with sharpening their clinical awareness and identifying the nuances of their clients' symbolic language. In addition, they learn to recognize personal issues, separate them from client concerns, and create a way to handle the complexities of cotransference.

I remember feeling quite inadequate as a developing sandplay therapist when an 11-year-old boy repeatedly created fighting scenes in the sand. Although his parents were happy with his progress, I was alarmed by what appeared to be a lack of resolution to his internal conflicts. By examining his sandplay photos, my supervisor was able to see the subtle shifts in his psyche as the inner tensions of parental abandonment and subsequent adoption were released and healed. With the help of this skillful supervisor, I recognized a core complex I carried of not feeling good enough, and then was able to avoid confounding the therapeutic relationship with my own psychological scars.

Supervising expressive art students involves the unique and creative task of educating students in non-verbal and symbolic language. This education takes place throughout the supervisory relationship with each case that is presented. It is also developed when students share their personal sandplay and art experiences, and the complex feelings and attitudes that arise with their work. I am reminded of an art therapist intern whose daily practice was creating a morning mandala. When she brought these into the supervision session, she was able to identify a certain tension that was visible in her work. This realization stimulated a deeper sharing in her supervisory sessions which became the foundation for further professional development. Her personal experiences with mandalas inspired her to introduce mandalas to her clients and allowed her to understand more accurately the messages contained in their imagery. In another situation, a student created her own sandplay after each client session. These images became a powerful and direct way of exploring transference issues as well as identifying personal and professional concerns. Sandplay, in particular, reveals issues hidden in the unconscious that otherwise might not come to light, thus providing a way to expand consciousness.

Although sandplay, art, music, and movement are all expressive arts, the concerns and issues arising for sandplay supervisors are unique. Knowing and understanding the symbolic significance of sandplay miniatures is as important as learning the vocabulary of a foreign language. Finding creative ways to expand a student's symbolic vocabulary is an essential aspect of sandplay training.

Sandplay therapists see transformation and healing manifest in the sand. Archetypes and images from the personal and collective unconscious mingle with ideas from consciousness to create complex representations of the psyche. Therapists hold a safe space for these images to emerge and receive the messages they communicate in both conscious and unconscious ways. Being grounded in Jungian theory, they understand sand scenes as the psyche's movement toward wholeness. Contrary to other forms of therapy, sandplay is a client-oriented process where therapists avoid active interpretations or directive interventions. Learning to respond to clients in such a spacious way can be difficult, and students often struggle with staying connected and not interfering or amplifying their client's experience. Sandplay supervision is important for mastering this approach. By being accountable to a supervisor, students deepen their ability to establish and maintain a safe and protected space for their clients. Mindfulness meditation and spiritual practices are also helpful, as well as continuing resolution of internal tensions. Although interacting with the psyche is largely invisible work, sandplay allows it to become visible. A client's relationship to the sand is as important as his or her relationship to the therapist. It provides a neutral place in which client and therapist meet. A student and supervisor interact to explore the intricacies of each case, open avenues for deeper understanding, and facilitate awareness and healing.

I have found it most beneficial for students to present sandplay photos or artwork in chronological order, along with their understanding, questions, and concerns about particular cases. It is helpful to project sandplay images on a large screen where patterns, feelings, and impressions can be explored together, and a more concrete analysis of case material can occur. Session-by-session art and sandplays can be discussed, looking for themes and messages contained in the material, relating these to the client's present situation and therapeutic issues, and exploring the deeper dynamics and overall direction of the case. While working in this way, suggestions for student research or personal exploration can be made, and student questions, personal sharing, and cotransference concerns can be addressed. Follow-up about previous assignments and suggestions needs to be included. Although supervision is an organic process that flows in response to student needs, there is an underlying structure and format that is well thought out and followed.

During supervision, students are encouraged to ask questions and share their research and study, particularly in the area of symbolic language development. They may be asked to keep a journal, produce art work, or use sandplay to develop proficiency and deepen understanding. Periodically I ask students to "read" sandplays without providing any case information. This is a stimulating and challenging way to develop confidence and intuition in understanding symbolic language. Then background information is shared to validate and clarify what has been seen discussed. For these experiential learning situations, small groups (three or four students) are most effective. Students learn from each other's cases and establish strong bonds of personal and professional support.

Issues of confidentiality and containment are important in any supervisory relationship, particularly when material from the unconscious is exposed directly and personally. Supervisors are strongly connected to the unconscious of a student's clients through their sandplay and art, and confidentiality issues are crucial to maintain a safe and protected container for healing. Because symbolic language cloaks personal feelings and attitudes, it is easy to forget how sensitive and revealing it can be. The way visual material is discussed, though, can have a tremendous impact on clients, both consciously and unconsciously. I became particularly aware of this dynamic during an unusual supervisory session many years ago. I am often associated with figures from *The Wizard of Oz*, because my great grandfather wrote the book over a century ago. During an international consultation, I was intrigued when this student's client used the Oz figures immediately following our consultation session. The client had no direct knowledge of me, the Oz story, or the consultation, yet chose Oz figures to represent an issue that was emerging in the sand. This unexpected synchronicity made me aware of the power of the unconscious to communicate without conscious awareness. I was reminded how important it is to treat sandplay and art work with respect and sensitivity, because a supervisor's reactions and attitudes may directly influence a client's psyche.

In summary, one of the unique advantages in supervising expressive art therapists is being able to view client sandplays and art work directly. This direct view provides an immediate way to understand case dynamics, stimulate student learning, and suggest effective interventions. Learning symbolic language with a skillful supervisor teaches a student to navigate the inner world of the psyche successfully. In the best of circumstances, supervision clarifies client issues, stimulates personal growth, and develops professional competency. In addition, students are encouraged to explore their inner worlds so their ability to create healing spaces expands and deepens. Mentors, supervisors, and more experienced therapists have an opportunity to share their wisdom by providing spaces for healers to learn, develop, and grow. In the following poem, Cecil Burney expresses the power of this healing transmission within the intimate and unique relationships of colleagues (Unpublished poem, Cecil Burney, 1975).

The Legacy after the Fact
Who will heal the healers,
If not the healers themselves?
    Knowing each other
    Trusting each other
    Touching each other
    Finding each other
    Again and again with tenderness

Who will heal the healers,
If not the healers themselves?
    Putting aside the demands of the profession
    And healing each other not with power but with love

Who will heal the healers,
If not the healers themselves?
    Music itself is healing for them.
    Lame Chiron taught Asklepios to heal
    But he also taught music:
    "He educated them to be physicians
    And turned their minds to music
    And made them into just men."

Who will heal us,
If we do not heal each other?
    With love
    And with companionship
    And with empathy
    And with joy

We enter the play of our life together
And become whole
        Singing and playing and loving and healing
        There is justice for us where we venture to go

Chapter 19

Supervision in sandplay: the art therapist as sandplay supervisor

Lenore Steinhardt

Introduction

The relationship between therapist, client, and image in sandplay may be represented symbolically as a triple spiral, a continuous long thread that spirals in and out of three interconnected centers: one representing the therapist's development and growth, one the client's development and growth, and one the developing sandplay process. Similar to the energies present in the therapeutic encounter, the thread connects the therapist's countertransference to the client and to the sand picture, the client's transference to the therapist and to the image, and the image born within this relationship to both therapist and client. The sandplay setting can be envisioned as a circle holding the unending triple spiral in continuous flow within it. Supervision can be envisioned as an outer second circle containing this unit (Figure 19.1).

In this chapter I discuss sandplay supervision informed by an art therapy orientation. As a child, I was a devoted beach sandplayer. As an adult, I became an artist, an art therapist, sandplay therapist, and supervisor. The points of view expressed in this chapter have evolved over time, influenced by a continuous process of learning that has led me from art-making and teaching into art therapy, sandplay, and a Jungian understanding of the creative process. But the stable center from which I approach my therapeutic work is the sense of knowing the importance of: (1) creating visual imagery with concrete materials; (2) struggling with uncertainty; and (3) the sense of fulfillment when an effortless flow of imagery occurs.

As an art therapist, I try to enable others to allow their visual imagery to unfold non-judgmentally and securely. As my observational skills developed, my verbal interventions focused on reflecting the artwork in process more fully. Now, after the artwork is done, I try to enable the art-maker to experience what the image conveys and, if necessary, make immediate changes in the work as I observe, sometimes in the presence of an art therapy group.

While working through the image, the art-maker may be moved to physically touch areas of the work or use body movement or sound.

Figure 19.1 Triple spiral symbol enclosed within a double circle. The triple spiral represents the therapeutic interaction, each part representing either therapist, client, or image. Each spiral extends an arm to the other two just as the energies in the therapeutic encounter flow into each other. The circle holding the triple spiral symbolizes the setting, and the outer circle symbolizes the supervisory container of the process

Therapists who have successfully "worked through" a visual image will be able to enable clients to use materials and sandplay freely for self-expression. They may also be able to use experiential means in supervision to "open the door to the pre-verbal world that was experienced through images and sensations" (Kielo, 1991, p. 14). All this is deepened and enhanced by the verbal discussion of the client's background and behavior, the transference and the countertransference.

A visual image can be viewed as a surface upon which marks are made, analogous to ourselves as a surface on which the environment – family, friends, and others – also makes marks. The relationship between the surface (paper, clay, sand, etc.) and the marks made on it (pencil, crayons, paint, forming and incising, adding objects, etc.) can reveal pain and the need for healing, or show concealment, or pleasure and satisfaction, and promote growth and self-esteem (Steinhardt, 1995).

As therapist-observer trying to understand the art-maker's visual language, I mirror the image in words and verbalize its aura, spatial relations, and the internal relationships between color, form, and texture (Arnheim, 1974). This mirroring affirms the artwork as an image in its own right, even as it also reflects the art-maker.

As supervisor, the supervisee and I observe images in the same way and engage the "artist's eye," which "has the potential to produce a deepening of the therapeutic relationship as well as illuminating all the complexities inherent in the relationship" (Franklin *et al.*, 2000, p. 106).

For me, coming from the "culture of art-making" into the "culture of sandplay" was at once familiar and unfamiliar. Beach sand had been my first serious creative medium, and sandplay can be experienced rather like a spontaneous bas-relief or assemblage, containing sculptural elements and a choice of ready-made found objects (miniatures) (Steinhardt, 2000). It was, however, unfamiliar in the experience of an immediate plunge, taking me into my own personal story, surprising me with the relevance it had to my life, and transforming obscure, physically felt urges into autonomous visual images. The emphasis given to archetypes, symbols, and myths was unfamiliar and yet wonderfully familiar. Initially, the sandplay therapist's silence seemed artificial to me. As an art therapist, I may speak very little but I do relate, at times, to the image-in-process or to the final state with carefully chosen words. I am now aware that in sandplay my inner sense of participation expands greatly as I relate to and experience the sandplay event by silently recording the process and by making a drawing (rather than a diagram) of the work as it progresses. I sense the movement and relationship between the hands of the client and the sand and wait in anticipation of choice and placement of objects. I participate without touching, listen and observe without intrusive response. I photograph and disassemble the sand picture sometimes with a sense of regret that it cannot remain. And sometimes when the work seems so "right" and actually familiar, I wonder "Whose sandplay is it?" or "How much of the room or the therapist is in the sandplay?" There are some sandplays that I leave intact, if possible, for a few hours or more, until the felt presence of numinosity has evaporated and the objects and sand can return to their unintentional states, until they are engaged in a new interaction.

Sandplay training aims to integrate theory and experiential practice with a prerequisite that the trainee is willing to understand experientially who he or she is. Experiential understanding cannot be theoretically conveyed, just as one does not learn to swim by taking a correspondence course. A personal experiential process is central to image-making based therapies. The trainee copes with the unpredictability of spontaneous creative processes and experiences the position of being a client and meeting the deeper psychic structure of which he or she is rarely aware until it is discerned in the visual image. This training enables a therapist to help others find the balance between creative focusing and a relaxed flow, as they witness their hands create an image in the sand.

Sandplay occurs in a setting created by the therapist. Its structure reflects the therapist's personality, personal sandplay experience, and knowledge of many sandplay processes from observation and theoretical study. In this chapter I view sandplay supervision in terms of a visual appreciation of image-making. I review the visual awareness stressed in art therapy supervision and relate this to observing the sandplay client and images-in-process, or to viewing sandplay photos in supervision. I discuss the tangible sandplay setting as an image the therapist creates to hold the therapeutic relationship, and I suggest a sequence of steps in supervision aimed at grounding the therapist in visual apperception as a way of comprehending the client's needs and sandplay expression, and giving consideration to the image on its journey.

The art therapy supervision model

In art therapy, group experiential training promotes awareness of one's own and others' artistic creative styles that reflect differences in personality and background. In addition to education and theory, support and empathy, the supervisor encourages self-awareness and clarifies how the interaction between therapist and client, and the use of materials to form an image, is therapeutic. This training also facilitates integration and understanding of a client's background, behavior, and creative process, as well as transference and countertransferential reactions. In addition, students may use supervision to learn to deal with administrative factors, including boundaries and staff interaction. Experienced art therapists who have attained a sense of professional identity are more likely to use supervision as a process of professional growth, deepening self-awareness, self-reflection, and an expansion of knowledge (Wilson et al., 1984; Kielo, 1991; Edwards, 1993).

An art-making experiential component is also used in supervision (Durkin, Perach, Ramseyer, & Sontag, 1989; Fish, 1989; Kielo, 1991; Franklin, 1999; Ireland & Weissman, 1999). An art therapy supervisee may draw how it feels to be in a session or a symbol of him- or herself and a particular client in relationship. The supervisee may also draw the felt sense of the client's attitude to him- or herself, or to the therapist, or react in a drawing toward the client's artwork, or draw the space or ground in which the therapeutic relationship unfolds (Franklin, 1999).

In group supervision, participants reflect on or draw their reactions to the artwork of one person's client, without prior information about the client. Each participant's reaction may be different and reveal aspects of the therapeutic encounter that the therapist might overlook. After this, the supervisee can provide the group with information about the client's history, behavior, and the process of therapy. The client's imagery that was created in the "potential space" between therapist and client is processed in supervision through an experiential component – a graphic reaction, reinforced by factual and theoretical understanding (Ireland & Weissman, 1999).

When supervision is exclusively verbal, the visible concrete image – artwork or sandplay photograph – can be used to ground the imagination of the supervisee or group members from flying too far into fantasy. Focus then returns to the client and the therapist, and the imagery that fills the potential space between them.

Coming to sandplay supervision from art therapy

Sandplay supervision is a relationship between two experienced therapists, one of whom has attained the status of sandplay supervisor. Within the diversity of countries, languages, and cultures where sandplay is practiced, and the different therapeutic orientations of supervisors and supervisees, assumptions and expectations about sandplay practice may differ. A supervisory relationship may have to take into account both the supervisor's and the supervisee's previous therapeutic orientation and sandplay training in order to establish a common base of reference between different cultural and/or therapeutic languages.

A sandplay supervisor forms his or her body of reference about sandplay process in three ways: (1) by completing an experiential sandplay process; (2) by viewing many sandplay case histories reinforced by studying theory, symbols, and mythology; and (3) by accompanying many clients on their individual sandplay journeys. Since the personal sandplay process is experienced alone with a therapist, most sandplay trainees never see anyone else's work, except in case slides, until they begin their own sandplay practice with clients. In comparison, art therapists train experientially in groups, and, as mentioned previously, group members are aware of concurrent processes of others, as well as their own.

One art therapist entered an individual sandplay process after recovery from a severe accident. She had never seen anyone create a sandplay and appealed to me to give some direction and meaning to her work. One day she arrived at her session amazed that one of her child clients had noticed a sand tray in her clinic and had spontaneously begun to sift the sand and become deeply involved without direction from her. She said, "I think that's what you want for me" – and proceeded to do her most authentic work yet. When the client is deeply involved in making a sandplay, yet with no conscious direction, it becomes a symbolic picture of the psyche, similar to what Schaverien (1992) calls an "embodied" image that needs no words to explain it, and actually cannot be explained, only observed.

I have developed two types of sandplay programs. One is a four-day intensive workshop designed to introduce sandplay to experienced creative arts therapists and is based on an expressive therapy model that combines personal experiential work and theory (Steinhardt, 2004). The workshop room has 20 standard-size wooden sand trays, painted medium cerulean blue inside and filled with fine white sand from a local beach. The trays stand on tables around the walls of the room so that each person works individually.

Participants wishing to become sandplay trainees enter a personal one-to-one sandplay process, while the group experience enables a wider glance at the many roads people take in sandplay and may diminish any preconceived idea of sandplay that is based primarily on one's own personal process (Steinhardt, 2004).

The second program trains sandplay therapists according to the International Society for Sandplay Therapy (ISST) guidelines. The requirements regarding the learning of Jungian theory, the stages of development according to Neumann, and mythology are taught by a Jungian analyst. I illustrate sandplay theory with case studies of children and adults of all ages (Kalff, 1980; Neumann, 1983, 1988; Weinrib, 1983; Bradway *et al.*, 1990; Ammann, 1991; Ryce-Menuhin, 1992; Mitchell & Friedman, 1994; Bradway & McCoard, 1997). This group also experiences sandplay together in three five-hour sessions per year for two years.

Our knowledge of basic sandplay theory has increased through books that contribute relevant new information from the fields of art therapy and couple or group work to neurobiology, numbers, chakras, and world mythology – directions that were unpredictable 10 or 15 years ago (Cooper, 1978; Steinhardt, 1997, 2000; Baum and Weinberg, 2002; Eastwood, 2002; Markell, 2002; Morena, 2005; Turner, 2005). The format of a training program can be enhanced by these additional contributions without relinquishing the basic approach.

As a sandplay supervisor, I usually supervise art therapists who include sandplay in their practice and who may themselves be supervisors. Our common base of reference includes appreciation of the influence of the visual setting, knowledge about creating with materials, and seeing the setting as a visual image created by the therapist and the therapist as part of it. Even so, the task of sandplay supervision changes with each supervisee and respects differences in personality, training, therapeutic experience, and cultural background.

In both sandplay training and supervision, we explore (1) how our setting and art-making orientation encourage the use of sand as base and form; (2) penetration of the surface; and (3) symbolic representation of water or the use of real water (Steinhardt, 1998, 2000). Miniatures are studied as a language of symbols that relate to the collective unconscious and as cultural and personal expressions. The animals that appear in the sand tray, as helping instincts, are viewed in terms of their evolutionary and biological survival, the legends and mythology in which they appear, and their connections to shamanic powers (Cooper, 1978; Sams & Carson, 1988; Gallegos, 1990; Bennett, 1993).

Students in the training program research symbols that appear in their clients' sandplay work. For example, one group presented the following symbols: bridge, labyrinth, mandala, volcano, cave, the temples of Malta, the Middle Eastern goddess Astarte or Ishtar, ambulance, table, boat, elephant, stag, Mickey Mouse, and mice, cat, whale, lizard, and turtle. Research in the literature and on the Internet can access pictures and information that greatly enrich our understanding of the symbolic powers with which we dialogue in the form of miniature objects used in sandplay. For example, the turtle is related to the 13 cycles of the moon, having 13 plates or scutes in the central area of its carapace (outer shell), and 27 or 28 marginal scutes in the peripheral circumference that, like a lunar calendar, represent the days of each month. The moon pulls the ocean's tide, influences animal mating ceremonies and human female menstruation, connecting to the turtle's role in Native American lore as keeper of the water and to Turtle Island as the first mother earth (Sproul, 1979; Steinhardt, 2000; www.shannonthunderbird.com).

Forming of a concept of sandplay supervision

Margaret Lowenfeld (1935) and later Dora Kalff (1980) intuitively let the new therapy of play with sand, water and miniatures develop around the needs of the children who used it, and then they organized guidelines for therapeutic practice. In today's sandplay training, one's concept of sandplay as a therapeutic modality is impacted by the personal sandplay process, theoretical sandplay training, attitudes cultivated in one's original therapeutic orientation, and by the particular population with whom one works. Although there are approximate guidelines for constructing the sandplay setting (Kalff, 1980; Mitchell & Friedman, 1994), it is shaped by the therapist's personal preferences, both conscious and unconscious, combined with the actual space available. The sandplay space is meant to invite clients to enter a symbolic universe and provide the invisible keys that open their own treasure chests containing unforgettable treasures, such as love, power and fate (Bachelard, 1994). As container of the therapeutic relationship, the setting should enable the client to play freely, to accept the psyche's mystery as it points out direction, first as a kind of diffuse awareness, until a sense of clarity is reached.

As a supervisor, one's personal concept of sandplay impacts what one wishes to convey, considers important, and enjoys. But the purpose of supervision is not to create a group of people who think just like the supervisor, which could hinder development of the supervisee and block transformation of the client. Weinrib captures the true purpose of supervision:

> In sandplay, the therapists bring their intellectual understanding to the dynamics in the tray. But much more important than that is the feeling of picking up the message, of receiving in an emotional way the impact of a sandplay picture that's been made by the patient. And that impact on the psyche of the therapist prepares the way for the next step.
>
> (Weinrib, 2005, p. 42)

A 38-year-old woman undergoing fertility treatments for a second pregnancy asked to do some sandplay because it had previously helped her. In her second sandplay, on an island in the center of a large blue pool, she placed a fertility goddess and three sprays of fresh flowering rosemary (used in purifying ceremonies). Six paired objects circled the island in the blue symbolic water: a dolphin opposite a whale, two turtles opposite each other, and a round gold-colored clam shell opposite a large bronze fish. Beyond immediate interpretation of the symbolic meanings of island, goddess, whale, dolphin, fish, turtle, or shell, I picked up a visual message: the two turtles and shell were round, perhaps an egg symbol, and the three others, whale, dolphin, and fish, had long sperm-like shapes. I silently imagined the six objects in the water swimming as if the fish-sperm shapes would fertilize the turtle. As a supervisor, I would like the supervisee to experience picking up messages in this way in addition to theoretical understanding of the tray.

Enacting sandplay supervision

In supervising art therapists working with sandplay, it is essential to differentiate between the therapist's interventions as an art therapist and the role of sandplay therapist, taking into consideration the type of facility in which the therapist is practicing, i.e., a psychiatric facility, a medical hospital, a public clinic, or a private studio. The ideal setting is a room used only for creative therapy, with areas for painting, clay work and various materials, puppets and musical instruments, and an area designated for sandplay trays and shelves with miniatures that will not be removed from the room.

Children and adult clients are often referred to art therapy with sandplay included because they cannot verbally express feelings or because they are overly verbal and intellectualize. In public facilities, art therapists may be supervised by psychiatrists and psychologists whose focus is the therapeutic relationship, with artwork or sandplay sometimes seen as diagnostic or as a catalyst enabling the client to verbalize. They may appreciate the client's symbolic expression and press the therapist to discuss symbols with the client that represent his or her conflicts.

To counterbalance the verbal and cognitive approach, sandplay supervision has to support facilitation of the unconscious process and delayed interpretation within the "free and protected space." Jumping too quickly into discussion and interpretation could shock the client and damage the therapeutic process. The understanding that visual symbols are close to consciousness but are certainly not part of conscious awareness must sometimes be conveyed by the sandplay therapist to other staff. Sandplay therapists in private practice can seek Jungian supervision or sandplay supervision according to their needs.

In supervision, I have found that sandplay therapists have different priorities when presenting their cases. Some supervisees immediately present sandplay photographs and want theoretical understanding and guidelines for continuing the client's process, perhaps in terms they can use with their co-workers and staff at a public clinic or hospital. Some wish to explore their countertransference as "a helpful tool for exploring clients' projection as well as the therapist's perceptions" (Kielo, 1991, p. 14) and leave the client's work to the last minute. Some emphasize the client's history and the reason for referral to art and sandplay therapy, leaving little time for attention to the therapy process and the work itself.

As a sandplay supervisor, I try to ground the supervision in two ways: (1) the supervisee is asked to describe the sandplay setting, placement of materials, furnishings, sand trays, the object collection, light sources, and seating, and clarify choices made in setting it up (the concept of "setting" is further defined below); and (2) we observe photographs of the sandplay images without description of the sessions and with little information about the client. We try to glean a maximum of information from each photograph, and examine the use of sand, water, and miniatures as this develops in a series of sandplays. Photographs that show territorial map placement from above (from where the sandplayer sits) and from the side to show the distance between forms and objects or things hidden may be helpful.

The psyche expresses its material in parts. It may be that the first and second sandplay together show a balance between feminine and masculine. It may be that the first three sandplays reveal a sequence that will repeat itself in the next series of three but with changes that begin to define the journey.

With intense observation, we begin to reverberate with the imagery as it fills the room with its symbolic potential. The therapist-supervisee will begin to realize how much there is to observe and, during the therapy session, observation skills will be sharpened. In the silent field between client and therapist, each one's unconscious will "pick up" the sense of collaboration, and this mutual perception furthers the work (Samuels, Shorter, & Plaut, 1986).

After this period of observing, factual material is introduced: The supervisee presents the client's history and recounts the sessions. We return to the image as mirror of the client–therapist dyad and relate this to the client's body language and verbalization throughout the session. We begin to understand the client's feelings in the light of what is done with the sand and miniatures. Dynamics of the sandplay session are then discussed, such as entering and parting rituals (which become fixed boundaries of warm-up and closure), recording the sandplay process accurately in writing or drawing, and the therapist's seating and distance from the sand tray (which can change with the client's need for autonomy or support). It is essential to consider the client's reaction to these aspects of the therapist's role and differentiate between what actually happened and one's interpretation or feelings about it.

A supervisee, "Helen," brought a series of eight sandplays and some drawings of shaky houses by a 6½-year-old boy, after three months of therapy. She observed, in the boy's first four sandplays, that whole communities of objects (e.g., cars and people) were left buried under the sand as large tractors, trucks, and strong men were placed on the sand above. The boy called these strata "upper world" and "lower world" and said he knew everything that was buried, although it was now invisible.

Without referring to biographical information, we examined the concept of burying, concealing, and covering in the photos, in contrast to the very visible large surface. In the fourth sand picture the boy repeated the division between surface and buried lower world, but constructed on the surface a new division between left and right sides. The right side was "round, wet, clean, and contained," featuring a mandala made by pouring water on the sand and the placement of a well and two ordinary people, washed clean. The left side was "rectangular, dry, dirty, and porous," containing a round sieve the same size and shape as the well on the right, and a tray filled with cars dirtied with sand. The purifying water on the right could indicate development of a positive transference to the therapist, with the dry, dirty left side as a description of pre-verbal experience, a sieve that could hold no sand and the tray of unwashed cars.

In the following sandplays a large central pond was the focus, and buried objects began to emerge into visibility. Now we could relate to the boy's referral to therapy (parent's divorce and the boy's violent behavior), his image-making behavior, and verbalization. The boy and his mother lived with a large extended family in an agricultural settlement where almost everyone had the same family name. The blurred boundaries between his family and his many cousins and uncles and aunts were confusing. His absent father rarely visited, leaving him "buried" in a matriarchal society. The boy's buried anger and resentment toward both parents took all his energy, leaving him limited in his social interactions. In the next four sessions, he relinquished the act of burying within the positive transference to the therapist.

The inclusion of sandplay in a studio setting that offers art materials may seem, on the one hand, to diminish sandplay's uniqueness in the light of other creative choices. But, on the other hand, the studio setting offers an opportunity for identifying sandplay's unique ambience, process, and outcome, and allows a client to oscillate between different levels of concrete expression and different levels of the psyche.

Materials elicit varying behaviors and emotions from conscious and unconscious levels of the psyche. Play with the natural materials of sea sand and water can access a deep level of the collective unconscious and enable metaphorical contact with the ancient womb of life, the salt sea.

Clarification of the differences in therapeutic understanding and ways of fulfilling the role of sandplay therapist enables new learnings for both supervisor and supervisee.

Points for consideration

The sandplay setting, theory and practice

As a supervisor I find it useful to have a mental picture of the setting that the supervisee has arranged for conducting therapy, and how therapist and client move in this space. I want to understand the range of materials and objects available, their variety and placement, and how a client moves among the activities of sandplay, art, relating dreams, and discussing actual life events. Sometimes the verbal content presented at the start of a session falls into place in relation to the created imagery and observation of it toward closure.

The sandplay area is an extension of the therapist's personality and reflects his or her sensibility and predisposition to arrange certain configurations of furniture and objects. The therapist's eye is selective, just like that of clients suddenly noticing for the first time an object that has been on the shelf for years. The therapist's preferences are expressed consciously or unconsciously in the display or minimization of the content of the sandplay environment. The way materials are provided may, in a sense, sanction what a client will express and experience in doing sandplay. The setting is at once an autonomous area for the client and yet subliminally an extension of the therapist. Therefore, content and arrangement of the setting should be addressed.

In visits to clinics of other sandplay therapists, I found that I can quickly feel comfortable about working in that setting, or not. As a visually oriented person, I notice windows and lighting and where sand trays and shelves with their contents are placed. In some places white shelves seemed to clearly set forth the miniatures, whereas wooden shelves, although warm and reassuring, "swallowed" their colors and shapes. The types of objects included in the miniature collection interested me, their variety and quality, whether breakable or made for hard use, and their display on shelves or in containers. I noticed that some shelves (6 inches wide) seem precariously narrow to support miniatures. An 8-inch-wide shelf feels secure to me.

In several sandplay settings blended into art therapy facilities, a considered use of cerulean blue inside the dry sand tray and medium cobalt blue inside the damp sand tray created pleasantly subtle distinctions between the two trays (Steinhardt, 1997, 2000). In one children's clinic a transparent bluish plastic container revealed the inner sand and provided less of a felt sense of containment, which might influence the act of play. In another clinic the wooden tray had been painted blue inside and outside, so that inner and outer space were not visually separate – a contradiction to the container itself. I felt distinctly uneasy in one sandplay room seeing how the tray's inner blue surface had long been chipped and worn away.

The color and texture of sand in various settings ranged from a grainy uninviting deep ochre, to lifeless artificial sand that, for me, had no connection to the sea, to the pale beige-white fine sea sand from the Mediterranean shore that has its own inner light. In one room in a public facility, two sand trays stood in the center of the room opposite the door, surrounded by narrow shelves lining all four walls, with infinite standing miniatures and no other creative materials. For me this did not encourage focusing or provide a sense of warmth and intimacy. In another setting, a preponderance of many kinds of miniature people, in proportion to other types of objects in the miniature collection, felt like a subtle directive to choose people-objects; perhaps the therapist assumed them to be most important.

An unexpected sandplay setting that intrigued me was one in which the sand tray and shelves were placed quite low near the floor, and the object collection was both ordered and in some places chaotic, so one could rummage. The ambience was fascinating, intimate, and immediately inviting.

In my small studio the two sand trays stand at right angles near different walls, separated by a cupboard. Above each are shelves with freestanding miniatures and miniatures of one kind (babies, horses, houses, etc.) in clear plastic containers. My own assumptions about the setting may sometimes be challenged. One client, a young dancer who usually worked in the damp sand tray, used only the miniatures on the shelves above it. After several months, she asked if she could use the miniatures above the dry sand tray even if she did not work in that tray, as if each sand tray and the shelves above it were one unit. I had not thought to question her concept of territory in her choice of objects, and after her comment, learned to notice the client's use of the whole setting as well as clarifying my introduction to sandplay and sometimes relocating miniatures. After a year in therapy, she began to use heavy metal coils to represent frightening force and violence. The next year the same coils, together with other metal objects such as small containers taken from shelves in different areas, were used to represent her strength and growing ego.

Silence and witnessing

The therapist's ability to contain the process in silence and the Kalffian principle of delayed interpretation augment the witness aspect of the therapist and heightens the client's autonomy, both of which open the door to image-making directed by the Self. The experience of ego deferring to the Self's guidance is sometimes stronger in sandplay than in art therapy, where verbalization of different kinds is acceptable at different stages. One art therapy training program (Franklin, 1999) integrates art therapy, yoga philosophy, and meditation. Franklin sees the presence of the witness in the Self, in the artwork as mirror, and in the external other, the trusted person of the therapist: "Rather than aligning ourselves with the fragmented, limited thoughts about ourselves (ego), alignment with the Self and the presence of the Witness – the neutral watcher within us – creates an expansive world view. In Witness awareness, our experiences continue to unfold" (p. 5).

The sandplay therapist is, of course, witness to each client's unfolding sandplay process. Another aspect of witnessing seems to imprint images on the therapist's unconscious or imbue sand or miniatures with active energy, so that certain forms and objects appear in the work of several people throughout the day.

Once I threw a long red ribbon into a box of string and wool on a fairly concealed shelf. Four people, three working during that day and another the following day, found this ribbon and let it wind through their sand landscapes. Once a client, herself a therapist working in a psychiatric ward, felt overwhelmed being in a group of chronic clients. She flattened the sand and made a series of rows of holes and placed an object in most of them. The next client in my studio also flattened the sand, made rows of holes, and placed objects in these, as if the process of constructing these sandplays had been autonomously witnessed and confirmed as a holding structure. Both women dealt with fear in a confusing environment, but the details of their stories differed. These synchronicities are frequent, and I record them in my notes as I wonder what else fills the role of witness besides myself.

The need to create an image

Art historian Ellen Dissanayake (1988, 1992) discusses art-making as a fundamental universal or biological human-species characteristic – a normal and natural behavior that is part of human nature, like language, sex, sociability, and aggression. Art developed in human societies as a form of behavior notably in conjunction with ritual ceremony essential for group survival. Sand art ceremonies for healing are still practiced by Native Americans and by Tibetan monks. Dissanayake points out the human need to "make special" those things about which one cares deeply.

Making a sandplay artistically special creates a boundary between the mundane and the extraordinary. In art therapy, or sandplay therapy, a special image is created in the presence of a therapist or therapy group. The sharing of an image with the therapist or with the group places the image-maker in a vulnerable position. The group circle and therapist must contain the sharing so it becomes a communal event of emotional importance for everyone (Steinhardt, 2004). Sharing the client's sandplay image with a supervisor is also a vulnerable moment for the supervisee. An empathic containing supervisor (the circle around the setting and the therapist–client–image triple spiral) must hold this emotionally important event in which both supervisee and supervisor try to understand the client's visual expression and share the fascination of exploring conscious and unconscious expressions of the psyche and its unending creativity.

Conclusion

The therapist's creation of a free and protected sandplay setting is the gift of containment, the circle around the triple spiral of therapist, client, and image. Whatever the therapist's theory and experience, these are contained in the center of his or her spiral and flow unconsciously into the spirals of clients, their images, and their centers, because that is the route of this never-ending snake-like thread that in other instances represents life, death, and rebirth. Supervision, the outside containing circle, helps hold this image as a way of understanding how the history of a client, the events of a client's sandplay, and the therapist's presence and creativity flow in and out of each other in the therapeutic interaction.

References

Ammann, R. (1991). *Healing and transformation in sandplay: Creative processes become visible*. LaSalle, IL: Open Court.

Arnheim, R. (1974). *Art and visual perception: A psychology of the creative eye*. Berkeley, CA: University of California Press.

Bachelard, G. (1994). *The poetics of space*. Boston, MA: Beacon Press.

Baum, N., & Weinberg, B. (Eds.) (2002). *In the hands of creation: Sandplay images of birth and rebirth*. Toronto: Muki Baum Association.

Bennett, H.Z. (1993). *Zuni fetishes*. San Francisco, CA: Harper.

Bradway, K., Signell, K.A., Spare, G.H., Stewart, C.T., Stewart, L.H., & Thompson, C. (1981/1990). *Sandplay studies: Origins, theory and practice*. Boston, MA: Sigo Press.

Bradway, K., & McCoard, B. (1997). *Sandplay: Silent workshop of the psyche*. London: Routledge.

Cooper, J.C. (1978). *An illustrated encyclopedia of traditional symbols*. London: Thames & Hudson.

Dissanayake, E. (1988). *What is art for?* Seattle, WA: University of Washington Press.

Dissanayake, E. (1992). *Homo aestheticus: Where art comes from and why*. New York: Basic Books.

Durkin, J., Perach, D., Ramseyer, J., & Sontag, E. (1989). A model for art therapy supervision enhanced through art making and journal writing. In H. Wadeson, J. Durkin, & D. Perach (Eds.), *Advances in art therapy* (pp. 390–432). New York: John Wiley & Sons.

Eastwood, P.S. (2002). *Nine windows to wholeness*. Honolulu, HI: Sanity Press.

Edwards, D. (1993). Learning about feelings: the role of supervision in art therapy training, *The Arts in Psychotherapy*, *20*, 213–222.

Fish, B. (1989). Addressing countertransference through image making. In H. Wadeson, J. Durkin, & D. Perach (Eds.), *Advances in art therapy* (pp. 376–389). New York: John Wiley & Sons.

Franklin, M. (1999). Becoming a student of oneself: activating the witness in meditation, art and super-vision, *The American Journal of Art Therapy*, *38*, 2–13.

Franklin, M., Farrelly-Hansen, M., Marek, B., Swan-Foster, N., & Wallingford, S. (2000). Transpersonal art therapy education, *Art Therapy: Journal of the American Art Therapy Association*, *17*, 101–110.

Gallegos, E.S. (1990). *The personal totem pole*. Velarde, NM: Moon Bear Press.

Ireland, M.S., & Weissman, M.A. (1999). Visions of transference and counter-transference: the use of drawings in the clinical supervision of psychoanalytic practitioners, *American Journal of Art Therapy*, *37*, 74–83.

Kalff, D.M. (1980). *Sandplay*. Boston, MA: Sigo Press.

Kielo, J.B. (1991). Art therapists' countertransference and post-session therapy imagery, *Art Therapy: Journal of the American Art Therapy Association*, *8*, 14–19.

Lowenfeld, M. (1935). *Play in childhood*. London: Victor Gollancz Ltd. (Reprinted 1991, London: MacKeith Press.)

Markell, M.J. (2002). *Sand, water, silence: The embodiment of spirit*. London: Jessica Kingsley.

Mitchell, R.R., & Friedman, H.S. (1994). *Sandplay: Past, present, and future*. London: Routledge.

Morena, G. (2005). Language of imagery: language of connection, *Journal of Sandplay Therapy*, *15*, 67–76.

Neumann, E. (1983). *The great mother*. Princeton, NJ: Princeton University Press.

Neumann, E. (1988). *The child*. London: Karnac.

Ryce-Menuhin, J. (1992). *Jungian sandplay: The wonderful therapy*. London: Routledge.

Sams, J., & Carson, D. (1988). *Medicine cards: The discovery of power through the ways of animals*. Santa Fe, NM: Bear.

Samuels, A., Shorter, B., & Plaut, F. (1986). *A critical dictionary of Jungian analysis*. London: Routledge.

Schaverien, J. (1992). *The revealing image: Analytical art psychotherapy in theory and practice*. London: Routledge.

Sproul, B.C. (1979). *Primal myths: Creating the world*. New York: Harper & Row.

Steinhardt, L. (1995). The base and the mark: a primary dialogue in artmaking behavior, *Art Therapy: Journal of the American Art Therapy Association, 12*, 191–192.

Steinhardt, L. (1997). Beyond blue: the implications of blue as the color of the inner surface of the sandtray in sandplay, *The Arts in Psychotherapy, 24*, 455–469.

Steinhardt, L. (1998). Sand, water and universal form in sandplay and art therapy, *Art Therapy: Journal of the American Art Therapy Association, 15*, 252–260.

Steinhardt, L. (2000). *Foundation and form in Jungian sandplay*. London: Jessica Kingsley.

Steinhardt, L. (2004). Relationship in large group experiential sandplay training, *Journal of Sandplay Therapy, 13*, 29–42.

Turner, B.A. (2005). Neurobiology and the sandplay process, *Journal of Sandplay Therapy, 15*, 99–112.

Weinrib, E.L. (1983). *Images of the self*. Boston, MA: Sigo Press.

Weller, B. (2005). A conversation with Estelle Weinrib, *Journal of Sandplay Therapy, 15*, 35–50.

Wilson, L., Riley, S., & Wadeson, H. (1984). Art therapy supervision, *Art Therapy: Journal of the American Art Therapy Association, 1*, 100–105.

Index

thinking symbolically 15, 140
vocabulary 194
see also image symbol formation
    project 152
synchronicity, of interweaving themes
    13, 195, 210

"talk(ing) therapy" 113, 139, 149
Tarasoff 77, 85–6n1
temenos 17, 152, 164, 183, 184
    see also container; "free and
        protected" space
therapist, *see* supervisee
training
    best foundation for 111
    cost of 68
    differentiating levels of 164–5
    diversity in 156–57
    examples of 203–4
    personal development in 161
    truth 164
transference 5, 27
    in case example 77
    with children 181
    dissolution of 69
    field, expanding notion of 95
    idealizing 100
    and parallel process 73–4
    positive 128, 207
    revealed in sandplay 194
    of supervisee 88
    triple spiral image of 198, **199**
transindividual field 95
trauma
    interventions/response 151, 167
    training in treatment of 154–5
    war, complexes difficult to treat 110
triad
    concept of field and 96
    engaging 99
triple spiral 198, **199**, 211
trust(ing)
    and collective concern about
        boundary violation 67
    the process 75
    rebuilding 133
typology, mismatches in 75–6, 77, 80

uncertainty, tolerating 14, 16, 100,
    198
unconscious (processes)
    anxiety inhibiting connection to 48
    communicating dynamics 100–2
    "confrontation with the unconscious"
        170
    cultural 99–100, 108
    facilitation of 206
    factors of supervisee 90
    key aspect of sandplay 169
    mysterious movement/power of 96,
        143, 195
    racial 98
    sand creations reveal 4
    symbols as language of 4
    wisdom of 144–7

Valencerina, Madalaine 124
values
    culture-based 155
    felt 162
venting 163
verbalization
    in art therapy 210
    sandplay vs. 113–14
visualization, 141–2
vulnerability 26, 27, 211

Weinrib, Estelle 6
Weller, B. 205
Williams, Frank 124
Winnicott, D.W. 82–3
witness(ing) 178, 210
Wizard of Oz, The 195
Wolkenfeld, F. 96, 100
wonder 181
World Technique 172
wuwei 170–1

Xian 175n1

yin/yang 172, **173**

Zhou Dunyi 172, **173**
Zhuang Zi 169